# The Sociology of Organizations

## Themes, Perspectives and Prospects

MICHAEL I. REED

*Lancaster University*

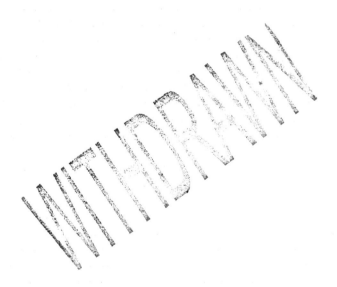

HARVESTER
WHEATSHEAF

New York   London   Toronto   Sydney   Tokyo   Singapore

First published 1992 by
Harvester Wheatsheaf,
Campus 400, Maylands Avenue
Hemel Hempstead,
Hertfordshire, HP2 7EZ
A division of
Simon & Schuster International Group

Typeset in 10/12 pt Trump Medieval
by Columns Design and Production Services Ltd., Reading

Printed and bound in Great Britain by
Billing & Sons Ltd, Worcester

British Library Cataloguing-in-Publication Data

Reed, Michael
    The sociology of organizations: Themes, perspectives
and prospects
    – (Studies in sociology series)
    I. Title   II. Series
    302.5

    ISBN 0-7450-0774-0
    ISBN 0-7450-0775-9 (pbk)

1  2  3  4  5    96  95  94  93  92

*For Ceris, Cara and Christopher*

# CONTENTS

## Contents

# PREFACE

If there is one thing which sociologists interested in the study of work organizations are agreed on is that their field of study is in a state of considerable flux and uncertainty. They may have differing opinions as to the nature and extent of this condition of instability and unpredictability. They may violently disagree as to the factors which have brought it about and the way in which it should be handled. But there is almost universal agreement within the field that, over the last two decades or so, the sociology of organizations has experienced a series of profound changes as to the way in which its subject matter is defined and the manner in which it is researched.

In this respect, both the way in which the phenomenon of 'organization' is characterized and the theoretical and methodological equipment thought most appropriate to its analysis have undergone a series of highly significant transformations over the period. This has resulted in a field of study which may seem barely recognizable to that existing in the 1960s. Across a range of fundamental issues – subject matter, theory, research, methodology, policy implications and underlying values or knowledge interests – the nature of and prospects for the sociology of organizations have been the focus for debate and controversy.

The purpose of this book is to survey these developments – or, as some would see them, metamorphoses – and to assess their implications for the present condition of and future prospects for the sociology of organizations as it is presently constituted. Consequently, the underlying objective of the book is in part descriptive and in part prescriptive; that is, it purports to provide both a detailed exposition of the most significant intellectual developments which have occurred over the past twenty years or so and a grounded appreciation of where these developments might be leading.

The first chapter provides an outline of those general sociological perspectives – Marxist, Weberian and Durkheimian – through which the growth and diffusion of formal or complex organizations within modern societies have been analyzed. In exploring the contribution which the advance of complex organization has made to the process of modernity, the chapter establishes the broader historical and institutional background against which more focused and selective research on the practices and structures most closely associated with the 'organizational phenomenon' must be set.

Chapter 2 identifies the more deep-seated thematic continuities which continue to shape and direct the sociology of organizations. At a time when discontinuity and rupture with the past is pre-eminent, this chapter traces the underlying 'master themes' or 'unit ideas' that have structured the field's, intellectual development since the second half of the nineteenth century. These leitmotifs are seen to provide the analytical and moral threads holding the sociology of organizations together as an intellectually coherent and practically relevant endeavour.

Having set the wider historical and thematic context in which contemporary organizational analysis needs to be situated, Chapters 3 and 4 focus more selectively on the analytical frameworks and research programmes that have framed the agenda for dialogue and debate since the 1960s. Chapter 3 provides a detailed specification of the major analytical frameworks that have been developed to pursue research on complex organizations since the intellectual dominance of positivist/functionalist orthodoxy began to be challenged and alternative perspectives gathered support. Chapter 4 looks at the particular theory groups and research programmes that coalesced around these analytical frameworks and the research priorities which they have highlighted. It is a relatively long chapter which provides a detailed review and evaluation of the particular research programmes carried through by a number of theory groups that have dominated the sociology of organizations over the last twenty years or so. The thesis which this wide-ranging exposition advances suggests that the sociology of organizations has undergone a series of theoretical shifts during this period which signify a clear break with the environmental or structural determinism that was in the ascendant for much of the 1950s and 1960s. In this respect, the research programmes reviewed in Chapter 4 have pulled the sociology of organizations towards forms of theoretical analysis and empirical inquiry in which the social construction and reconstruction of 'organizational reality' emerges as *the* strategic research interest. The overall impact of these programmes, in producing a field of study characterized by theoretical trajectories pressing in the direction of increasing plurality, diversity and controversy, is also assessed.

Chapters 5 and 6 bring the story up to date by adumbrating the substantive issues which are most prominent in shaping current research and analysis, as well as outlining the developmental strategies for future intellectual advance that are on offer at the present time. The book concludes with the argument that the most likely source of a 'progressive narrative' within the sociology of organizations is to be discovered in those studies which focus on the strategic role of modern organizations in providing the social technologies whereby the 'reflexive monitoring of system reproduction and change' is facilitated in advanced capitalist societies. The latter find themselves caught up in the drive towards a form of globalization which damages and fragments established structures and routines, while at the same time reinforcing the strategic role of complex organizations as mechanisms of surveillance and control. Indeed, the belief that we are living through a period of profound instability and disorganization has crystallized into something of a 'new orthodoxy' which has exerted a dramatic influence on current thinking and research within the sociology of organizations.

While this book is mindful of the very significant structural and intellectual developments which have occurred over the last two decades, it argues against the thesis that these changes are leading us into a 'postmodern' or 'post-Fordist' world in which all the established epistemological ground

rules and organizational forms have been so radically transformed that we need to start anew in terms of basic
theoretical presuppositions and institutional rationales. In
direct opposition to these 'radical' interpretations of irreversible intellectual rupture and institutional fragmentation, the
case argued in this book suggests that we need to formulate
and debate a much more considered appreciation of the
balance between continuity and discontinuity than has often
been the case in more recent interventions. Only by doing
this, will the sociology of organizations be adequately
equipped to make its full contribution to a better understanding of the times in which we live and the direction in which
they may be leading.

Consequently, this book cautions against a too easy
acceptance of the 'new times' ethos and theories. The latter
seem to suggest that we are living through a period in which
history is at an end and rational dialogue between contending
epistemological positions and institutional analyses has been
overtaken by a cacophony of voices and images that drowns
out the possibility of shared dialogue based on negotiated
ground rules. Instead, the overriding emphasis is on the lack
of any collective or shared sense of meaningful historical
development and the intellectual heritage that it bequeaths.
Discontinuity, rupture and disjuncture are highlighted at the
expense of any deeper appreciation of the underlying continuities in thematic focus, theoretical development and
policy concerns that can be discerned beneath the swirling
eddy of contemporary intellectual discontent and polarization.

While clearly recognizing the upheavals and travails of the
last twenty years or so, this book attempts to introduce a
much greater degree of historical balance, theoretical sensitivity and institutional realism into current assessments of
the sociology of organizations. In doing so, it argues a case for
the 'reclaiming' of the concept of organization as referring to
strategic social practices and technologies which will in-
delibly shape the institutional transitions that are currently
taking place and the structures which they will produce.
By restating the value of seeing modern organizations as
crucial mechanisms facilitating the planned, but contested,

reproduction and transformation of social systems, this book reasserts the continuing significance of the central problematic which has directed the development of the sociology of organizations since Weber. As Weber clearly recognized, the relentless dynamism and unrivalled capacity of modern organizations to shape the institutional landscape of the social world which we inhabit must form the substantive core of any sociology of organizations worthy of that name. The analysis and recommendations outlined in this book follow in that tradition; a tradition which may be in need of substantial revision, but still speaks to present concerns and anticipated futures.

## / 1 /

# ORGANIZATIONS AND MODERNITY

### INTRODUCTION

The widespread acceptance of structures and processes normally associated with bureaucratic or formal organization was a key development in the transition to modern industrial society. While pre-industrial, agrarian societies had centralized state structures and military systems which displayed some of the characteristics of bureaucratic organizations,[1] the latter only reached its fully developed form in industrial capitalist societies.

In this respect, the structural principles and operational practices associated with bureaucratic organization constitute a primary institutional carrier of modernization in so far as they indicate the growth and diffusion of an integrated set of social practices required for technologically induced economic growth[2]. As Berger *et al.*, argue: 'Modernization, then, consists of the growth and diffusion of a set of institutions rooted in the transformation of the economy by means of technology. . . . Bureaucracy presupposes general and autonomous organization ability. In principle everything is organizable in bureaucratic terms.'[3]

Complex organizations provide a mechanism or instrument through which the rational control over and deployment of scarce resources – such as time,[4] space and energy – could be realized and directed to the achievement of continuous technological advance and sustained economic growth. They constituted a social technology through which material and human resources could be effectively combined and geared towards the accumulation of capital on a regular and stable basis. By establishing the administrative practices and cognitive frameworks through which individual behaviour could be routinely subjected to disciplined calculation and control, bureaucratic systems facilitated the acceptance and diffusion of an 'organizational culture' in which attitudes and behaviour were naturally adapted to the rhythms of collective enterprise.[5]

What this entailed above all else was a massive extension of instrumental rationality – as a behavioural norm and organizing principle – into every area of economic, social, political and cultural life.[6] Instrumental rationality embodied a form of reasoning and an associated set of social practices dedicated to the employment of the most effective technical means to the achievement of valued social ends such as maximizing profitable production or reducing operational costs.[7] Bureaucratic organizations were seen as the primary institutional expression of the cognitive dominance of instrumental rationality in modern societies. Their underlying principles of functional differentiation and hierarchical coordination were dedicated to the rational calculation and control of behaviour in minute and specific detail. As Weber put it:

Already now rational calculation is manifest at every stage. By it, the performance of each individual worker is mathematically measured, each man becomes a little cog in the machine and, aware of this, his one pre-occupation is whether he can become a bigger cog.[8]

In this way, bureaucratic organizations seemed to provide the right combination of cognitive instrumentality, moral anonymity and technical effectiveness that secured the necessary prerequisites for the successful transition from a social order based on custom and tradition to one founded on rational calculation and control.

The purpose of this chapter is to review and assess the contribution that sociological analysis has made to our understanding of modern organizational forms and the role which they have played in the development of advanced industrial societies. We will begin by examining in greater depth and detail the general respects in which formal or complex organizations are carriers of modernization. This is followed by a review of the particular analyses and interpretations of modern organizational forms which have been offered by exponents of three influential general perspectives in sociological theory: first, a Marxist analysis of the changing nature of managerial control strategies over the labour process; second, a functionalist interpretation of modes of corporate management and control in industrial societies; and third, a Weberian explanation of conflict regulation in the corporate state.

These analyses provide the context in which more recent accounts of longer term institutional trends and their organizational implications – as found in the theory of post-industrial society and the postmodernist interpretation of organizational culture – can be located and evaluated. Taken as a complete package, the exegesis and evaluation of the most significant contributions that have been made to improving our appreciation of the symbiotic links between organizations and modernity provided in this chapter will establish the historical and theoretical background against which the more analytical treatment of 'thematic continuities' explored in Chapter 2 can be located.

As Giddens[9] has recently argued, organization theory has the potential to make a crucial contribution to the analysis of the institutional structures and processes which constitute the foundations of modern society. Unfortunately, that potential has yet to be realized in full. At least two reasons can be adduced for this relative failure. First, mainstream organizational analysis tends to offer a conceptualization of 'organization' that rips the social structures and processes normally associated with such a form of collective action from their location within wider institutional configurations.[10] Second, the 'history' of organization theory is presented in a decontextualized way, denuded of its intimate connections to a much wide-ranging debate over the nature and significance of modern organizational forms for the development of Western civilization.[11] This usually leads – either implicitly or explicitly – to a Whig interpretation of organization theory's history as entailing unstoppable progress towards explanatory theories and methodological protocols that map the true condition of modern organization. However, the price to be paid for accepting this view is a sanitized account of organization theory's history and a technocratic reading of its purpose and procedures which conveniently forgets that:

Arguably a liberal modern state interferes in the lives of its citizens far more than a traditional pre-industrial despotism. The complexity and interdependence of society, and this dependence on an overall infrastructure, make its members docile and habituated to obedience to bureaucratic institutions. In one way, the striking thing about Nazi-dominated Europe is not the brutality of its camps, but the amount of obedience it could expect without even deploying such brutality. People co-operated in the various stages of their deportation and eventual annihilation. Submission to bureaucratic orders is habitual, normal and inevitable. If the final step of a series of conformities to instructions leads to the gas chamber door, it is then too late to resist.[12]

It is time that this 'darker' side of modern organization – and of organization theory's history – be recovered so that Weber's insight into the terrible process whereby technical means are applied to the most immoral of ends can be rediscovered and its full implications for the study and management of organizations be more clearly developed.

## COMPLEX ORGANIZATIONS AND MODERN SOCIETY

Organizations are containers and mobilizers of material and human resources which provide the infrastructure of administrative control and regulation required for the effective function of highly differentiated and interdependent social systems. They hold and pump the vital resources or 'powers' through which the assembly and integration of diverse and heterogeneous activities undertaken within modern societies can be economically achieved on a routine basis. The competing demands for functional differentiation within and between social units to be pushed to its fullest extent – in order to cope with increased environmental complexity and to maximize productive efficiency, and for structural integration to be made as effective as possible, in order to realize overall coordination – can only be met through the mechanisms and processes embedded in bureaucratic organization. The reproduction of the social systems associated with modernity – that is, urban–industrial complexes functioning within centralized political structures – depends upon the mechanisms and processes constitutive of complex or formal organization.[13]

Giddens has suggested that organizations involve the storage and direction of two basic types of resources: first, allocative resources as entailed in land, capital, machinery and manpower; and second, administrative or authoritative resources as entailed in ideologies, information and devices that structure geographical space and social time in such a way that detailed surveillance of, and control over, interdependent activities can be maintained.[14] He argues that the former have tended to attract the lion's share of the attention within organization theory, but that the latter are more significant to the extent that they provide the means through which surveillance is intensified within modern societies:

There are two aspects to surveillance. One is surveillance as the accumulation coding and retrieval of information; the other is surveillance as the direct supervision of the activities of some individuals or groups by others. The collation of information is vital for the generation of administrative power, because of the control over time–space which it generates – particularly control over the timing and spacing of the activities of individuals whose behaviour is then made a part of the organization. One of the most important connections between the two forms of surveillance is the relation between the accumulation of 'organizational history' and that of personal histories or personal data.[15]

It is the capacity of modern bureaucratic organizations to generate and deploy administrative power which, in Giddens' view, makes them so central to the reproduction of the social systems most closely associated with modernity such as urban–industrial complexes and the centralized nation-state.

The administrative power that they generate and deploy – through devices such as documentary archives, timetables, filing systems and rule books – makes it possible to accumulate and manipulate knowledge about the physical and social world in such a way that self-reflexive control over institutional change and development can be maximized:

A timetable is one of the most significant of modern organizational devices, presuming and stimulating a regulation of social life by quantified time in a manner quite unknown to prior types of society. Timetables are not just means of using temporal differences in order to identify and specify regularized events – the arrival and departure of coaches, trains, buses or planes. A timetable is a time–space ordering device, which is at the heart of modern organizations. All organizations, up to and including the world system today, operate by means of timetables, through which the sequencing of activities in time–space is choreographed.[16]

In this way, organizations engage in a temporal and spatial structuring to ensure that their members and clients internalize rhythms and norms that fit individual behaviour to the pattern of sequences demanded by modern industrial life.[17] Consequently, the problem of controlling the multifarious activities of large numbers of people becomes much more manageable to the extent that they automatically accept the discipline instilled by a socio-economic order which is geared to economic efficiency and profitability.

The latter point reminds us of the need to link the authoritative resources and administrative power of modern organizations to their material base. As Giddens acknowledges, all forms of organizational surveillance and control exercised through the mobilization of administrative power are backed by coercive sanctions of one type or another. Within modern industrialized societies, this is most often achieved through the economic compulsion to work for a living and the organizational and ideological control practices which support it. The strategic role that modern organizations play in generating and allocating economic resources to different segments of the population, through the implementation and monitoring of highly sophisticated reward systems, gives them a powerful source of leverage over the 'life chances' and opportunities of large numbers of people who are dependent on their largesse. Indeed, the detailed recording and storage of the life histories and performances of organizational members and clients is directly and indirectly linked to the material and social rewards that they receive as a result of acceptable participation and engagement. The 'dead hand' of economic compulsion is a much more economical and stable mechanism for securing compliance with instructions and ensuring the internalizing of expected behavioural norms than the whole paraphernalia of physical threats and coercions more common within traditional societies.[18] When economic compulsion is combined with the sophisticated monitoring and control systems made available by modern organizations, an extremely formidable regime of administrative governance is established.

In general terms, bureaucratic organizations facilitate 'centrally directed and supervised, hierarchically structured routine administration on a scale so large that it must be conducted on the basis of rules, files and delegated but formally limited, authority that is related to the functions of each office'.[19] As such, they provide a unique integration of administrative and economic power through synchronized control over authoritative and allocative resources, which provides the necessary organizational means for the effective management of institutional reproduction in modern societies.

However, the manner in which the specific dynamics and structures of modern organizations have been analyzed within the sociology of organizations has been subject to considerable theoretical variation – depending on the particular frame of reference in which it has been pursued. One of the most currently influential theoretical approaches is that which analyzes the contribution that modern organization makes to the maximization of profit and sustained capital accumulation within the capitalist mode of production. The nature and implications of this perspective will be explored as a preliminary to an exposition of analyses that have been developed as a critical response to the putative inadequacies of the former.

## INDUSTRIAL CAPITALISM AND THE LABOUR PROCESS

From a Marxist standpoint, the development of modern organizational structures has to be related to the changing structure of capitalism and the 'control imperatives' which different regimes of accumulation impose on managers and workers.[20] The drive to maximize profits and the need to procure the basis for sustained capital accumulation establish the structural parameters within which organizational control strategies and practices emerge. Thus, both at the level of the economic system as a whole and at the level of individual companies and workplaces within it, the development of organizational forms has to be related to structural constraints embedded within the capitalist mode of production. There may be considerable variation in organizational structures and practices within and between each of these levels of analysis.[21] Nevertheless, overall trends in the systems and techniques through which the organization of productive activity is realized are accounted for in terms of the underlying dynamics of capitalist development.[22]

At the level of political economy, Marxist writers have highlighted a set of interconnected structural changes that have driven capitalist societies in the direction of 'monopoly capitalism'.[23] The latter describes a much more integrated and coordinated structure than that prevailing under earlier – liberal or entrepreneurial – forms of capitalist production and exchange in which a relatively small number of large corporations have come to dominate the economy. Within this structure, the financial institutions play a central role in coordinating and controlling subordinate production units through centralized financial groups of interlocking directorships and other types of financial holding arrangements. They are supported by the state intervening directly in the management of the economy so as to protect and enhance the international competitiveness of big business and financial institutions.

Indeed, a number of Marxist commentators have referred to these developments in terms of the shift towards a form of 'organized capitalism' in which the economic, political, administrative and cultural spheres have become much more tightly knit and functionally interdependent.[24] Here, industrial capitalist economies are seen to be developing in the direction of concentrated capital ownership and centralized bureaucratic management as a result of the intensification of international competition and the greater coordination and regulation that national economic success demands. Lash and Urry characterize organized capitalism as entailing a number of structural innovations at both the macro and micro levels that are linked together by intermediate organizational mechanisms:

> Organization at the top here includes, for example, the concentration of industry, increasing inter-articulation of banks, industry and the state, and cartel formation; organization at the bottom includes, for example, the development of national trade union bodies, working class political parties, and the welfare state.[25]

These changes in capitalist organization and industrial relations were integrated – in an extremely loose and fragile way – by a set of state-sponsored or supported organizations (such as employers' federations or public sector agencies) that coordinated policy and regulated conflicts between the key producer groups. Thus, a pattern of interrelated institutional changes such as the concentration and centralization of capital, the separation between private ownership and bureaucratic managerial control and the growth of collective organizations in industry and labour markets, culminated in the development of a form of organized capitalism in North America and Europe[26] that was strategically dependent on the administrative coordination provided by modern bureaucracy.

These macro-level developments seemed to encourage a more coherent alignment between the formulation of corporate strategy by the dominant coalition of directors and senior managers and its implementation at the level of the workplace by lower-level management. Scott has argued that the formulation of corporate strategy can be understood as a struggle for control over the strategic decision-making agenda between directors and top-level managers whose actions 'are shaped by the network of intercorporate relations in which the enterprise is embedded and, beyond this, by the actions of the state and other political agencies'.[27] The control strategies and systems implemented and administered by lower-level factory managers are conditioned by the priorities imposed by directors and senior managers as members of the intercorporate networks that dominate organized capitalist economies.[28] The latter translate the changing organizational requirements for profitable production into appropriate corporate policy that provides the framework of constraints within which the coordination and control of the production process itself has to be achieved.

However, research on the managerial practices through which production is actually organized suggests that the integration between a centrally determined and coordinated strategy of capital accumulation and the manner in which workplace control is secured is much more tenuous than the above analysis indicates.[29] While managers must construct a control apparatus to ensure that the productive potential inherent within labour power is translated into actual performance, the specific organizational practices through which they achieved this are open to considerable variation.[30] In general terms, research on the historical development of labour process organization indicates a shift from personalized and direct methods of control to indirect techniques in which administrative and ideological controls become much more prominent.[31] Dependence on internal subcontracting or the foreman system – both of which constituted control systems based on direct supervision – gradually gave way to automated production technologies and extended managerial hierarchies. Within the latter, the mobilization of allocative and administrative resources was facilitated though the deployment of organizational mechanisms which allowed managers to realize 'control at a distance' – that is, to monitor and correct labour performance through means remote from the actual production process itself.[32] Consequently, the growing sophistication of advanced information technologies and methods of organizational selection and socialization (in which the inculcation of attitudes and behaviour consistent with prevailing corporate culture was the primary objective for management[33]) seemed to provide owners and managers with a more integrated control apparatus. This would allow a much tighter alignment between corporate strategy and labour process management than had been possible under cruder regimes of accumulation. Developments such as these, have prompted some Marxist writers to identify the emergence of an 'internal state' within the modern corporation which mirrors the growth of organized capitalism within the political economies of Western industrial societies.[34] The increasing importance of internal labour markets (where labour is allocated and rewarded on the basis of firm-specific rather than external market criteria), formalized plant and company-level collective bargaining systems and sophisticated processes of cultural socialization generate 'factory regimes' that successfully obscure the intensification of labour exploitation. The rise of these 'hegemonic regimes', which rely on ideological control and bureaucratic rationalization to tie workers' interests to the fortunes of their employers, is seen to signify the dominance of a 'new despotism' entailing 'the rational tyranny of capital mobility over the collective worker . . . to mobilize consent to increased productivity'[35] and to carve out arenas in which workers' opposition will be effectively pre-empted.

Yet, the institutional developments associated with the rise of organized capitalism and hegemonic factory regimes have been articulated and analyzed in very different terms to those provided by Marxist commentators. Indeed, they have been interpreted as constituting a pattern of institutional development that undermines any Marxist-based analysis of the dynamics and outcome of capitalist development. Instead, they point to an organizational revolution that fundamentally transformed the institutional foundations and ideological superstructure of liberal capitalism, which must be accounted for in terms of the move to a generic social order that radically breaks with the latter – that is, the shift to 'industrial society'.

INDUSTRIAL SOCIETY AND THE CORPORATE ECONOMY

The concept of industrial society provided the theoretical resources from which an alternative (i.e. non-Marxist) interpretation of the process of modernization and the typical social structures that it produced could be constructed. It promulgated a narrative account of modernity and its major organizational features that challenged the appropriateness of an analysis which treated private ownership of the means of production and the drive for profitability as the overriding universal imperatives within which institutional development had to be explained. In direct contrast, the theory of industrial society[36] focused on technological and organizational imperatives that were independent of the mode of property ownership and its underlying economic dynamic. A production system that was organized on the basis of rational methods of calculation and control – rather than the maximization of profit and the exploitation of labour power – was presumed to constitute a shared socio-technological base that would determine the institutional structure of all industrial societies, whatever their particular political and ideological configuration.[37] The cognitive essence of modernization lay in a form of calculative instrumentalism which would impose itself on all industrial societies whatever their specific historical and cultural identities.[38] The clearest institutional expression of the global diffusion of this cognitive principle was to be found in the allocative mechanisms and administrative practices constitutive of rational bureaucratic organization. Technological and organizational rationalization, rather than class power, was the cognitive driving force of modernization.

Both the increasing scale and complexity of industrial production were seen to generate a form of administrative organization and control that could not be contained within the short-term economic interest of private owners and the ideological rationalizations through which these sectional concerns had been projected as social benefits for the community as a whole. The spreading of share-ownership within all industrial societies[39] beyond a tiny minority of family owning groups or powerful industrial magnates reinforced the movement towards a system of professional managerial control through organizational mechanisms that were geared to a wide range of competing socio-economic interests beyond the narrow confines of profit maximization and sustained capital accumulation.[40] Effective corporate power was seen to pass out of the hands of private owners into the laps of managerial technocracy that was forced to attend to the impact of their policies on a diverse, and often bewildering, array of interest groups which had to be moulded into a coherent and sustainable public constituency. The dominance of the capitalist class was giving way to the increasing power of a managerial technocracy.

In these respects, all economically advanced societies were deemed to have structural and cultural characteristics which they shared, irrespective of whether the means of production remained in private hands or was under state control.[41] Industrialization and modernization entailed certain universal organizational imperatives that had to be met if individual countries were to be successful within the world-wide system of pluralistic industrialism.[42]

Ruling elites within particular countries may exert some minimal influence over the trajectory of modernization which their nations followed. But the role of human values and strategic choice was seen to be subordinate to the organizational requirements of large-scale factory production. While Marxists and industrial society theorists agreed that the development of modern societies necessarily entailed a dramatic extension of administrative power within the enterprise and the workplace, they fundamentally disagreed as to the causes and consequences of this enhancement of organized coordination and control. For the Marxist, it is a manifestation of the much more subtle and sophisticated forms of class domination and control prevalent in advanced capitalist societies in which the dull compulsion of economic necessity and industrial discipline has been sublimated within a complex infrastructure of ideological indoctrination and cultural assimilation. The theorists of industrial society, on the other hand, regarded the increasing organizational sophistication and technological rationalization concomitant with industrialization as establishing the institutional foundations of a social democratic political system in which ideological polarization and class conflict would be more effectively regulated and eventually eradicated.[43] Representative democracy was 'functional' for industrial society in so far as it provided the political infrastructure through which economic growth and organizational efficiency could be maximized.

As such, we can identify three interrelated analytical components to the theory of industrial society; first, the separation between formal private ownership and effective managerial control within the modern corporation; second, the strategic role of managerial elites in directing the organizational apparatus that more advanced technology demands; and third, the development of a technocratic culture and politics which removes any remaining traces of ideological conflict.

Scott[44] argues that the separation between ownership and control within the large-scale business corporation provides the theoretical backbone to the industrial society thesis. It treats the dispersal and decomposition of private share-ownership within the corporate economies of all advanced societies as providing the structural precondition for the rise of modern management to a position of organizational dominance. As the extended managerial hierarchy typical of the large corporation becomes more differentiated and bureaucratized, power passes out of the hands of private capital into the control of an 'organized intelligence' – that is, an expanding stratum of administrative, scientific and technical experts who direct the long-term development of the economic system as a whole,[45] and provide the cognitive, technical and informational resources through which administrative power is generated and directed to the most efficient and effective use of allocative resources. Economic decision-making within the business corporation becomes a much more complex affair in which short-term profit maximization gives way to long-term corporate growth and stability as the overriding consideration. Managers come to exercise a trust or fiduciary role on behalf of the collective interests of the community as a whole; the interest of private owners in profit and capital accumulation becomes one amongst a range of competing demands that managers have to take into account.[46] As a result of these changes, the force of ideologically based conflicts between capital and labour is substantially moderated. The 'age of ideology' fades, to be replaced by an 'age of realism'; 'the benevolent political bureaucracy and the benevolent economic oligarchy are matched with the more tolerant mass'.[47]

The theory of industrial society projects a modern social order in which technological change, organizational functioning and political direction demand a high degree of decentralized economic control, balanced by a large measure of centralized administrative coordination by the state. Capitalism sows the seeds of its own destruction to the extent that it revolutionizes its economic structure from within to create a highly bureaucratized control system in which socio-economic change is directed by a depersonalized organizational apparatus that destroys the technical function of, and ideological justification for, the property owning class.[48] An unstoppable process of 'creative destruction' transforms liberal or entrepreneurial capitalism into managerial capitalism; it undermines the economic and cultural foundations of the bourgeois as a class and the bourgeois family as the key economic unit of capitalist society. Within this process of institutional transformation from within, modern organizations play the strategic role in so far as they become the primary carriers of an instrumental rationality and an apparatus of administrative control which are ideally suited to the imperatives of deliberately planned change.[49] Scientifically based social engineering and technical expertise rather than natural evolution and the rights of private property become the dominant organizational practices and ideological legitimations of the industrial society which has emerged 'pheonix like' out of the ashes of liberal capitalism.

Above all else, industrial society is an 'organized society';[50] it depends on large-scale bureaucratic organizations mobilizing and directing administrative power towards the coordination and control of the highly specialized and complex activities which automated factory production demands. Organizations become the central social units through and around which the rhythms and patterns of modern urban industrial life are regulated and controlled. They effectively combine the administrative preconditions for continuous technological progress and sustained economic growth with the social and cultural mechanisms necessary for effective moral integration within a collectivized order. They constitute the paramount social technology through which the simultaneous, but conflicting demands, for social differentiation and administrative integration could be met and directed towards the achievement of collective goals dominated by the drive for national economic success within an increasingly competitive international system.

Organizations were 'the grand device for transforming human irrationalities into rational behaviour'.[51] By providing the administrative structures and cultural mechanisms through which individual behaviour could be automatically subjected to disciplined calculation and control, organizations established the technical apparatus and cognitive foundations on which modern social life depended. The continued functioning of advanced industrial societies – whatever their particular political arrangements and cultural traditions – was totally dependent on the diffusion and operation of an organizational technology that controlled and manipulated material, human and symbolic resources on the basis of an instrumental rationality that valued the norm of methodical calculation over all others.[52] This technology would counteract the 'anomic' tendencies which Durkheim identified as the major social problem in modern industrial societies.

Within this cluster or network of bureaucratic organizations on which industrial societies had become dependent for their survival, the centralized state was accorded functional pre-eminence. It was the major agent of technologically led rationalization and it regulated the tensions and conflicts which would unavoidably arise between the various sectional interest groups that struggled for power within a pluralistic industrial order.[53] Thus, the rise of the modern industrial state to a position of institutional dominance and ideological pre-eminence within the organizational infrastructure of industrial societies could be explained in terms of its strategic role in managing social conflict through a process of bureaucratic regulation and containment.

The analysis of the central state as a network of organizations through which the governance of civil society can be realized has attracted particular attention from those who offer a corporatist interpretation of long-term institutional development within industrial societies.

## THE CORPORATE STATE AND CONFLICT REGULATION

During the course of the 1970s[54] a growing body of opinion seemed to indicate that the regulation of social conflict between the major organized producer interest groups within industrial society – that is, employers, managers and workers – by an increasingly interventionist state, heralded a move towards a socio-economic system and political order that was fundamentally different from that prevailing under liberal capitalism.[55] The dominant position of the state within a socio-economic system characterized by functional specialization and hierarchical coordination was reinforced by the need for an administrative mechanism and supporting political ideology which would contain and diffuse the social conflicts that seemed to be threatening the institutional foundations of modern industrial societies.[56] The state itself had matured into a reasonably coherent and integrated network of organizations which provided both the formalized mechanisms and informal processes necessary to achieve a restructuring of the relationships between producer groups so that they operated within the policy guidelines that the former laid down.

The strengthening of the long-term trend towards a more powerful central state that attempted to coordinate and manipulate the interaction between producer groups in the interests of national policy had its institutional and ideological roots in the mobilization of nation-states for war.[57] However, this trend had been accentuated by the repeated failure of the state apparatus in a number of Western industrial societies to deal with the distributional conflicts which bedevilled the latter from the late 1960s onwards.[58] This failure of state-directed coordination and control seemed to be undermining the organizational foundations and ideological coherence of industrial societies as the fragmenting effect of distributional conflict intensified. The problem of effective conflict management was proving to be far more complex (and seemingly intractable) than had been envisaged by the theorists of industrial society who had assumed a degree of ideological consensus over distributional issues and an effective system of conflict regulation that were much easier to define in theory than to achieve in practice:

> What the theorists of industrialism implicity assumed, so far as the Western world was concerned, was that the development of improved techniques of economic management ... and with the growing readiness of governments to apply such techniques, the problem of regulating capitalist, or mixed economies, were essentially solved; and that for the conceivable future, therefore, economic stability and dynamism would be reconciled and guaranteed ... the functional viability of pluralistic industrialism was greatly overestimated through a neglect of the generally damaging effects of interest group activity on the operation of market mechanisms ... significant corporatist tendencies should be regarded primarily as a response to problems of economic management.[59]

As Goldthorpe notes, this response took the form of incorporating organized interest groups into the process of policy formation, with the assumption that they would be prepared to accept responsibility for, and have the capacity to implement, centrally agreed policies. In particular, the emergence of a more interventionist and directive state – through the mobilization of enhanced administrative power by formal and informal means – which took responsibility for the management of the economy, presupposed that sectional interests would be subordinated to the 'general good' – as determined by central government. Both the theory and practice of corporatist governance depended on the coherent and stable organization of the state apparatus and a restructuring of the organizational capacities and ideological predilections of major interest groups. They were the necessary institutional prerequisites for the effective implementation of a policy-making process and a structure of conflict regulation that would deal with the severe economic problems of stagflation and recession which were besetting industrial societies from the late 1960s to the early 1970s onwards.[60]

In this sense, the shift towards corporatist forms of interest intermediation and concentration in the 1970s took the 'organizational revolution' highlighted by the theorists of industrial society a stage further. It strengthened the administrative power and control of the state considerably further than had been envisaged by the latter, to an extent that the line between the state and civil society became virtually impossible to draw. The extension of state control over economic management and conflict regulation was attempted through administrative mechanisms of a covert and indirect kind which radically undermined any remaining belief in open parliamentary government or independent private interest decision-making. As Winkler put it:

Corporatism, therefore, will tend towards indirect, unformalized non-public and covert forms of administration.... The state effectively delegates enforcement ... This is why strategic control can work; private organizations become the administrative agents of the state.... Our contemporary word for this is participation ... Under many other names 'participation' has always been the cunning ruler's form of social control: to make the people believe that they rule themselves ... incrementally, state control of the economy expands and the discretion of private groups correspondingly diminishes.[61]

Under this kind of administrative regime, the state attains a degree of directive control, through covert forms of surveillance and regulation, far in excess of anything that is envisaged within the industrial society thesis. It becomes the major collective actor within a structure of interorganizational networks consisting of all the major producer interest groups in industrial societies. This structure becomes the effective policy-making and implementing mechanism within the political economies of the latter. It entails a degree of external intervention in processes of 'private' or intra-organizational decision-making – over investment, pricing, location, wage claims and bargaining tactics – through a mix of direct and indirect controls that drastically limit the autonomy of constituent members.

The extent to which particular countries were able to achieve the institutional and ideological preconditions necessary for successful implementation of a corporatist regime varied considerably.[62] In addition, these institutional structures had to be supported by a political culture and an ideological tradition that mitigated the worst excesses of distributional conflicts and their prejudicial impact on national economic performance. But corporatism – both a theory of governance and a political practice – was above all else an organizational phenomenon; it required and promoted an enhancement of collective incorporation and administrative power – through a complex infrastructure of informational, supervisory and ideological controls directed by a central state apparatus – far more extensive and sophisticated than anything anticipated by the theorists of industrial society. Organizations become the crucial locations of, and carriers for, collective interest formation and representation[63] within a political economy that is structured around an ideology of national unity. Their interaction is located within a hierarchical system of regulation in which the state delegates responsibility for policy implementation to 'voluntary' interest groups or associations that remain formally independent, while retaining directive control over policy formulation and reserve powers of enforcement through an elaborate infrastructure of surveillance and monitoring devices.

Consequently, the corporatist strategies and structures which were developed in a number of industrial societies in the 1970s could be seen as a response to the economic problems and related political crisis generated by an unfavourable conjuncture between intensified international competition and escalating labour movement demands.[64] The need for stabilized labour costs and continuous increases in productive efficiency came into conflict with a trade union movement which was reluctant to forgo the material advances which they had achieved since the Second World War and equipped with the organizational capacity to resist state intervention in collective bargaining.[65] At the same time, the organizational arrangements necessary to make corporatist strategies of intermediation and incorporation minimally viable – that is, the existence of three national and reasonably coherent organized interest groups consisting of the state, labour and employers – were in place. The increasing directive role assumed by the state, and the evolution of an administrative and control system required to operationalize this role in practice, reinforced the tendency towards policy initiatives and organizational structures which eroded the liberal-democratic foundations of industrial societies even further. Indeed, they seemed to signal the move towards a socio-economic system that pushed the inherent logic of industrialization and technological advance towards a more tightly integrated structure of centrally directed interdependent organized interests even further.

The industrial society thesis of the 1950s and 1960s was giving way to the post-industrial society futurology of the 1970s.

### POST-INDUSTRIAL SOCIETY

The theory of industrial society explained the rise of large-scale bureaucratic organizations to a position of institutional dominance in terms of a technological and economic rationality or logic that imposes a universal set of functional imperatives which have to be met by social structure. All modern and modernizing societies were converging around a common institutional package of 'pluralistic industrialism', driven by the organizational demands that large-scale production imposed on socio-political and administrative structures. The elite ruling groups and pre-industrial cultures of particular societies would exert some directional influence over the trajectories of industrialization which they followed. But the inherent developmental logic of industrialism ultimately determined the socio-political systems that all modern societies would adopt.[66] Social action and values were subordinated to a technologically driven process of institutional transformation in which bureaucratic organizations inevitably became the dominant social units in all areas of socio-economic and political life.

The theory of the corporatist state also accounted for the move towards a more highly organized socio-economic system in terms of an underlying logic or dynamic which imposed itself on social action. But rather than looking to the organizational imperatives imposed by mass production technology and economic rationality for an explanation of long-term institutional change, the theorists of corporatism identified a political logic or dynamic which accounted for the drive towards enhanced central coordination and control. While the theorists of industrial society traced the source of the organizational revolution undergone by all modern societies to technological and economic forces contained in their material base, supporters of the corporatist thesis assigned causal primacy to the political logic underlying the emergence of the central state as the most powerful collective actor within the former. They argued that the dominant position and role of the state in all advanced industrial societies could only be explained in terms of their shared need for a directive agency and administrative apparatus that would provide effective organizational mechanisms of social integration and conflict regulation.[67] The long-term survival of modern societies as coherent political entities and viable economic units was ultimately dependent on these state-initiated and directed mechanisms. Politics, rather than economies or technology, was the overriding integrative and regulative force in all modern societies, and this would increasingly be the case as the organizational revolution which the central state directed became more firmly established. The corporate state was the only political and administrative institution strong enough to contain the centrifugal forces at work in modern industrial societies.

However, during the course of the 1970s another interpretation of the nature and direction of institutional transformation in modern societies emerged that promised to provide a synthesis of both the industrial society and corporate state scenarios – that is, the theory of post-industrial society. The foremost exponent of the latter was the American sociologist Daniel Bell,[68] but a more radical twist to the post-industrial thesis has been provided by Touraine.[69] Bell's analysis is more significant to the extent that it provides a synthesis of selected elements of both industrial society and corporate state perspectives.[70] It reworks these interpretations within an analysis of institutional transformation in modern societies that highlighted the strategic role of organized knowledge and of those groups who produce and use it to control innovation and change.

Bell argues that the organizing principles of all modern

societies can be described in terms of three interrelated components: first, a socio-economic structure that allocates scarce material, human and symbolic resources on the basis of economic efficiency and profit maximization; second, a political system that mobilizes and directs scarce resources according to utilitarian criteria of improving the general standards and quality of living for the mass of the population; and third, a cultural framework that facilitates conditions conducive to individual fulfilment and self-development. Transformations in the technological base and economic structure of all modern societies, he maintains, are pushing in the direction of a post-industrial society in which – in the changed interrelationships between social structure, political order and cultural system – they are generating a qualitatively different form of institutional framework from that envisaged by conventional social science.

Bell suggests that the transition from an industrial to a post-industrial society can be described in terms of five interrelated dimensions: first, the change from a manufacturing to a service-based economy; second, the increasing economic and political dominance of a professional-come-technical class; third, the centrality of theoretical knowledge and knowledge-producing institutions in the policy formulation and implementation process; fourth, a 'future-orientation' on the part of decision-makers and the development of an information-based technology to achieve long-term planning and control; and finally, the creation of a new 'intellectual technology' that will guide and manage socio-economic development.[71]

For Bell, the most important of these developments are the primacy of theoretical knowledge and the pre-eminence of a professional, managerial and technical class that produce and apply their expertise to direct the course and outcome of social change. Thus, post-industrial societies are organized around the generation and application of specialized knowledge geared to the realization of social control and the directing of innovation and change. Theoretical or abstract knowledge becomes more important than experientially based knowledge. It is the strategic intellectual resource that will provide the basis for planned social change and for the emergence of a new elite that will impose the discipline of 'rational action' on political decision-making. The industrial corporation will lose its place as the pre-eminent institution to the university, research institute and other organizations providing the social foundations for the new 'intellectual technology'. The management of 'organized complexity' emerges as the central problem of post-industrial society; that is,

the management of large-scale systems, with large numbers of interacting variables, which have to be co-ordinated to achieve specific goals. . . . The goal of the new intellectual technology is, neither more nor less, to realize a social alchemist's dream – the dream of ordering the mass society.[72]

Bell's model of post-industrial society may be seen as the apogee of the organized society; that is, an analysis which maintains that development of the cognitive capabilities and institutional sophistication of modern society have reached a stage where the rational direction and control of large-scale innovation and change has become a practical goal. The rise of a new 'knowledge elite' with its own organizational apparatus, which replaces the ownership of property and control over political power as the basis for social control, held out the promise of a modern social order that would achieve a degree of conscious planning of and control over, technological change (and therefore a reduction of indeterminacy about the economic future) which was unknown to previous societies.[73]

On one reading, Bell's vision of the post-industrial society envisages a much greater degree of social integration and institutional harmony than had been achieved under a manufacturing-based industrial economy.[74] However, this does not entail the disappearance of all sources of sociopolitical tension within the new post-industrial order. The central clash within the latter revolves around the confrontation between the technological determinism flowing from an organized technocracy and the emergence of a cultural system in which the demands for individual freedom and collective participation in political decision-making receive enhanced legitimacy.[75] These value systems clash because the practice of collective planning and control rests on an ideology of technical expertise that excludes non-expert opinions; the philosophy of direct participation denies expert knowledge any privileged control over decision-making and calls for a dramatic widening of access to the latter process.[76] It is out of these gaps and tensions between the management of organized complexity and the growing demands for participatory politics and individual freedom that social change is likely to emerge in a post-industrial society. The latter may have the organizational equipment and technical capability to manage the conflict between bureaucratized collectivism and market individualism which is unavailable to industrial societies, but this does not entail the eradication of this problem. Indeed, Bell's vision of a post-industrial future seems to incorporate many of the tensions and conflicts inherent in industrial societies, such as declining political legitimacy for democratic government, economic poverty and widespread alienation from existing political institutions.[77] We seem to be back where we started – with the problems that modernization inevitably generates as it spawns an organizational technology which comes to dominate every aspect of economic, political, social and cultural life within the 'brave new world' it has created.

## THE CONDITION OF MODERNITY

Each of the analyses of modernity outlined in the previous section of this chapter gives the central role in directing institutional transformation to the rise and dominance of bureaucratic systems of organization and control as the primary carriers of modernization. They provided the essential mechanisms through which the process of modernization could be achieved and stabilized. Bureaucratic organization of and control over technological rationalization and economic production established the institutional infrastructure through which the effective integration of a highly complex division of labour could be realized. They also established the cognitive style and cultural framework required to diffuse the 'moral anonymity' characteristic of modern consciousness:

In bureaucracy, anonymity is intrinsically defined and morally legitimated as a principle of social relations ... bureaucracy, like technological production, imposes control upon the spontaneous expression of emotional states ... while technological production may be viewed as a basic structuring force of modernity, modern man commonly copes with its impact on his own everyday life via various bureaucracies.[78]

Considered in these terms, bureaucratic organization engenders a dynamic of its own at the level of social action and consciousness which creates a depersonalized symbolic and cultural universe inhabited by an amorphous and anonymous mass of people who have to be organized. It becomes the 'institutional prototype for the emerging rationalized society';[79] that is, a mass society dominated by the drive for ever more effective means for realizing disciplined control over all aspects of modern life. Within this institutional setting, the principles of calculability, predictability and control become embedded in an organizational culture that secures compliance through socialization into collective norms which value individual conformity above all other considerations.[80] Bureaucratic or complex organizations are the primary institutional carriers of a cognitive style and cultural order which demands social homogeneity and individual conformity in public life, allowing – if not encouraging – a much greater degree of hedonistic diversity in the private or domestic sphere.

Yet, the analyses which we have previously reviewed also begin to reveal the underlying contradictions of modernity and the tensions and conflicts that they inevitably generate. A number of social critics have pointed to the 'totalitarian' or 'normalizing' tendencies inherent in the theory and practice of the industrial or post-industrial society, even at a time when it was at the zenith of its academic popularity.[81] The critics argued that the latter produced an apparatus of cultural, political and organizational control that subordinated all human needs and values to the pervasive and insidious demands of technical and bureaucratic necessity. The majority of the population in industrial societies were indoctrinated into a 'one dimensional' thought pattern and a system of technocratic management and control which excluded any debate over the substantive values and morality that 'ought' to inform the process of institution building in a modern democratic society. Instead, technical reason and bureaucratic structures imposed themselves on the policy-making process and largely suppressed alternative values and ideologies which had the potential to challenge the cultural domination of crass materialism and homogenized individualism.

In sharp contrast, other commentators suggested that modern industrial societies were beset by economic and political crises which could not be effectively managed by the technological and organizational apparatus on which the former depended for its survival and legitimacy.[82] This second group argued that the economic prosperity and socio-political stability envisaged by theorists of industrial or post-industrial society was much more precarious and ephemeral than they believed. The growing complexity and power of the highly centralized administrative and political system in all modern societies created as many problems as it solved. This was true to the extent that it stimulated unrealistic expectations about sustained economic growth and political maturity which could not be delivered by an expanding administrative apparatus that was unable to manage itself, much less the diverse and specialized activities taking place in a modern society. The more complex and remote this bureaucratic system of centralized coordination and control became, the more extreme its problems of effective conflict management and cultural legitimation also became; rather than providing a precise instrument of functional organization and control, modern bureaucracy seemed to make the task of efficient and effective decision-making more intractable. Far from operating like perfectly calibrated and maintained machines, large-scale bureaucratic organizations were a battleground for conflicting sectional interests and values in which the 'rationality' of decision-making was severely compromised and the capacity to deliver a better standard of living for everyone substantially weakened. In turn, this produced widespread alienation from the materialistic and individualistic values on which technological production and bureaucratic organization rested:

That this 'rationality – economistic and calculative – embodied in large-scale organization could produce an equal degree of irrationality, as a necessary consequence of its principle of action, was something already seen and feared by Weber. But he considered this to be something the modern world would have to live with. . . . Were he to return today he might not be so sure that the price is worth paying. Internally and externally to the organization, the pile-up of dis-amenities in terms of economic and social costs, environmental destruction, personal frustration, and individual powerlessness and alienation, all seem to suggest that the balance sheet needs to be inspected more critically.[83]

The cumulative impact of these underlying contradictions and tensions seemed to undermine the moral legitimacy and social foundations of modern industrial society. They engendered a series of interrelated economic, political and cultural crises that irreparably damaged the position and status of bureaucratic organizations as the primary carriers and protectors of a technical rationality that would guarantee economic well-being and social integration for the mass of the population.[84] By the late 1970s/early 1980s the technological optimism and determinism which seemed to drive so much of the analysis of modernization in previous decades had been replaced by forms of social analysis highlighting the intellectual exhaustion and moral bankruptcy of the 'organized society'. The 'darker side' of modernism has reasserted itself and set about demythologizing the scientific and ideological pretensions of the modernist project with a vengeance. The modern condition may be a condition of organized rationality, but this had degenerated into an insidious disciplinary technology in which the mundane and everyday world of 'formal institutions becomes part of the grotesque side of life'.[85] The focus of attention switches to the 'disciplinary society' in which the techniques and practices through which human beings subject themselves to the cultural and ideological controls required by modern organizations become the central theme.[86] The shift to an 'internalized' form of discipline, in which the inculcation and acceptance of normal bureaucratic attitudes and routines can lead to large-scale destruction and genocide, replaces economic progress and social integration as the reference points for an analysis of the organized society. Formal organizations are seen to be engaged in the construction and propagation of institutionalized myths that cover their irrational practices and techniques with a veneer of scientific rationality in the hope of maintaining their dominant position within a social order which is still clinging to the fading promise of technological progress.[87]

The critical reaction against the totalizing and normalizing impulse of modernity, with its unbridled celebration of technological progress and organized rationality, was not entirely negative. It identified a number of resistance points and 'counter-culture' movements which seemed to offer some kind of challenge to a naive belief in a scientifically managed utopia where organized rationality reigned supreme.[88] Yet, this critique of the naive optimism and pretentious scientism underlying so much of the modernist project also reflected and confirmed the sustained cultural power and political strength of an ideology that eulogized the economic benefits and social progress which modern technology and industrial bureaucracy had delivered. Modern society was an industrial, technological and scientifically managed system in which the strategic significance of organized knowledge, and that class of specialists which produced and used it to direct long-term social change, was unchallengeable. Modernity constituted a belief system and a way of life that valued the rational pursuit of economic growth, individual opportunity and technological progress above all else; it asserted the moral primacy of materialistic and individualistic values against the humanitarian and communal values extolled by cultural and social movements which rejected the cloying embrace of bureaucracy. Organizations provided the specialized social practices through which the myriad of complex activities required of men and women in modern societies could be assembled to form coherent structures that instilled automatic discipline and obedience. Whatever discontents and frustrations remained, the triumph of modernity and of the organizational structures which made it possible seemed complete. Organizations had emerged as the institutional pillars of modernity and all that the latter entailed in terms of a form of life which regarded collective discipline and control in the economic sphere as a necessary and unavoidable price to pay for enhanced personal freedom in non-work activities.

## CONCLUSION

In this chapter we have reviewed and assessed a number of meta-narratives which attest to the triumph of modernity and the strategic role of bureaucratic organizations in providing the primary institutional carriers of the social structures and cultural orders which are constitutive of modern society. These stories establish the larger intellectual canvas on which the development of the sociology of organizations can be painted in subsequent chapters. They provide the intellectual capital and vision on which different schools of thought in the sociology of organizations would draw for inspiration and direction while pursuing their own theoretical projects.

However, faith in the ultimate triumph of modernity has waned in recent years. Currently, there is much talk of a 'crisis of modernity' in both capitalist and socialist societies; a crisis not only in the belief that rational bureaucratic structures will provide the technical means required for a better standard and quality of life, but also in the commitment to modernization as a process and collective project that all societies ought to follow.[89] Indeed, centralized and hierarchical organizations are now seen as one of the most spectacular failures of modernity; they establish a social technology that has produced many of the most unattractive features of modern life, such as widespread work alienation and bureaucratic amorality.[90]

Yet, it should not be forgotten that declining faith in modernity and an unravelling of foundational beliefs in the inherent goodness and progress of modern science and technology that informs so much of the contemporary debate about complex organizations has to be set in a wider historical context. In so far as modernity was based on 'a belief in linear progress, absolute truths and rational planning of ideal social orders and the standardization of knowledge and production',[91] then it was grounded in an ideology that was positivistic, technocratic and rationalistic. This ideology came to dominate socio-political thought from the latter half of the nineteenth century onwards and exercised a formative influence over the development of organization theory in the twentieth century.[92] Above all else, it imbued formal or complex organizations with an institutionalized rationality that would become the dominant cultural hallmark and social condition of modernity. The diffusion of this institutionalized rationality throughout all modern societies was also interpreted as constituting a dramatic extension of human mastery over, and control of, the natural and social environment which was unheard of in previous historical epochs.

It is to these 'master themes' of rationality and power that we must turn in the following chapter. They provide the intellectual continuity of shared preoccupations and themes that gives the study of organizations a coherence which is often belied by its disputatious character and the fragmentation that this generates.

## REFERENCES

1. Kamenka, E., *Bureaucracy* (Blackwell, Oxford, 1989).
2. Berger, P.L., Berger, B. and Kellner, H., *The Homeless Mind* (Penguin, Harmondsworth, 1974).
3. *ibid.*, pp. 15–51.
4. The current focus on time as a key resource in the process of organizing will be discussed in more detail in Chapter 6.
5. Foucault, M., *Discipline and Punish: The birth of the prison* (Penguin, Harmondsworth, 1979).
6. Hindess, B., 'Rationality and the characterization of modern society' in Whimster, S. and Lash, S. (eds), *Max Weber, Rationality and Modernity* (Allen and Unwin, London, 1987).
7. Luckmann, T., 'On the rationality of institutions in modern life', *Archives Europeans or Sociology*, vol. 26, 1975, pp. 3–15.
8. Quoted in Mayer, J.P., *Max Weber and German Politics* (Faber and Faber, London, 1956), p. 127.
9. Giddens, A., *Social Theory and Modern Sociology* (Polity Press, Cambridge, 1987).
10. For a recent example of this see Donaldson, L., *In Defence of Organization Theory* (Cambridge University Press, Cambridge, 1985).

11. Reed, M., *Redirections in Organizational Analysis* (Tavistock, London, 1985).
12. Gellner, E., *Plough, Sword and Book: The Structure of Human History* (Collins Harvill, London, 1988), p. 234.
13. Giddens, A., *op. cit.* (1987).
14. Giddens, A., *The Nation State and Violence* (Polity Press, Cambridge, 1985).
15. Giddens, A., *op. cit.* (1987), p. 154.
16. Giddens, A., *op. cit.* (1985), p. 174.
17. Blyton, P., Hassard, J., Hill, S. and Starkey, K., *Time, Work and Organization* (Routledge, London, 1989).
18. Thompson, E., 'Time, Work-Discipline and Industrial Capitalism', *Past and Present*, no. 38 (1967), pp. 56–97.
19. Kamenka, E., *op. cit.* (1989), p. 158.
20. Aglietta, M., *A Theory of Capitalist Regulation: The US Experience* (New Left Books, London, 1979).
21. Reed, M., *The Sociology of Management* (Harvester Wheatsheaf, Hemel Hempstead, 1989).
22. Rueschemeyer, D., *Power and the Division of Labour* (Polity Press, Cambridge, 1986).
23. Braverman, H., *Labour and Monopoly Capital* (Monthly Review Press, New York, 1974).
24. Habermas, J., *Legitimation Crisis* (Macmillan, London, 1973); Offe, C., *Disorganized Capitalism* (Polity Press, Cambridge, 1985); Lash, S. and Urry, J., *The End of Organized Capitalism* (Polity Press, Cambridge, 1987).
25. Lash, S. and Urry, J., *op. cit.* (1987), p. 4.
26. Lash and Urry make a point that different societies will 'disorganize' at different rates and through varying institutional forms. However, they all share in a general process of 'disorganization'. This issue is discussed in greater detail in Chapter 6.
27. Scott, J., *Corporations, Classes and Capitalism* (Hutchinson, London, second edition, 1985), p. 180.
28. Littler, C.R., 'The Labour Process Debate' in Knights, D. and Willmott, H., *Labour Process Theory* (Macmillan, London, 1990), pp. 46–94.
29. Thompson, P., *The Nature of Work* (Macmillan, London, 1983).
30. Edwards, P.K., *Conflict at Work* (Blackwell, Oxford, 1986).
31. Reed, M., *op. cit.* (1985).
32. Storey, J., 'The Means of Management Control', *Sociology*, vol. 19, no. 2, 1985, pp. 193–211.
33. Child, J., *Organization: A Guide to Problems and Practice*

(Harper and Row, London, second edition, 1984); Axtell-Ray, C.A., 'Corporate Culture: The Last Frontier of Control', *Journal of Management Studies*, vol. 23, 1986, pp. 287–98.

34. Burawoy, M., *The Politics of Production* (Verso, London, 1985).

35. *ibid.*, pp. 150–1.

36. Aron, R., *Eighteen Lectures on Industrial Society* (Weidenfeld and Nicolson, London, 1968); Dahrendorf, R., *Class and Class Conflict in Industrial Society* (Routledge, London, 1959); Schumpeter, J., *Capitalism, Socialism and Democracy* (Allen and Unwin, London, 1943); Galbraith, J.K., *The New Industrial State* (Hamish Hamilton, London, 1967).

37. Kerr, C., Dunlop, J.T., Harbison, H. and Meyers, C.A., *Industrialism and Industrial Man* (Penguin, Harmondsworth, second edition, 1973).

38. Brown, D. and Harrison, M.J., *A Sociology of Industrialization* (Macmillan, London, 1978).

39. Child, J., *The Business Enterprise in Modern Industrial Society* (Collier-Macmillan, London, 1969).

40. Nichols, T., *Ownership, Control and Ideology* (Allen and Unwin, London, 1969).

41. Goldthorpe, J.H., 'Theories of Industrial Society; Reflections on the Recrudescence of Historicism and the Future of Futurology', *Archives Européennes de Sociologie*, vol. 12, 1971, pp. 263–88.

42. Kerr, C., *et al.*, *op. cit.* (1973).

43. Bell, D., *The End of Ideology* (Free Press, New York, 1960).

44. Scott, J., 'Ownership and Employer Control' in Gallie, D. (ed.), *Employment in Britain* (Blackwell, Oxford, 1989), pp. 437–64.

45. Wilson, T.H., *The American Ideology: Science, Technology and Organization as Modes of Rationality in Advanced Industrial Societies* (Routledge, London, 1977).

46. Scott, J., *op. cit.* (1989).

47. Kerr, C., *et al.*, *op. cit.* (1973), p. 265.

48. Schumpeter, J., *op. cit.* (1943).

49. Faunce, W.A. and Form, W.H., *Comparative Perspectives On Industrial Society* (Little Brown, Boston, 1969).

50. Presthus, R., *The Organizational Society* (Random House, New York, 1962).

51. Wolin, S., *Politics and Vision* (Allen and Unwin, London, 1961), p. 380.

52. Luckmann, T., *op. cit.* (1975).

53. Kerr, C., *et al.*, *op. cit.* (1973).

54. Williamson, P.J., *Corporatism in Perspective: An Introductory Guide to Corporatist Theory* (Sage, London, 1989).

55. Winkler, J.T., 'Corporatism', *Archives Européenes de Sociologie*, vol. 17, 1976.
56. Goldthorpe, J.H., *Order and Conflict in Contemporary Capitalism* (Clarendon Press, Oxford, 1984).
57. Middlemass, K., *Politics in Industrial Society: The Experience of the British System since 1911* (André Deutsch, London, 1979).
58. Crouch, C. and Pizzorne, A. (eds), *The Resurgence of Class Conflict in Western Europe since 1968*, vols I and II (Macmillan, London, 1978).
59. Goldthrope, J.H., *op. cit.* (1984), pp. 317–25.
60. Cox, A., 'Corporatism as Reductionism; Analytical Limits of the Corporatist Thesis', *Government and Opposition*, vol. 16, 1981, pp. 78–95.
61. Winkler, J.T., 'The Corporate Economy: Theory and Administration' in Scase, R. (ed.), *Industrial Society: Class, Cleavage and Control* (Allen and Unwin, London, 1977), pp. 43–58.
62. Cox, A. and O'Sullivan, N., *The Corporate State: Corporatism and the State Tradition in Europe* (Edward Elgar, Aldershot, 1988).
63. Williamson, P.J., *op. cit.* (1989), pp. 92–94.
64. Lash, S. and Urry, J., *op. cit.* (1987), pp. 279–84.
65. Crouch, C., *Class Conflict and the Industrial Relations Crisis* (Heinemann, London, 1977).
66. Goldthorpe, J.H., *op. cit.* (1971).
67. In this respect, sociological versions of corporatist analysis have their theoretical and ideological roots in Durkheim's sociology. However, the actual analysis which they provide is more strongly influenced by Weber's work on bureaucratic power and control. For an elaboration of this point see Eldridge, J.E.T. and Crombie, A., *A Sociology of Organizations* (Allen and Unwin, London, 1974). It is the Weberian character of corporatist analysis which is being highlighted in this chapter.
68. Bell, D., *The Coming of Post-Industrial Society* (Basic Books, New York, 1973).
69. Touraine, A., *The Post-Industrial Society* (Wildwood House, London, 1974).
70. Encels, S., 'The Post-Industrial Society and the Corporate State', *Australian and New Zealand Journal of Sociology*, vol. 15, no. 2, 1979, pp. 37–44.
71. Bell, D., *op. cit.* (1973).
72. *ibid.*, pp. 107–10. For a highly critical assessment of this view

see Ross, G., 'The Second Coming on Daniel Bell' in *The Socialist Register* (Spokesman Books, London, 1974), pp. 331–48.

73. Leggat, T., *The Evolution of Industrial Systems* (Croom Helm, London, 1985).
74. Kumar, K., *Prophecy and Progress: The Sociology of Industrial and Post-Industrial Society* (Allen and Lane, London, 1978), pp. 198–9.
75. Bell, D., *The Cultural Contradictions of Capitalism* (Heinemann, London, 1976).
76. Dickson, D., *Alternative Technology and the Politics of Technical Change* (Fontana, Glasgow, 1974).
77. Leggat, T., *op. cit.* (1985), pp. 22–3.
78. Berger, P.L., Berger, B. and Kellner, H., *op. cit.* (1974), pp. 53–61.
79. Wilson, T.H., *op. cit.* (1977), p. 146.
80. Whyte, W.H., *The Organization Man* (Simon & Schuster, New York, 1956); Presthus, R., *op. cit.* (1962).
81. Ellul, J., *The Technological Society* (Knopf, New York, 1964); Marcuse, H., *One Dimensional Man* (Sphere Books, London, 1968).
82. Habermas, J., *op. cit.* (1973); Kumar, K., *op. cit.* (1978).
83. Kumar, K., *op. cit.* (1978), pp. 176–7).
84. The postmodernist critique of 'mainstream' organizational analysis is examined in greater detail in Chapter 6.
85. Cooper, R. and Burrell, B., 'Modernism, Post-Modernism and Organizational Analysis: An Introduction', *Organization Studies*, vol. 19, no. 1, 1988, pp. 91–112.
86. O'Neill, J., 'The Disciplinary Society; From Weber to Foucault', *British Journal of Sociology*, vol. 37, no. 1, 1986, pp. 42–60.
87. Meyer, J.M. and Rowan, B., 'Institutionalized Organizations: Formal Structure as Myth and Ceremony' *The American Journal of Sociology*, vol. 83, no. 2, 1977, pp. 340–62.
88. Roszack, T., *The Making of the Counter-Culture* (Faber and Faber, London, 1970).
89. Bauman, Z., 'From Pillars to Post', *Marxism Today*, February 1990, pp. 20–5.
90. Jackall, R., *Moral Mazes: The World of Corporate Managers* (Oxford University Press, Oxford, 1988).
91. Harvey. D., *The Condition of Post-Modernity* (Blackwell, Oxford, 1989), p. 9.
92. Wolin, S., *op. cit.* (1961).

# / 2 /

# THEMATIC CONTINUITIES

## INTRODUCTION

In recent accounts of organization theory's intellectual development overriding emphasis has been given to the conflicts and disagreements between competing perspectives; the focus has been on what divides and separates different schools of thought or approaches.[1] Consequently, organization theory's history has been written within a frame of reference which stresses the sharp discontinuities between schools of thought holding radically divergent views as to the nature of organization and the manner in which it should be analyzed.[2] These discontinuities in basic philosophical assumptions, problem focus and conceptual frameworks are seen to generate deep-seated fissures in the intellectual fabric of organization theory. The latter tends to be viewed as a highly fragmented field of study lacking any overarching intellectual coherence or sense of historical direction.[3]

Earlier interpretations of organization theory's history tended to present an evolutionary account of its development in which there is a progressive movement towards a more theoretically advanced and empirically inclusive explanatory framework.[4] Underlying conflicts and disagreements are overcome through a higher-level synthesis of competing approaches. This synthesis establishes a shared conceptual vocabulary and a set of universal cognitive principles and procedures that makes the routine production and evaluation of general theoretical explanations possible.[5] Thus, the process of intellectual development in organization theory was characterized as a linear progression towards a 'general theory of organizations' that would explain a much wider range of empirical phenomena in a more economical and simplified way than any preceding theory.[6]

However, this evolutionary or progressive interpretation is no longer fashionable. Instead, the appropriate image or metaphor for understanding organization theory's history seems to be a veritable 'tower of babel' in which a cacophony of voices squabble over what remains of its shared intellectual inheritance. Rather than celebrate ineluctable progress towards a logically coherent and analytically powerful general theory, contemporary interpretations suggest that the grand narrative of scientific progress is in a state of terminal decay.[7] The only certainty is the uncertainty and ambiguity inherent within a disputatious field of study occupied by warring camps of 'paradigms warriors' intent on emasculating, if not destroying, the accumulated intellectual resources and powers of the opposing factions. Controversy, confusion and crisis now become the ineradicable hallmarks of a field of study that has lost any residual belief in its existence and status as a unified scientific discipline. In place of a narrative account of organization theory's history founded on the belief in an irreversible trend towards a general theory which would reveal more and more about the 'objective truth' of organizations, we are offered a vision of competing discourses or language games that vie for our attention. The capacity to mobilize and deploy intellectual resources in a struggle for cultural power and hegemony – rather than rational argument and logical coherence – becomes the essential prerequisite for gaining acceptance and support within the scientific community and wider society.[8]

Yet, there may be another way of looking at organization theory's intellectual history that offers an alternative viewpoint to the grand narrative of scientific progress promulgated by positivism or the series of ultimately indecisive and destructive cultural conflicts highlighted by relativism. Both of these viewpoints lack any sense of organization theory's intellectual history and the recurring themes through which it is structured. Positivism focuses on the 'technical' questions and problems which seem to dominate organization theory's development; that is, the problem of designing organization structures which will maximize operational efficiency and effectiveness.[9] Relativism on the other hand, dissolves history into a babble of squabbling factions which speak different languages and are unable to communicate with each other, much less share any sense of genuine intellectual continuity and community.[10] Neither of these interpretations is equipped to recover and retrieve the deep-seated and recurring themes which serve to frame the preoccupations that have given organization theory a sense of intellectual direction and historical coherence.[11]

The latter can only be achieved if we situate debate and controversy within the wider dialogue or conversation which has unfolded through the development of a continuously evolving grammar and vocabulary of concepts that signify and symbolize a continuity of preoccupations.[12] Organization theory does possess a coherent intellectual history. However, it can only be understood and appreciated if the underlying 'problematics' or 'master themes' that have shaped and guided its development are surfaced. This is the objective of this chapter; that is, to identify and elaborate the overarching concerns which have structured the intellectual development of organization theory since the latter half of the nineteenth century. An exposition of the analytical narratives which have been woven around these general themes will provide a more informed appreciation of the wider intellectual context in which the debate over the organizational preconditions and consequences of modernity, reviewed in the previous chapter, needs to be contextualized. It will also provide a broader canvas on which the specific theoretical perspectives and research programmes outlined in the following chapters can be discussed and assessed.

The general themes outlined in this chapter have exerted a governing influence on the intellectual development of organization theory and possess a number of characteristics: first, they have attained sufficient generality to be reflected in the works of a wide range of contributors; second, they exhibit a sufficient degree of continuity to be regarded as recurring concerns in organization theory's past and present phases of development: third, they are distinctive in the sense that they exert a lasting impact on the field's evolution as an identifiable area of intellectual endeavour; and finally, they constitute frameworks or perspectives within which vision and fact unite to form coherent analytical narratives accounting for the nature and significance of organizational phenomena.[13] In short, the themes outlined in this chapter provide rudimentary intellectual structures through which the analytical and moral preoccupations of organizational theorists coalesce to form 'a field of phenomena which yields problems for investigation'.[14]

Four themes will be discussed; rationality, alienation, anomie and power. An initial specification of each theme will be followed by an exposition of the manner in which it has been carried through by subsequent analysis, and the way in which it continues to inform current controversy about the nature and significance of complex organizations in modern society. Taken together, the themes provide a set of interrelated focal points for enduring debates in the historical development of organizational analysis as a field of study and as an intellectual practice.

## RATIONALITY

The status of complex organizations as exemplars of the drive to diffuse formal or instrumental rationality as the dominant cognitive principle on which the institutional development of modern industrial society was to be founded has been explored in the previous chapter. However, the historical significance of this theme for the long-term intellectual growth of organization theory and its contemporary relevance still needs to be established.

Weber's analysis of the process of rationalization in Western industrial societies must be given pride of place in highlighting the interrelated material and cultural transformations that implanted formal or instrumental rationality as a regulative principle in the development of social systems.[15] This principle entailed a number of linked components in a complex process of socio-cultural change that integrated the application of rational decision-making procedures with economic and technical progress. Above all else, the diffusion of formal rationality into all spheres of modern life imposed a decision-making calculus which required that the choice between alternative means to the attainment of given ends was made on the basis of rules permitting precise and deliberate assessment of consequences.[16] Bureaucratic organization – in economic, political and administrative life – was the most pervasive institutional expression of formal or instrumental rationality; it established an objective decision-making mechanism, based on impersonal rules and specialist knowledge, which excluded all subjective, moral or similarly irrational considerations:

The fully developed bureaucratic apparatus compares with other organizations exactly as does the machine with the non-mechanical modes of production. Precision, speed, unambiguity, continuity, unity, strict subordination, reduction of friction and of material and personal cost – these are raised to the optimum point in the strictly bureaucratic administration.[17]

The belief that bureaucratic organization was based on the categories of instrumental rationality which imposed itself in an impersonal and objective way on the individual behaviour and collective action of its members and clients exerted a very powerful influence on the historical development of organization theory.[18] As Wolin argues, this belief was the conceptual loadstone within a larger movement in social thought which become intellectually dominant from the second half of the nineteenth century onwards. This movement promulgated the doctrine

that there exist discoverable 'laws' governing social phenomena; that the operation of these laws was 'necessary' in the sense that to resist them was to invite social calamities; and consequently, these laws carried presumptive injunctions to which men ought to conform – all these added up to a view of society which left no room either for politics and the practice or political art, or for a distinctively political theory.[19]

The above view legitimated the demand for a science of organization which would discover and codify the logical principles on which the development and management of large-scale complex organizations must be founded.[20] This quest for an abstract and universalizable body of knowledge concerning the underlying principles governing the functioning and design of formal organizations became the overarching theme in organization theory's evolution as a distinctive field of study well into the twentieth century.[21] By identifying and codifying the rational principles embodied in the hierarchical structures and differentiated decision-making processes of all formal organizations, organization theory would provide the technical expertise required to manage 'the machine' more effectively.[22] It would also facilitate the creation and implementation of specific practices or techniques – such as cost accounting, budgeting, job design and personnel selection – through which recalcitrant and wasteful human beings could be transformed into governable and efficient organizational members.[23]

Thus, the instrumental rationality inherent in the generic structures and practices of complex organizations seemed to signify the emergence of a form of social organization based on cognitive recipes and design principles which successfully excluded all emotional, moral and ideological 'distortions' from the decision-making process. The triumph of bureaucracy signalled the overwhelming cognitive power and technical superiority of an inner organizational logic and mechanism which eradicated the ineluctable conflict between fundamental values and beliefs that had been the hallmark of traditional societies.[24] Organization theory became the discipline through which this 'inner logic' could be revealed and conveyed to a sympathetic, if uniformed, audience. This emerging discipline projected an image of organization as a social unit possessing 'its own distinctive logic and motivation towards the attainment of some organizational goal'.[25] It treated the concept of organization as an analytically distinct social unit oriented to the achievement of predetermined objectives through the application of rational decision-making rules and the technical knowledge on which their systematic functioning depended. The organization was defined as a deliberately constructed instrument or tool for attaining goals that are defined or given in advance.[26] Precise and systematic analysis of the organizational apparatus through which predetermined objectives were to be achieved would provide professional managers and administrators with the knowledge base from which they could realize effective control over complex operations.[27] In this way, organizational analysis would unite theory and practice in a body of knowledge and techniques founded on the powerful cultural legitimacy that scientific rationality provided.

Yet, the limitations and inadequacies – not to say inherent contradictions – of this approach have been recognized. From the 1950s onwards there has been a growing body of empirical research and successive waves of theoretical reformulation which attest to the paradoxical nature of the rational model of organization. Nevertheless, the intellectual shadow of the rational or goal paradigm hangs long over more recent debates and developments.

Weber's analysis of bureaucracy as the organizational epitome of formal rationality has been criticized on a number of counts.[28] In particular, he has been accused of providing an account of bureaucratic rationalization, based on a logic of cultural determinism, that produces an excessively formalistic and mechanistic model of bureaucratic organization.[29] Recent empirical research on the actual functioning of bureaucratic organizations suggests that the realities of organizational behaviour deviate substantially and consistently from the formal principles and procedures of instrumental rationality.[30] As a result, bureaucratic organization loses its machine-like character and is now seen as a social unit in which subjectivity, emotions, ideology and conflict play a central role in shaping the 'objective' structures through which formal rationality is instantiated in social practice.[31] Indeed, the neutral or objective character of the formal rationality which is presumed to inhere in organizational structures has now been transformed into a cultural or ideological resource that is mobilized by various interest groups in their struggle for power with opposing factions.[32] Far from constituting a rational instrument or tool for the achievement of generally accepted objectives, bureaucratic organization is now redefined as a power resource for the attainment of conflicting sectional interests and values.[33]

Simultaneously with the above development, there has been a long retreat from the belief that organizational structures can be viewed as the outcomes of a decision-making process which rationally aligns internal arrangements with external conditions.[34] The origins of this move away from 'strong' versions of organizational rationality lay in the work of writers such as Simon,[35] Cyert and March,[36] and Lindblom.[37] Taken together, the contributions of these writers indicated that the actual practice of organizational decision-making diverged sharply from that envisaged in the model of formal or instrumental rationality. Rather than a logical and systematic selection between alternative courses of action based on an informed and calculated assessment of potential consequences, the practice of organizational decision-making was limited or bounded in various ways by imperfect informational inputs, partial technical knowledge and constrained cognitive capacities. More than this, the very fabric of the decision-making process – from the initial formulation of 'agendas' to the making of final choices – was pervaded by political and ideological considerations that determined both the course and outcome of collective deliberations.[38] Divergent, and usually conflicting, rationalities are at work in the process of organizational decision-making and they are intimately related to distributions of power and authority. Coherent and sustainable organized action in turbulent and uncertain environmental conditions seems to call for strong ideologies and cultures that are patently 'irrational' in terms of the formalized decision-making calculus prescribed by theories of instrumental rationality.[39] Not only is the concept of 'organized rationality' transformed from a universal principle into a cultural variable, but it is also subordinated to a political logic of action rationality driven by ideologically-mediated interests and substantive moral values.

As such, the foundational assumption that formal organization structures and decision-making processes are necessarily designed with operational efficiency and long-term goal achievement as their dominant priorities dissolves into a plethora of subjective interpretations and political evaluations.[40] 'Rationality' becomes a symbol or icon to be mobilized or projected as a critical resource in the continuing struggle to legitimate certain sectional interests and values as the only proper basis for organized action and to deny that crucial aura of legitimacy to opposing ideologies.[41] Its status as a universal principle of collective action now becomes metamorphozed into a cultural and ideological gloss on sectional interests which are masquerading as the 'general good'.

Yet, however radical these more recent departures from the conventionally accepted theory of instrumental rationality may be, they are still formulated and promulgated within a narrative which is focused on 'organized rationality' in all its different forms and permutations. They are contextualized within a problematic or tradition which speaks to the limits of organized rationality as a, perhaps the, cognitive and cultural core of modern society. They take on meaning and significance within a view of organized rationality – however badly distorted and compromised in real life – as the axial or guiding principle of social action and organization in Western industrialized societies. Their reference point is still the functioning of organized rationality as the regulative cognitive principle and dominant integrative institutional practice of societies which have developed an advanced division of labour and a technological base that makes sustained economic growth achievable. Conceptual reformulation and theoretical innovation within an accepted frame of reference that has structured debate over certain preoccupations and predicaments during a long period of intellectual maturation are the defining features of this process.

However, the division of labour and bureaucratic organizations – in all their diverse forms – not only play a regulative and integrative function; they also fragment and divide humanity.[42] They separate 'workers' from ownership of, and control over, the means of production, distribution and exchange. Inevitably, they impose a set of organizational control systems and norms based on specialization and hierarchy which entail compliance with, if not commitment to, the coercively perceived demands and constraints of large-scale production. In this context, the concept of organized rationality begins to look more like a 'ruling illusion'[43] or an official philosophy that mystifies and obscures the realities and distortions of governing institutions based on exploitation and subjugation. It is at this point that the theme of alienation enters the story.

## ALIENATION

If the dominant theme or unifying concept in the history of organization theory is rationality, then the more pessimistic, not to say darker, sub-plot within which the onward march of rationalization has been narrated can be captured in the notion of alienation. Weber's ambivalence towards rationalization is clearly evident in his vision of a deep-seated and widespread alienation in modern societies that emanates from an inversion of rationalism. Having emasculated, if not totally destroyed, all traditional, religious and communal values, organized rationality becomes an end in itself – unable to provide any moral spiritual or ethical foundations for social action. All that remains is a monolithic, secular and utilitarian bureaucracy that legitimates social action on the basis of a rule-bound formalism, open to repeated exploitation by various sectional power groups bent on enhancing their narrow economic and political interests:

It is not disorganization any more than it is catastrophe that Weber fears, but, rather, over-organization; a future sterilized of the informal and the use-and-wont contexts within which personality takes on the stuff of resistance to mass-mindedness and cultural uniformity. The rationalization that made democracy and capitalism triumph over the social systems which preceded them will, if not freshly inspired, bring about a society in which democracy and capitalism themselves will not survive, in which only caricatures of these systems will exist, with man converted from his modern Faustian character to a demon-ridden creature of apathy and fear.[44]

In this way, Weber is giving vent to his vision of a future society in which bureaucracy overwhelms individuals – whether they are workers, managers, clients or customers – and leaves them helpless in the face of the mechanistic control systems and amoral cultural orders in which they are trapped. The diffusion of bureaucratic norms and structures throughout modern industrial societies encourages the spread of a cultural uniformity and passivity in which isolated individuals are powerless to exert any influence, much less control, over an organizational apparatus that excludes any serious consideration of the moral values which ought to inform behaviour. In place of morality, custom or tradition, modern organizations offer a soulless utilitarianism which raises the norms of productive efficiency and operational effectiveness to overriding status. These seem to gel with a highly individualistic and hedonistic culture in which material self-interest and social well-being are assumed to be synonymous. A sense of individual identity and purpose in life becomes entirely dependent on organizational membership and the economic, cultural and social rewards that it provides. But that membership is itself experienced as a meaningless process in which the struggle for individual survival, in a hostile and threatening environment, demands calculated engagement in forms of action that negate any expression of honest human feelings and values.[45] Nowhere is this more clearly reflected than in the bureaucratic power struggles in which managers are routinely required to engage – conflicts in which cynical manipulation of structures, practices and appearances to protect and/or enhance one's position within the organization's power structure is the key to survival and success:

For most managers, especially for those who are ambitious, the real meaning of work – the basis of social identity and valued self-image – becomes keeping one's eye on the main chance, maintaining and furthering one's own position and career. This task requires, of course, unrelenting attentiveness to the social intricacies of one's organization. One gains dominance or fails depending on one's access to key managerial circles where prestige is gauged precisely by the relationships that one establishes with powerful managers and by the demonstrated favour such relationships bring. . . . But self-rationalization, even for those willing to open themselves up fully to institutional demands, produces its own discomforts and discontents. . . . managerial work requires . . . a willingness to discipline the self, to thwart one's impulses, to stifle spontaneity in favour of control, to conceal emotion and intent, and to objectify the self with the same kind of calculating functional rationality that one brings to the packaging of any commodity.[46]

Whereas Marx characterized and explained alienated labour in terms of the exploitative imperatives embedded within the division of labour under capitalism,[47] organizational analysis has tended to follow Weber and extend the concept to account for the lack of meaning and control engendered by rational bureaucracy, irrespective of property relations:

> In Weber's thesis, any form of organization which has a hierarchy of authority can become subject to a process of 'expropriation': for the Marxian notion of the 'means of production' Weber substitutes the 'means of administration'. Oversimplifying somewhat, it might be said that Weber gives to the organization of relationships of domination and subordination the prominence which Marx attributes to relationships of production.... in Weber's eyes the progression of bureaucratization increasingly reveals a tension between the demand for technical efficiency of administration on the one hand, and the human values of spontaneity and autonomy on the other.[48]

From the 1950s onwards, a voluminous body of theorizing and empirical research in organizational analysis set out to identify the social psychological syndrome associated with the alienating effects of bureaucratic organization and related factors such as assembly-line technology.[49] The cumulative impact of this literature was to transform the concept of alienation from a moral and political critique of the authoritarian and amoral power structures prevailing under rational bureaucracy into a temporary psychological condition that found behavioural expression in high levels of job dissatisfaction and poor work performance. Consequently, alienation was treated as a 'feeling of disappointment with career and professional development, as well as disappointment over the inability to fulfil professional norms. Alienation from expressive relations reflects dissatisfaction in social relations with supervisors and fellow workers.[50] Its source lay in the highly centralized and specialized organization structures prevailing under rational bureaucracy; these reduce job discretion to a minimum and generate strong feelings of powerlessness and meaningless amongst workers. The latter become diffused throughout the organization, effecting white-collar, professional and managerial employees as much as blue-collar, shopfloor workers. Various programmes of organizational reform were suggested through which the inherently alienating propensities of hierarchical structures and specialized divisions of labour could be counteracted and eventually overcome by more flexible and participative decision-making processes in relation to job design and authority systems.[51]

The overall thrust of this literature was to produce a neutralized, indeed depoliticized, reading of alienation and its explanatory significance for organizational analysis. The critical intent and polemical edge of Weber's original analysis is sublimated, and eventually submerged, within a technocratic ideology and positivistic research apparatus that purposively neglects the structural sources of worker discontent in favour of a psychologistic interpretation of the concept's meaning and implications. Far from providing critical insight into the demoralizing and degrading effects of bureaucratic domination and control, the concept of alienation is transformed into a social–psychological contingency that can be contained and managed through more sensitive organizational engineering. A more balanced relationship between organizational demands and individual needs through more socially skilled and sensitive managerial interventions would remove the scourge of alienation from modern organizational life.

However, alienation also provided a crucial ideological and theoretical reference point for another tradition or school of thought within organization theory which attacked bureaucracy much more directly. These writers focused upon the bureaucratic structures of organized societies and traced their alienating consequences to the logic of institutional development on which the process of rationalization was based.[52] Thus, writers such as Illich,[53] Reich,[54] and Rozak[55] argued that the instrumental or functional rationality imposed by bureaucratic organizations is a negative and destructive force which mystifies and distorts real human needs, such as the desire for communal association and convivial working practices:

The institutions of modern society (whether capitalist or communist) are no longer harnessed to the social improvement of the individual and the community. Rather the opposite has occurred: the organization is transcendent. Societies are vulnerable to a process of institutional overgrowth. Ultimately, morality and life itself may be destroyed by developments in organizations originally intended to foster their improvement. Technically rational, organizations are substantively irrational. . . . Alienation will be heightened in such a society. The individual will not merely be alienated in terms of his organizational experience – he will be made use of as a recipient of professional 'treatments' over which he will have no control.[56]

The only way in which alienation can be combated and eventually overcome is by reversing the logic of institutional development within modern industrial societies which is uncontrollably pushing in the direction of increased bureaucratic centralization and enhanced technological rationalization. An alternative conception of rationality must be found to provide the cognitive equipment and ideological vision of a 'counter-cultural' movement which rejects the 'taken-for-granted' assumption that unrestrained economic expansion, technological rationalization and bureaucratic centralization will necessarily lead towards the 'good society'. This alternative is likely to be grounded in a set of values expounding the virtues of smaller-scale and simpler forms of life. The latter, it is argued, will provide a supportive organizational context in which the rigidities and constraints of bureaucratic hierarchies and specialized divisions of labour are superceded by more natural, flexible or 'organic' systems of organization.[57]

Whatever the theoretical limitations and practical inadequacies of this anti-bureaucratic tradition within organization theory, it reveals the continued intellectual and ideological significance of concepts such as alienation. The latter cannot be purged of its critical and evaluative connotations. It continues to provide a common reference point through which shared concerns about the condition, character and direction of modern industrial society can be brought together to form a coherent dialogue stretching over time, place and context. This dialogue evolves an analytical focus and a narrative structure which convey a shared sense of intellectual history and moral concern.

As Lukes maintains, a continuing interest in the nature, causes and consequences of alienation can only be sustained if moral vision and social analysis (carried out at different levels of conceptual abstraction) are bonded together to form coherent, if contestable, conceptions of modern industrial societies and their trajectories of institutional development.[58] These conceptions involve a potent intellectual view of competing doctrines about human nature and empirical hypotheses concerning the social conditions in which innate human potential has the best chance of being fulfilled. The reformist wing of organization theory looks to improved organizational climate and enhanced structural flexibility for effective antidotes to the corrosive impact of work alienation on the quality of life. The radical wing advocate a fundamental restructuring of organizational life and the materialist ideology on which it rests. Both rely on a mixture of moral philosophy and empirical knowledge to legitimate their preferred solutions. While the latter may be poles apart, they draw on a shared intellectual and cultural capital to give their diagnoses and prognoses coherence and direction.

Alienation clearly conjures up images of a social condition in which organizational existence is characterized by an overwhelming sense of powerlessness to influence, much less manage, the bureaucratic mechanisms through which individual performance is co-ordinated and monitored. At the same time, this vision seems to resonate with a view of long-term institutional development in industrial society as necessarily entailing social disintegration, moral decay and general demoralization.

ANOMIE

If the concept of alienation evokes a vision of organized societies as dominated by oppressive bureaucratic structures that entrap individuals within dehumanized and amoral systems of control, the notion of anomie suggest that disorganization, rather than over-organization, is what we most have to fear. Rather than posit an organizational future in which socio-economic and political life is excessively regulated by bureaucratic rule, the concept of anomie projects a scenario in which uncontrolled competition, intense class conflict and mindless, degrading work produces a breakdown of normative order. As a result, social anarchy ensues. The latter is seen to be brought about by the speed and scale of economic and technological change outpacing the development and maturation of social institutions that would contain and regulate the disruptive upheavals and divisive conflicts which the former unavoidably generate.

As Durkheim[59] saw the situation, industrial societies had so far failed to develop appropriate intermediate groups and institutions which would counteract the anomie tendencies inherent within their logic of institutional growth and development. The latter seemed to be inexorably leading in the direction of intensified competition, rancorous distributional conflicts and unregulated ideological struggle. Technological progress, and the relative material cornucopia which it had made available, had not been matched by the widespread diffusion and acceptance of normative controls that would instil discipline in an increasingly avaricious, competitive, materialistic and individualistic society. Indeed, industrial society had swept away all the social and ethical restraints embedded in traditional social structures, but had put nothing substantial in its place to regulate the egotistical behaviour encouraged – even required in the competitive struggle for individual survival – by a culture and economic system that valued material success above all other considerations.

Durkheim was reasonably confident that this state of 'anomie' – in which moral regulation and social control in industrial societies was at best limited and at worst non-existent – was a temporary phenomenon. The development of a more mature and proactive centralized state that effectively managed interest-group conflict, combined with the proliferation and strengthening of intermediate occupational and professional strata which integrated isolated individuals into a wider social network, would together provide the social interdependence so desperately lacking in industrial societies:

European industrial societies are then portrayed by Durkheim as being in a state of moral crisis. What is required is an institutional order which would provide a new basis of social cohesion, and hence the framework in which individuals would be bound by ties of interests, ideas and feelings. . . . In this new system of regulation, he envisages employers and employees represented on the governing body (and possibly elected separately given the conflicts of interests between them on many questions), and concerned with such matters as wages, details of the labour contract, working conditions, and the regulation of industrial disputes. . . . The social consequences of rapid industrial change posed both a threat and a possibility. The threat was the total breakdown of industrial civilization. The possibility was that men might, by taking thought, reconstruct the social order. For Durkheim, this demanded not the imposition of a Leviathan but the encouragement of all tendencies which promoted organic solidarity.[60]

However, modern organization theory has been far less sanguine about the capacity of state-led and professionally supported social reconstruction to combat the anomic tendencies of advanced industrial societies. Rather than look to external social and political agencies – such as the state or occupational associations – as a basis for social integration, organization theorists have focused on the employing organization and its management as the strategic locale and agency for combating moral disorder and institutional fragmentation.

An extremely influential school of thought in organizational analysis has consistently maintained that modern bureaucratic organizations – if left to their own devices – are destructive of moral regulation and social integration. The central structural features of modern organization – hierarchy, specialization, rationalization and atomization – necessarily produce an organizational setting and climate in which individuals are unable to achieve any meaningful sense of belonging or association. The imposition of formal or instrumental rationality imposes a dominant set of social values and norms that excludes any consideration of moral, spiritual or communal needs. Impersonality, objectivity, control and calculation become the strategic organizing principles on which modern organizations are constructed and managed. This destroys any remaining internalized residues of 'pre-modern' patterns of associates – such as the craft guild, the village commune or the family-based work unit – and the communal and cooperative norms that they entailed. In short, modern organization involves the unqualified imposition of a form of rationality and type of social structure that destroys the 'traditional' norms and practices which previously provided the framework for social integration and moral regulation.[61]

The destruction of social cooperation wrought by the organizational principles and structures inherent in modern industrial production had not been counteracted by the political and managerial elites which exercised effective power in this 'brave new world':

It was argued that industrialism and urbanism were destroying the small, close-knit, traditional communities within which every man had an acknowledged place and function . . . social needs were being ignored in modern work organizations. Management, in failing to direct planned effort towards the creation of the right social conditions of work, was denying employees all sense of identity, of belonging, and of participation in a group or community purpose. . . . Management itself must meet these social needs in a consciously organized manner and recruit group affiliations for its own ends. . . . Properly and imaginatively interpreted and applied, such a strategy could, it was felt, construct for the atomized and isolated individuals of industrial society a social context at the workplace within which they could reknit the social bonds they needed and live satisfying lives.[62]

A strategy of managerially led and controlled reform of work organization so that it established the normative context and social conditions through which anomie could be effectively counteracted was only viable if a number of theoretical assumptions were borne out in practice. First, that modern corporate management had both the will and the way to carry such a programme of organizational reform through to successful completion. Second, that a great many of the disagreements and conflicts that characterized modern industrial life were largely the expression of defective organizational practices, rather than endemic to the social, economic and political structures of corporate capitalism. Third, that the wider institutional context in which work organizations were embedded could be ignored in favour of a reform strategy that exclusively concentrated on the 'internal' rationalities, norms and systems which produced social fragmentation and normative deregulation. The acceptance of these assumptions legitimated a reform strategy which could safely ignore political action directed at the democratization of decision-making structures – in particular, centralized state power – in the wider society.[63] Instead, social action could be understood and managed in terms of 'the efforts of men to find in large-scale organizations the values of status and security which were formerly gained in the primary associations of family, neighbourhood and church'.[64]

This set of assumptions constituted an emerging managerial ideology directing a programme of applied research on organizational behaviour which continued over a period for several decades and still continues to shape significant trends in organizational analysis to the present day.[65] As Bendix[66] has argued, the ideology was collectivist in so far as it entailed the deliberate manipulation of norms and values associated with group membership and teamwork in order to incorporate a mass of previously unorganized and isolated workers within a coherent corporate 'personality'. The research programme was driven by the imperative to discover a viable and coherent package of organizational practices and techniques that would dramatically extend and buttress the moral basis of compliance within modern organizations. Obedience in the modern workplace would become progressively less dependent on external coercive control and more reliant on internalized attitudes and norms. The latter would be congruent with the interests of management in achieving effective control over an increasingly complex and recalcitrant industrial system. The modern industrial corporation would be transformed into a 'cooperative enterprise' in which politically enlightened and socially skilled managers would propagate robust collective moral codes for socializing workers and integrating them into a larger social unit.[67]

At the same time, the key figures carrying forward this research programme envisaged a series of interrelated organizational changes which would revivify decaying managerial authority within the wider society and combat the disintegrative forces undermining social cohesion. These changes took a number of different forms and were directed at a wide range of organizational problems: the redesign of jobs to make them more satisfying and motivating; the restructuring of decision-making processes at the point of production to encourage more widespread participation and involvement; the reskilling of managerial leadership and supervision within the workplace so that it was more sensitive to the social and emotional needs of employees. Their overall objective was to revitalize managerial authority within the work organization and, by extension, within industrial society, by 'capturing the enormous power of social groups and tethering them to the organization's norms and attitudes so that their power of enforcement over their members' action becomes almost absolute and unchallengeable'.[68] In this fashion, the concept of anomie established a common reference point through which organization theorists of the 1930s or of the 1960s could justify their endeavours in terms of a theoretical project and a practical concern which resonated with the problem of maintaining social order in an industrial society bedevilled by the destabilizing consequences of unplanned economic expansion and technological progress.

This abiding concern with the organizational sources of moral regulation and social integration within the rapidly changing and increasingly differentiated structures of modern industrial societies continues in contemporary debates over corporate cultures. The humanization of work has been replaced by the management of organizational culture as providing the most promising avenue for realizing more effective means of control within present-day work organizations:

the latest strategy of control implies that top management teams aim to have individuals possess direct ties to the values and goals of the dominant elites in order to activate the emotion and sentiment which might lead to devotion, loyalty and commitment to the company. . . . Resting within the concept of corporate culture is the notion of shared values and a heightened sense of collectivity; it implies commitment to the firm rather than to career or leisure activities.[69]

In this respect, the problem of corporate governance in conditions that unavoidably corrode and threaten the foundations of social and moral order within modern organizations continues to evoke a strong response within the organizational studies community. The dynamic of economic and technological change in Western industrialized societies seems to press in the direction of greater individualism and the fragmenting consequences that flow from a more competitive and privatized socio-economic system. Yet, at the same time, national or company-level economic success and social cohesion seem to be increasingly dependent on collective values and structures that tie the individual into a larger social enterprise which meaningfully integrates personal needs with organizational demands. The search for a form of organizational governance – in society and in the business firm – which will align prevailing cultural values, social expectations and personal ambitions is as strong in the 1980s as it was in the 1930s.[70] The problem of maintaining workable mechanisms of organizational integration and control in the face of rapid change is as acute in the closing decades of the twentieth century as it was when the decade opened.

The conceptual idiom through which these concerns are expressed may have changed, but the underlying problem of implanting 'strong' organizational cultures and 'participative' structures that will bind members into a social collectivity based on highly individualistic and utilitarian values remains the same. In the 1930s and 1940s the crisis of modern organizations was characterized in terms of the fragmenting and disintegrating effects of large-scale industrialization. The latter was deemed to have unleashed an unquenchable thirst for continual economic expansion that demanded a degree of socio-technical specialization and routinization within the work organization which was incompatible with moral involvement and social integration. The psychological and social needs of workers were being ignored by a philosophy and practice of industrial organization that imposed mechanistic structures and impersonal routines on a disoriented and demoralized population.

The response which the organization theorists of those times advocated was planned intervention on the part of an enlightened managerial elite possessing the socio-psychological expertise required to manipulate informal relationships in such a way that 'spontaneous' cooperation was built into the organization's social fabric.[71] By the 1960s, the focus of attention had moved on to the need for a rolling programme of organizational reform in leadership styles, job designs, group dynamics and personnel practices that would elicit much higher levels of commitment and involvement from the great mass of industrial workers.[72] In the 1980s the emphasis had shifted to a strategy of inducing subordinate cooperation by means of the control and management of collective beliefs and values which will produce genuine moral engagement with the organization.[73] The perceived failure of what Anthony calls 'the primary apparatus of control' in work organizations – rational bureaucracy and advanced technology – to elicit significant levels of normative commitment on the part of ordinary employees has led to a burgeoning interest in 'culture' as a resource or instrument which can be manipulated by managers to achieve genuine involvement.[74] This is directly linked to a repeated failure on the part of American and British management to realize the high levels of economic performance and organizational integration achieved by managers in south-east Asian countries such as Japan and South Korea.[75] The search for organizational cultures and practices which will effectively integrate the rank-and-file worker into the larger collectivity is driven as much by the need to discover forms of organization that guarantee economic success in an increasingly competitive world economy as it is by more altruistic motives.

The difficulties encountered in practising forms of sociopsychological engineering within modern organizations which will counteract the disintegrative and demoralizing effects that the latter inevitably generate has been a powerful theme in the history of organization theory. It resonates with broader cultural values – often, but not necessarily, of a conservative kind – and traditions that are profoundly sceptical, if not downright suspicious, of the supposed benefits that industrialization brings. Disorganization, moral turpitude and cultural breakdown, rather than technological progress and economic advance, are highlighted as the 'poisoned fruits' which massive industrialization and large-scale bureaucratization produce. Within this frame of reference, modern organizations are as much part of the underlying problem as they are of a potential solution.

While those writers who have directed their attention to the problem of anomie in an organized society have developed one of the most evocative themes in socio-political thought, their work also betrays a consistent blindness to the institutionalized structures of domination and control in which that problem must be located. In short, they have paid little or no attention to the intimate relationship between the problem of order and the realities of power in organized societies. For the most part, the tradition reviewed in this section tends to regard social conflict and power struggles as symptoms of the organizational abnormalities and pathologies produced by unplanned economic growth and unregulated social differentiation. The writers associated with it are unable or unwilling to see that conflicts of interests and values are endemic to the organizational structures and practices of all advanced industrial societies. Indeed, organizations are both the major arenas in which these struggles are carried on and the primary instruments through which power is exercised to achieve temporary resolutions of ongoing disputes.

## POWER

The concept of power has been of pivotal significance for an understanding and explanation of organizational structures and processes since Weber's work on the dynamics and consequences of bureaucratic rationalization in modern societies.[76] While the Durkheimian or functionalist tradition in organization theory tended to focus on the institutional mechanisms that regulate conflict and disorder, the Weberian strand of thinking has concerned itself with the organizational sources of power struggles and the organizational practices through which they are continued. For Weber, organization was power in so far as it constituted a structure of domination and control that translates the intentions of certain actors or agencies into practical accomplishments or outcomes when they are resisted and opposed by others.[77] In modern societies, complex organizations become the indispensable tools for mobilizing and directing resources in support of collective action directed to the realization of certain interests and values over others.

Of late, the Weberian conception of power has attracted a strong following within the sociology of work organizations.[78] However, the comparatively recent pre-eminence of Weberian analysis has to be set within a longer-term context in which Durkheimian or functionalist conceptualizations of organized power were predominant. A number of commentators[79] have argued that the intellectual roots of organization theory lie in a conservative reaction to the destabilizing consequences of political and industrial revolution within Western societies. Modern organizations were seen to provide an indispensable tool or mechanism through which established and emerging sources of authority and privilege – the landed aristocracy as much as the industrial bourgeoisie– could defend themselves against incipient instability and disorder:

Organization promised the creation of a new structure of power, a functioning whole superior to the sum of the tiny physical, intellectual and moral contribution of the parts. . . . As a system of power, organization would enable men to exploit nature in a systematic fashion and thereby bring society to an unprecedented plateau of material prosperity. The industrial order, by providing a new structure for society, a new principle of authority, a new form of integration, was to be a counter-revolutionary antidote to the agitation of the masses, the de-revolutionizing remedy for the present social agony.[80]

This conservative cast of mind encouraged an approach to the study of organized power in modern societies as a collective resource that is directed to the realization of shared objectives. This view was based on the presupposition of an underlying consensus as to the major problem of maintaining social order in the conditions of rapid change which such societies confront.[81] This legitimated a sustained analytical focus on organizational power as an institutionalized resource, authorized by a society's central value system, and formalized into hierarchical relations that are generally accepted by the great mass of organizational members.[82] Thus, the concept of organizational power became theoretically and substantively disengaged from its grounding within a continuous struggle over the basic structures through which economic, political and social life is organized. It was transformed into generalized resource or capacity that structured and stabilized social interaction for the benefit of society as a whole, rather than for any particular set of sectional interests engaged in conflict over organizational arrangements and the distributional outcomes which they produced. The concept of power was neutralized as an idea that highlighted the underlying divisions of modern society. It was transformed into a necessary collective force which kept the latter in one piece.

Nevertheless, the dynamics of organizational power have been analyzed in a way that challenges the conservative or functionalist tradition in organization theory. This view develops an approach that stresses the strategic role of 'organization' in destabilizing and undermining established structures of power and domination in modern societies.[83] It focuses on the significance of organization as a locale and mechanism for mobilizing and directing countervailing sources and forms of power which circumvent and fragment institutionalized structures of domination. Rather than theoretically privilege authorized and formalized structures of organizational power as generalized resources geared to system survival, the Weberian approach highlights the constantly shifting pattern of alliances between groups that struggle to control the wider networks of power through which domination can be secured. Within this perspective, organizational power is conceptually tied to the endemic conflicts of interest and value between groups, movements, elites and classes, as agencies that calculate and enact a strategic course of social action to realize their preferred outcomes.[84] It is also recognized that the formulation and implementation of power strategies by various agencies is constrained by an existing structure of power relations and the supporting ideological frameworks through which they are legitimated. But the stabilization and routinization of organizational power is always a temporary phenomenon. Organizational life necessarily entails a continuous, if often latent, conflict between actors to control the structures of domination through which collective action becomes organized.[85]

Each of these conceptions of power – the Durkheimian and the Weberian – entail very different views as to the relationship between strategic action on the one hand and structural constraint on the other. The Durkheimian or functionalist conception of organizational power stresses structural constraint and treats power as an institutional mechanism for regulating, if not determining, collective action. The Weberian or strategic conception focuses on the constitution of power relations through the unequally distributed capacities of actors to shape the structures of domination in which they are unavoidably implicated. For the former, organizational power is approached as a resource that facilitates structural control over potentially disruptive and destabilizing conflicts which have the potential to threaten social order. For the latter, organizational power is a relational capacity employed by competing agencies to create and maintain complex structures of social interdependence and coordination that privilege their interests and values over others.[86] Power as the ultimate expression of structural determination of and institutional control over, collective action, rather as an ongoing process through which the strategic interventions of agencies make and remake organizational order, is the fundamental issue at the heart of this dispute.

This supports Luke's view that power is an 'essentially contested' concept – as are all the other concepts discussed in this chapter – that inevitably involves fundamental disputes over its conceptualization, operationalization and interpretation.[87] Thus, any particular concept of power has to be interpreted and deployed within a wider frame of reference entailing contestable judgements as to the defining features of human nature, the constitution of society and the highly complex process through which 'interests' or 'values' are formulated.

The Durkheimian conception of organizational power rests on a view of human nature as an essentially unruly, but malleable or 'plastic', force which must be controlled by society in such a way that deep-seated conflicts of interest and value can be regulated and contained within institutionalized parameters supportive of social order. The Weberian conception emphasizes the uncontrollable, but infinitely creative, potential of human action as it strives to achieve mastery over a social environment constituted by conflicting ideologies and rationalities that defy any lasting attempt at reconciliation and synthesis.[88] One conception sees power as that fundamental collective resource through which a precarious stability and order is achieved; the other view engages with power as an unevenly distributed capacity directed to the realization of sectional interests and values which contend within a wider arena of struggle between competing world-views or *Weltanschaung* that is never at rest.

It is not too far from the truth to suggest that 'power' has come to be regarded as the leitmotif of organization theory's history, however chequered and disputatious the latter has proved to be in practice. Controversy and disagreement over appropriate conceptualization, methodology and interpretation has been evident throughout all the concepts and traditions that have been reviewed in this chapter. But these disputes are collectively incorporated within debates that stretch over many years of systematic speculation concerning the human condition and its institutional equipment. Such debates serve to coordinate a shared interest in a broad gamut of common preoccupations and to communicate a collective sense of engagement within a continuing discourse over the 'great transition' to a modern industrialized society in which organizations become the strategic nodal points directing the process and outcome of institutional transformation.

The concept of power has provided a vital intellectual conduit through which some of the most significant and far-reaching debates concerning the theoretical and methodological means by which organizational life can be properly understood could pass. It also established a tradition of discourse through which these, constantly developing and fructifying, concerns could be handed on to successive generations of scholars fascinated by the emergence of a novel institutional form and practice that seemed to signify a fundamental break and discontinuity with the past.

Continuing debate between competing conceptions of organizational power raise a number of basic questions concerning the 'dialectic of agency and structure' and its implications for our understanding of social life.[89] Lukes maintains that the major conclusion that has to be drawn from the recurring debate over the nature of power and its significance for social explanation is that:

social life can only properly be understood as a dialectic of power and structure, a web of possibilities for agents, whose nature is both active and structured, to make choices and pursue strategies within given limits, which in consequence expand and contract over time. Any standpoint or methodology which reduces this dialectic to a one-sided consideration of agents without (internal and external) structural limits, or structures without agents, or which does not address the problem of their interrelations, will be unsatisfactory. No social theory merits serious attention that fails to retain an ever-present sense of the dialectic of power and structure.[90]

Again, it would not be too much of an exaggeration to suggest that the problem of developing a theoretical framework and research methodology in which the 'dialectic of agency and structure' can be adequately captured and exploited to account for the most important aspect of complex organization that has stood at the centre of debate in organization theory over the last two decades.[91] The history of organization theory has been plagued by a series of dichotomies or dualisms that have revolved around the polarization between those who have conceptualized organizations in terms of 'objective' structures or systems which impose themselves on actors and those who have advocated a social ontology in which organizations are defined in terms of the 'subjective' meanings and interpretations through which they are constructed and maintained.[92] Debate over the nature and significance of the concept of power has crystallized this polarization to the extent that it has generated a shared discourse, grammar and language through which the dispute between 'objectivitist' and 'subjectivist' theories of organization can be articulated and sustained. It has also thrown up a shared belief that any contemporary theory of organization which looks for general support within the intellectual community must provide the conceptual resources for encapsulating and understanding the ever-present interpenetration of agency and structure through which organizational life is constituted.[93] The need to think through the various ways in which power structures are interwoven in the ongoing activity of organizational life has provided a focal point for debate and analysis within contemporary organization theory.

A never-ending conversation over the conceptual meaning and explanatory status of organizational power has permeated the intellectual foundations of organizational analysis in relation to the characterization of subject matter, the principles and procedures through which it is to be investigated and the logics of explanation which they legitimate. The problems which this conversation surfaces may not be amenable to any final resolution, much less solution. Yet, they signify and symbolize an intellectual struggle to come to terms with seemingly intractable issues which have to be confronted if organization theory is to retain any sense of itself as a collective endeavour that speaks to some of the most challenging predicaments which face men and women in the present era.

It is this struggle, as it works itself through in a number of different theoretical, methodological and ideological idioms, that provides the focal point for the contributions which are reviewed and assessed in subsequent chapters of this book.

CONCLUSION

The debates that have been reviewed in this chapter can be read as successive attempts to gain some explanatory leverage on the severe social dislocations engendered by the transition to an organized society and their continuing significance for our understanding of contemporary organizational life. The attempt to come to terms with the rapid and revolutionary changes initiated by the transition to industrial capitalism – both at an intellectual and political level – emerges as the underlying theme that informs the debates that have clustered around the unifying concepts highlighted in this chapter.

One of the most profound changes which this transition entailed was the emergence of complex organizations as the strategic social units through which the development and growth of modern societies was to be managed. Indeed, the arguments reviewed in this chapter and the previous chapter suggest that organizations provided the crucial social technology through which the continuous self-management and strategic administrative control of modern industrial societies was realized.[94] The dominance of formal or complex organizations in all areas of socio-economic, political and cultural life made available a highly sophisticated apparatus of administrative surveillance and control through which the reflexive monitoring and correction of individual and collective behaviour could be routinely carried out. It provided the organizational means through which administrative governance could be economically and effectively practised within modern nation-states.

However, the machinery of administrative surveillance and disciplinary control made available by modern organizations did not provide a blueprint for social order. As this chapter has demonstrated, the increasing role of bureaucratized systems of coordination and control in all areas of social life exacerbated many of the most deep-seated and far-reaching problems encountered in modern societies. Alienating work, amoral and normless administrative settings, intensified power conflicts and a stultifying decision-making rationality which stifled initiative and inbred a collective mentality resistant to change and adaptability, came to be regarded as the distinguishing features of modern organization. In addition, the growth of this innovative social technology seemed to signify the emergence and proliferation of 'discontents' which were constitutive of modern life. The drive to rationalize all aspects of individual and collective existence inherent in modern organizations seemed to generate a highly fragmented and angst-ridden form of life. All sense of social integration and cultural identity was lost in a miasma of remote, centralized corporate power and the unregulated competition and conflicts which it had let loose in modern societies.[95]

It is against the historical and analytical backdrop conveyed by these concerns, and the concepts through which they have been articulated, that the perspectives, programmes and trends discussed in subsequent chapters must be located. The former establish the context in which the latter are framed. The significance, implications and relevance of contemporary debates can only be evaluated against the backdrop of thematic continuities that stretch over time and place. To selectively rephrase Marx, 'organization theorists make history, but not in circumstances of their own choosing.'

Whether we like it or not, the sociology of organizations is directly implicated in the process of institutional building which has made, and will remake, modern industrialized societies. Both as an intellectual practice and as a social technology, systematic reflection on the nature, dynamics and consequences of complex organizations has become an integral feature of modernity. It is in this context that the theoretical developments, research programmes and longer-term trends reviewed in the following chapters must be set.

## REFERENCES

1. Benson, J.K., 'Innovation and Crisis in Organizational Analysis', *Sociological Quarterly*, vol. 18 (1977), pp. 229–49; Morgan, G. *Images of Organization* (Sage, London, 1986).
2. Burrell, G. and Morgan, G., *Sociological Paradigms and Organizational Analysis* (Heinemann, London, 1979).
3. Morgan, G., *Beyond Method* (Sage, London, 1983).
4. Pugh, D., 'Modern Organization Theory', *Psychological Bulletin*, vol. 66, 1966, pp. 235–51.
5. Scott, W. R., 'Theory of Organizations' in Faris, R.L. (ed.), *Handbook of Modern Sociology* (Rand McNally, Chicago, 1964), pp. 485–529.
6. Blau, P., *The Dynamics of Bureaucracy* (University of Chicago Press, Chicago, revised edition, 1963).
7. Gergen, K., 'Organization Theory in the Postmodern Era' in Reed. M. and Hughes, M. (eds), *Rethinking Organization: New Directions in Organization Theory and Analysis* (Sage, London, 1992).
8. Latour, B., *Science in Action* (Open University Press, Milton Keynes, 1986).
9. Donaldson, L., *In Defence of Organization Theory* (Cambridge University Press, Cambridge, 1985).
10. Reed, M., 'From Paradigms to Images: The Paradigm Warrior turns Post-Modernist Guru', *Personnel Review*, vol. 19, no. 3, 1991, pp. 35–40.
11. Perry, N., 'Recovery and Retrieval in Organizational Analysis', *Sociology* vol. 13, 1979, pp. 38–50.
12. Wolin, S., *Politics and Vision* (Allen and Unwin, London, 1961).
13. Nisbet, R.A., *The Sociological Tradition* (Heinemann, London, 1970).

14. Abrams, P., *Historical Sociology* (Open Books, Somerset, 1982), p. xv. For a similar approach to the one adopted here also see A. Dawe, 'Theories of Social Action' in Bottomore, T. and Nisbet, R.A., *History of Sociological Analysis* (Heinemann, London, 1979), pp. 362–417.

15. Albrow, M., 'The Application of the Weberian Concept of Rationalization to Contemporary Conditions' in Whimster, S. and Lash, S. (eds), *Max Weber: Rationality and Modernity* (Allen and Unwin, London, 1987), pp. 164–82.

16. Brubaker, M., *The Limits of Rationality* (Allen and Unwin, London, 1984).

17. Weber, M., *Economy and Society*, 2 vols (University of California Press, Berkeley, 1978), p. 973.

18. For an extremely detailed and insightful analysis of this belief on the development of American legal theory see Frug, G.E., 'The Ideology of Bureaucracy in American Law', *Harvard Law Review*, vol. 97, 1984, pp. 1279–379.

19. Wolin, S., *op. cit.* (1961), p. 360.

20. Waldo, D., *The Administrative State* (Knopf, New York, 1948).

21. Perrow, C., *Complex Organizations: A Critical Essay* (Random House, New York, third edition, 1986).

22. Albrow, M., 'The Dialectic of Science and Values in the Study of Organizations' in Salaman, G. and Thompson, K. (eds), *Control and Ideology in Organizations* (Open University Press, Milton Keynes, 1980), pp. 278–96.

23. Miller, P. and O'Leary, T., 'Accounting and the Construction of the Governable Person', *Accounting, Organizations and Society*, vol. 12, 1985, pp. 1–31.

24. Dawe, A., *op. cit.* (1979).

25. Georgiou, P., 'The Goal Paradigm and Notes Toward a Counter Paradigm' in Zey-Ferrell, M. and Aiken, M., *Complex Organizations: Critical Perspectives* (Scott, Foresman and Company, Illinois, 1981), pp. 69–88 (p. 82).

26. Thompson, J. D., *Organizations in Action* (McGraw-Hill, New York, 1967).

27. Massie, J., 'Management Theory' in March, J. (ed.) *The Handbook of Organizations* (Rand McNally, New York, 1965), pp. 387–422.

28. Beetham, D., *Bureaucracy* (Open University Press, Milton Keynes, 1987 Kamenka, E., *Bureaucracy* (Blackwell, Oxford, 1989).

29. Beetham, D., *Max Weber and the Theory of Modern Politics* (Cambridge University Press, Cambridge, second edition, 1985).

30. Reed, M., *Redirections in Organizational Analysis* (Tavistock, London, 1985).
31. Frug, G.E., *op. cit.* (1984).
32. Brunsson, N., *The Organization of Hypocrisy* (Wiley, New York, 1989).
33. Perrow, C., *op. cit.* (1986), pp. 258–78.
34. Bryman, A., 'Organization Studies and the Concept of Rationality', *Journal of Management Studies*, vol. 21, 1984, pp. 391–404.
35. Simon, H., *Administrative Behavior* (Collier Macmillan, New York, 1945).
36. Cyert, R.M. and March, J.G., *A Behavioral Theory of the Firm* (Prentice-Hall, Englewood Cliffs, NJ, 1963).
37. Lindblom, C., 'The Science of Muddling Through', *Public Administration Review*, vol. 19, 1959, pp. 77–88.
38. Pettigrew, A., *The Politics of Organizational Decision-making* (Tavistock, London, 1973).
39. Brunsson, M., *The Irrational Organization* (Wiley, New York, 1985).
40. The wider implications of this argument are discussed in greater detail in Chapter 5.
41. Pettigrew, A., *The Awakening Giant: Continuity and Change in ICI* (Blackwell, Oxford, 1985).
42. Gellner, E., *Plough, Sword and Book: The Structure of Human History* (Collins Harvill, London, 1988).
43. Skillen, A., *Ruling Illusions; Philosophy and the Social Order* (Harvester Wheatsheaf, Hemel Hempstead, 1977).
44. Nisbet, R.A., *op. cit.* (1970), p. 297.
45. Feuer, L., 'What is Alienation? The Career of a Concept', *New Politics*, vol. 1, no.4, 1962, pp. 116–34.
46. Jackall, R., *Moral Mazes: The World of Corporate Managers* (Oxford University Press, Oxford, 1988), pp. 202–3.
47. Anthony, P.D., *The Ideology of Work* (Tavistock, London, 1977), pp. 113–45.
48. Giddens, A., *Capitalism and Modern Social Theory* (Cambridge University Press, Cambridge, 1971), pp. 234–5.
49. This literature is reviewed in more detail in Eldridge, J.E.T., *Sociology and Industrial Life* (Nelson, London, 1971) and Thompson, P., *The Nature of Work* (Macmillan, London, 1983).
50. Aiken, M. and Hage, J., 'Organizational Alienation: A Comparative Analysis' in Grusky, O. and Miller, G.A., *The Sociology of Organizations: Basic Studies* (Collier Macmillan, New York, 1970), pp. 517–26.

51. These programmes are reviewed in Poole, M., *Towards a New Industrial Democracy* (Routledge and Kegan Paul, London, 1986).

52. Pitt, D., 'The End of Bureaucracy: The Beginning of Ideology?' *Public Administration Bulletin*, December 1979, pp. 4–9; Burrell, G. and Morgan, G., *op. cit.* (1979), pp. 310–25.

53. Illich, I., *Tools for Conviviality* (Calder and Boyars, London, 1973).

54. Reich, C.A., *The Greening of America*, (Penguin, Harmondsworth, 1972).

55. Roszak, T., *The Making of a Counter Culture* (Faber and Faber, London, 1970).

56. Pitt, D., *op. cit.* (1979), pp. 8–9.

57. The concept of 'organic' organizational systems will be further elaborated in the following chapter.

58. Lukes, S., 'Alienation and Anomie' in Lukes, S., *Essays in Social Theory* (Macmillan, London, 1977), pp. 74–95.

59. Lukes, S., *Emile Durkheim: A Historical and Critical Study* (Penguin, Harmondsworth, 1975).

60. Eldridge, J.E.T., *op. cit.* (1971), pp. 89–91.

61. Ackroyd, S., 'Sociological Theory and the Human Relations School', *Sociology of Work and Occupations*, vol. 3 (1976), pp. 379–410; Bartell, T., 'The Human Relations Ideology', *Human Relations*, vol. 29, 1976, pp. 737–49; Rose, M., *Industrial Behaviour* (Penguin, Harmondsworth, second edition, 1988).

62. Fox, A., *Man Mismanagement* (Hutchinson, London, second edition, 1985), pp. 88–9.

63. Wolin, D., *op. cit.* (1961), pp. 400–18.

64. Nisbet, R.A., *The Quest for Community* (Oxford University Press, Oxford, 1969), p. 49.

65. For overviews of this literature see Perrow, C., *op. cit.* (1986) and Rose, M., *op. cit.* (1988).

66. Bendix, R., *Work and Authority in Industry* (University of California Press, Berkeley, 1974), pp. 303–40.

67. Miller, P. and O'Leary, T., 'Hierarchies and American Ideals: 1900–1940', *Academy of Management Review*, vol.14, 1989, pp. 250–65.

68. Anthony, P.D., *op. cit.* (1977), p. 257.

69. Axtell-Ray, Carol, 'Corporate Culture: The Last Frontier of Control?', *Journal of Management Studies*, vol. 23 (1986), pp. 287–97. This issue is explored in greater depth in Chapter 6.

70. Miller, P. and Rose, N., 'The Tavistock Programme: The

Government of Subjectivity and Social Life', *Sociology*, vol. 22, 1988, pp. 171–92.
71. Child, J., *British Management Thought* (Allen and Unwin, London, 1969).
72. For general discussions of this programme see Mouzelis, N., *Organization and Bureaucracy: An Analysis of Modern Theories* (Routledge and Kegan Paul, London, second edition, 1975) and Perrow, C., *op. cit.* (1986).
73. Anthony, P.D., 'The Paradox of the Management of Culture or He Who Heads Is Lost', *Personnel Review*, vol. 19, no. 4, 1991, pp. 3–8.
74. Turner, B., 'The Rise of Organizational Symbolism' in Hassard, J. and Pym, D. (eds), *The Theory and Philosophy of Organizations* (Routledge, London, 1990), pp. 83–96).
75. Ouchi, W.G., *Theory Z: How American Business Can Meet the Japanese Challenge* (Addison-Wesley, California, 1981).
76. Beetham, D., *op. cit.* (1987), pp. 56–96.
77. Clegg, S., *Frameworks of Power* (Sage, London, 1989), pp. 72–5.
78. McNeil, K., 'Understanding Organizational Power: Building on the Weberian Legacy', *Administrative Science Quarterly*, vol. 23, 1978, pp. 65–90; Martin, R., *The Sociology of Power* (Routledge and Kegan Paul, London, 1977); Wrong, D., *Power: Its Forms, Bases and Uses* (Basil Blackwell, Oxford, 1979); Clegg, S., *Power, Rule and Domination* (Routledge and Kegan Paul, London, 1975).
79. Wolin, D., *op. cit.* (1961); Perry, N., *op. cit.* (1979); Reed, M., *op. cit.* (1985).
80. Wolin, D., *op. cit.* (1961), pp. 377–8.
81. Parsons, T., 'On The Concept of Political Power' in Bendix, R. and Lipset, S.M. (eds), *Class, Status and Power: Social Stratification in Comparative Perspective* (Routledge and Kegan Paul, London, second edition, 1967), pp. 240–65.
82. Clegg, S. and Dunkerley, D., *Organization, Class and Control* (Routledge and Kegan Paul, London, 1980), pp. 433–83.
83. This argument is developed at some length in Clegg, S., *op cit.* (1989).
84. Pfeffer, J., *Power in Organization* (Pitman, London, 1981).
85. Eldridge, J.E.T. and Crombie, A.D., *A Sociology of Organizations* (Allen and Unwin, London, 1974), pp. 143–9.
86. Wrong, D., *op. cit.* (1979); Lukes, S., 'Power and Authority' in Bottomore, T. and Nisbet, R.A. (eds), *op. cit.* (1979), pp. 633–76.
87. Lukes, S., 'Power and Structure' in Lukes, S., *op. cit.* (1977), pp. 3–29.

88. For an elaboration of the 'models of man' that underpin a wide range of social science theorizing see Hollis, M., *Models of Man* (Cambridge University Press, Cambridge, 1977).

89. This theme is explored further in the following chapter.

90. Lukes., S., *op. cit.* (1977), p. 29.

91. Reed, M., 'The Problem of Human Agency in Organizational Analysis', *Organization Studies*, vol. 9, no. 1, 1988, pp. 33–46; Knights, D. and Willmott, H., 'Power and Subjectivity at Work: From Degradation to Subjugation in Social Relations', *Sociology*, vol. 23, 1989, pp. 535–58.

92. Willmott, H., 'Beyond Paradigmatic Closure in Organizational Enquiry' in Hassard, J. and Pym, D. (eds), *op. cit.* (1990), pp. 44–60.

93. The extent to which this view has penetrated the intellectual community in the sociology of organizations is discussed in more detail in Chapter 6.

94. Held, D. and Thompson, J.N. (eds), *Social Theory of Modern Societies*, (Cambridge University Press, Cambridge, 1989).

95. The significance of this analysis for an understanding of modern organizational forms is assessed in Chapter 6.

# / 3 /

# ANALYTICAL FRAMEWORKS

## INTRODUCTION

The previous chapters have reviewed the competing socio-logical interpretations which have been offered of complex organizations as the crucial 'carriers' and 'products' of modernity. They have also located these overarching interpretations – and the controversies which they have generated – within a longer-term historical context constituted by recurring debates over the relationship between the individual and society in the organizational conditions and forms characteristic of modern industrial life.

In one sense, the story that these general sociological analyses tell is one of deep-seated change and discontinuity in social conditions, organizational forms and moral relationships. The transition from traditionalism to modernity is characterized in terms of an 'organizational revolution' which has swept away all vestiges of the moral foundations and primary social institutions that once integrated the individual into a wider community and provided the social bonds through which stable personal identities could be forged. In their place, the 'organized society' merely offers a never-ending power struggle between unattached and unfettered individuals for the material, political and cultural rewards which domination guarantees. Membership of and identification with a broader social or organizational collectivity is now entirely conditional upon the practical assistance it provides to isolated individuals competing for scarce material resources and the socio-political privileges which economic power bestows. Modern organizational life consists of a Darwinian struggle for survival minimally constrained by weak social norms and fragmented institutions.

Yet, at the same time deep-seated continuities in problems and approaches can be discerned underlying these indicators and symbols of fundamental discontinuity and transformation. Recurring concern over the corrosive, not to say destructive, impact of formal rationalization and bureaucratic centralization on social cohesion, political regulation and cultural integration is evident in the attempts made by successive generations of sociologists to understand and explain the major institutional dynamics and structures of modernity. Organization theory becomes both a celebration of and a warning against the structural transformations and cultural movements that modernity has let loose through a process of institutional transformation driven by the search for universal rationality, efficiency and effectiveness.

These concerns and debates provide the wider intellectual and historical context in which contemporary research and analysis must be situated. They constitute a 'coherent, powerful conversation that has direction'.[1] Together, these thematic continuities and the debates crystallizing around them provide the common intellectual focus and shared pattern underlying change and discontinuity.

The following two chapters will outline and assess the most important analytical frameworks and theory groups/ research programmes which have been developed in the sociology of organizations over the last twenty years or so. But it must be remembered that more recent work draws its sociological inspiration from an intellectual heritage which has its roots in a continuing struggle to grasp the complexities of institutional change and development which stretch over a century or more.

This chapter focuses, in a relatively formal and abstract manner, on the most influential analytical frameworks developed to pursue sociological research on complex organizations since the mid–late 1960s. The following chapter concentrates on the particular theory groups which have deployed these perspectives in pursuit of coherent and

relevant research programmes. The wider theoretical movements arising out of the interchange between these groups
will also be reviewed.

Analytical frameworks fulfil three crucial functions: first,
they provide a characterization of subject matter by identifying the conceptual components constitutive of 'formal' or
'complex' organizations; second, they bring these disparate
elements together within a coherent theoretical structure by
specifying and ordering the relationships between them;
third, they allow certain inferences to be drawn concerning the
implications of the latter for our understanding of the 'logic'
of organizational change and development. In their broadest
sense, analytical frameworks constitute 'a way of seeing
which, designates, to some degree, significant elements that
are thought to be appropriate to the patterning or order
inherent in organizations'.[2] They provide networks of
concepts which are structured around shared problems and
interests that arise out of the particular form of order or
patterning thought to be most crucial for our understanding
of organizational phenomena.

At their core, there lie some very basic assumptions about
the nature of organizations and of the social processes
through which they are produced and reproduced over time.
Around this core, a diverse, and often loosely coupled,
network of concepts are developed that allow the researcher
to identify the relationships between selected components
with greater clarity and to gauge their explanatory relevance
and weight with more precision. Over time, this network of
concepts becomes more complex as researchers attempt to
incorporate an extended range of phenomena within its
domain. This inevitably creates divergent interpretations and
more substantial theoretical disagreements between those
using and developing the framework. In turn, these generate
difficulties for maintaining a stable analytical focus and a
clear set of conceptual parameters which serve to distinguish
between distinctive approaches. Consequently, analytical
frameworks are never fixed and immutable; they necessarily
change over time to accommodate new ideas and empirical
findings, but this unavoidably threatens their distinctive

identity and the internal coherence that it supports. Conceptual change and development is a necessary evil; it secures continued theoretical vitality and relevance but at the risk of undermining core foundations or commitments and the separate identity that they provide.[3]

Each of the analytical frameworks discussed in this chapter will be reviewed within a common format. First, a general specification of each framework, in terms of core assumptions, theoretical structure and explanations of change, will be provided. Second, individual examples and illustrations of each of the frameworks 'in action' will be outlined. Finally, a brief assessment of the strengths and weaknesses of each framework will be formulated, with particular regard to the theoretical difficulties that they have experienced and the problems this has created for sustaining internal coherence and viability. Four analytical frameworks will be reviewed: first, that framework which views organizations as social systems; second, a perspective on organizations as negotiated orders; third, an approach which treats organizations as structures of power and domination; finally, a viewpoint that regards organizations as symbolic constructions. The penultimate section of the chapter will consider whether a partial synthesis between selected elements of each of these perspectives may be made available by conceptualizing organizations as social practices. A final section will provide an overview of the most significant theoretical debates and developments occurring in the sociology of organizations over the last two decades or so and their wider implications for a consideration of major theory groups and research programmes which follows in the next chapter.

## ORGANIZATIONS AS SOCIAL SYSTEMS

The core assumptions underpinning the systems framework in organizational analysis can be summarized in the following manner:

1. Organizations are social units directed to the achievement of collective goals or the fulfilment of institutional needs

for the wider society or environment of which they are a constituent part.

2. These externally derived goals/needs set the parameters within which the structural forms that organizations exhibit must function; organizational structures must facilitate the realization of collective goals/needs set by the environment if their longer-term survival and viability as 'going concerns' is to be secured.

3. Structural forms appropriate to the goals/needs set by the environment establish a framework of interrelated roles that integrate organizational members into a coherent and relatively stable social unit.

4. This set of roles imposes a pattern of behavioural and attitudinal expectations and norms to which individual members must display a minimal degree of obeisance.

5. Organizationally determined demands for compliance are often perceived as constraining, to some extent or in some degree, by individual members and exist in a state of permanent tension with their preferred wants/expectations.

6. The resulting tension between organizational demands and individual needs is a perennial source of conflict in organized systems and generates endemic instability and disequilibrium within structural designs that have to be coped with or managed in some way or another if organizational survival and effectiveness are to be secured.

7. The coping strategies undertaken by organizational management will, during the course of time, modify the organizations' relationship with the environment and the internal designs through which this relationship is mediated and developed.

Considered in these terms, the systems framework emphasizes the recurring and regularized properties that can be discerned as defining features of all formal or complex organizations as opposed to the relatively uncoordinated and poorly structured relationships prevailing within other social units such as social movements, classes and families. The defining characteristic of all formal or complex organizations is the systematic patterning in structural forms that arises out of the demand to satisfy or fulfil environmentally derived needs or imperatives. It is this consciously planned and coordinated patterning of relationships that sets organizations apart from other social systems. It allows us to assume that 'once firmly established, an organization tends to assume an identity of its own which makes it independent of the people who have founded it or of those who constitute its membership.'[4] Thus, the starting-point for the systems framework is a conception of organization as a goal-oriented, purposeful system constituted through a set of common underlying abstract variables or dimensions relating to structural properties which are geared to the functional needs of a more inclusive social system.[5] As social systems, organizations are seen to exhibit structural patterns of coordination and control – that is, of conscious planning and monitoring – in their own right that can be identified and analyzed independently of the actions of organizational members. These structural regularities are shaped by the wider environment in which organizations operate to solve certain functional problems for the larger social system in which they are embedded. What makes these problems or needs 'organizational goals' is that they have been authorized and institutionalized by a supra-individual collectivity represented by the decisions of top management or the corporate leadership:

Whilst it is true that only humans can define goals (future ideal states), and that organizational goals are defined by humans, what makes goals organizational is the process of their authorization and institutionalization. The latter process ensures that goals, once understood and shared, and perhaps backed by detailed plans and schedules, can survive the death of most of their architects. The process of authorization involves the organization giving its legitimacy to the objectives (just like the University of Oxford giving degrees). This makes the objectives the property of a supra-individual 'entity'. The institutionalization process, similarly, makes the objectives the property of a supra-individual collectivity.[6]

The existence of organizations as distinctive structural or supra-individual entities with collective goals or plans that have been authorized and institutionalized by the leadership group – and the socialization mechanisms which they rely on to secure general acceptance of 'their' policies – is predicated on the assumption that organizational systems are dependent on their environments for longer-term survival. It is only by effectively solving functional problems for the wider environment and society that organizations can secure the material, political and cultural resources required for their continuation as 'going concerns'. Organizational life persists because organizations evolve means – that is, structures – whereby they fulfil the functional needs 'which are either preconditions or consequences of organized social life'.[7]

The basic problem which directs the systems framework in organizational analysis centres around the forms of structural design most appropriate to the fulfilment of different functional needs and the environmental conditions under which they are most effective for dealing with the latter. At the most general level, these 'needs' can be defined in relation to the stability and maintenance of whole societies;[8] at a lower level of analysis, they can be identified in relation to the transactions and exchanges that organizations have with their more immediate 'task environments'.[9] While the former refer to a very broad range of functions centred on the adaptation, integration and governance of society in general, the latter are more focused and specific in relating to the resource inputs that the organization requires from its environment to function effectively and the means that it relies on to secure them. However, at either of these levels of analysis overriding emphasis is given to the external conditions in which organizations have to function and the demands or pressures that the former exert on the latter. Formal administrative structures are analyzed in terms of the capacity they provide to adapt organizations successfully to the immediate environmental circumstances or wider societal configurations in which they find themselves.

These internal structures establish a network of interlocking sub-systems consisting of role sets that integrate individuals into a more encompassing social unit by providing them with reasonably stable and coherent identities as 'organizational members'. Through the inculcation of behavioural and attitudinal norms appropriate to organizational membership and the wider cultural values from which the former draw to sustain their meaning and significance, organizations are able to rely on a minimally acceptable level of performance from their members. Though coercive sanctions of various types will be needed to punish serious deviance from established norms, organizations can usually rely on well-developed socialization mechanisms and processes to secure routine or habitual compliance with institutionalized norms. Yet, the latter are rarely completely effective in the degree of psychological and behavioural control which they realize; individual and group recalcitrance is a recurring problem that all organizations must face and respond to:

Social action is always mediated by human structures which generate new centres of need and power and interpose themselves between the actor and his goal. Commitments to others are indispensable in action; at the same time, the process of commitment results in tensions which always have to be overcome.[10]

The official or manifest demands that organizations impose on individuals often conflict with the latter's unofficial or latent preferred wants and expectations. But organizations have to rely on individuals to perform the roles required of them by their position within the formal structure. Individuals are an indispensable means to the realization of collective goals but they resist being treated as 'tools' and turn formal structures to their preferred ends. The resulting tension between 'formal' and 'informal' organization – between sanctioned controls and unavoidable deviance – generates instabilities and conflict that unsettle the prevailing balance or 'equilibrium' between the various segments or sub-systems within the overall structure. These will require responsive action on the part of management to ensure that this disturbed balance between the constituent components of the structure is readjusted in favour of a new equilibrium. In turn, this corrective managerial action aimed at reintegrating organizational structures and individual behaviour is likely to alter the organization's relationship with its environment. This will be the case in so far as it results in modifications to existing structural arrangements within the organization and to the behavioural expectations and attitudinal norms that they previously legitimated:

the organization is embedded in an institutional matrix and is therefore subject to pressures upon it from its environment, to which some general adjustment must be made. As a result, the organization may be significantly viewed as an adaptive social structure, facing problems which arise simply because it exists as an organization in an institutional environment ... there will develop an informal structure within the organization which will reflect the spontaneous efforts of individuals and sub-groups to control the conditions of their existence ... the adaptation is dynamic in the sense that the utilization of self-defensive mechanisms results in structural transformations of the organization itself.[11]

This core conceptualization of an organization as a purposive social system geared to the fulfilment of a relatively stable set of environmentally induced needs for security, integration, continuity and survival has formed the theoretical bedrock of the systems framework in organizational analysis. Around this core a veritable plethora of auxiliary concepts and theoretical innovations have been woven with the aim of making systems analysis more dynamic – that is, better equipped to explain the causes and consequences of organizational change.[12] This has encouraged the analytical shift towards an 'open-systems'[13] view of the organization in which it copes with change and uncertainty through managed exchanges and transactions with its task environment. The most influential expression of this approach in recent years has been contingency theory.

Contingency theory concentrates on the immediate pressures that organizations face in their task environments and the internal structural accommodations which they have to make to meet these challenges. Factors such as volatile market demand, technological change and political realignments within the environment are identified as key 'contingencies' which organizations have to respond to in the appropriate manner if they are to ensure their long-term survival.[14] Change in these external factors is likely to exert considerable pressure on the organization's production system to realign its goals and structures so that it maintains 'compatibility with its niche and to ensure continued satisfaction of the system's needs'.[15] Environmental change is seen to create new sources of uncertainty for the organization in that the course of future developments is unpredictable and the appropriate response required from the organization to meet the challenge posed by these changed circumstances becomes problematic. A mixture of rational managerial intervention in policy-making and unintended adaptive response to a new environmental situation usually shapes the pattern of organizational response elicited by changed environmental conditions that pose a threat to established structures:

The particular contribution of structural-functionalism to the explanation of organizational change is to point out which forms are best suited to which situations; and to identify the pressures which will lead firms to change; that is, which combination of context and structures will constitute a mismatch, a state of disequilibrium. The general structural-functionalist model of change is that it will occur when organizations disequilibrate and there will be a shift to a condition of equilibrium.[16]

The clearest expression of the general systems framework in organizational analysis and the more focused contingency approach which has been developed out of it has been provided by Thompson[17] and Lawrence and Lorsch.[18] In the late 1960s they provided a codification of the systems/contingency framework − based on empirical work and theoretical innovations undertaken in the 1950s and early 1960s − which was to direct and legitimate the contributions of other writers/researchers working within this perspective in the 1970s and 1980s.

Thompson's book provides a synthesis of the 'rational' and 'natural' viewpoints developed within the systems framework.[17] While the former emphasizes the deliberately planned and coordinated aspects of organization, the latter stresses the more spontaneous and unintended qualities of organizational processes. Thompson argued that these need to be synthesized within a conception of the organization as a social system interdependent with its environment and faced with the uncertainty which the latter presented but, at the same time, 'subject to criteria of rationality and hence needing determinateness and certainty'.[19] The problem of coping with uncertainty – that is, the extremely restricted capacity of all organizations to predict and control their environments – was Thompson's starting-point for analyzing the various structural designs that management selected to adapt, as best they could, to the capricious pressures and demands that their environments presented. As problem-facing, problem-solving, phenomena, all complex organizations needed to achieve a suitable balance between their internal operational core and their external environmental circumstances if they were to ensure their long-term survival and effectiveness. Here, management had a key role to play in designing, implementing and monitoring control mechanisms and information systems that would introduce a partial or 'bounded rationality' into organizational functioning.

Lawrence and Lorsch focus on the problem of how managers are to develop organizational structures and decision-making processes which will allow their organizations to deal effectively with different kinds and rates of environmental change, especially of technological and market change. They postulate that the structural designs which may be effective under one set of environmental conditions may not necessarily be so under changed circumstances. The basic problem that managers have to confront and solve is to achieve the appropriate balance between functional differentiation or specialization and structural integration or coordination which will equip them to adapt to the changing external environmental conditions they face. Their empirical research indicates that the more unstable, complex and demanding environments become – as indicated by the accelerating rates of market and technological change prevailing within the niches in which they operate – the more highly differentiated organizational structures have to become. The latter are held together and coordinated through deliberately planned mechanisms or processes which contain the fragmenting dynamic generated by intensified specialization. Less complex and more slow moving environments, on the other hand, required simpler organizational structures in which bureaucratic inertia and established routine were the major problems. This was the case in so far as they breed a degree of managerial complacency which could become positively dangerous in the much more uncertain and turbulent conditions introduced by environmental change. The more certain and settled managers were in their philosophy and practice of structural design, the less well-prepared they were to deal with environmental instability and change, once it gathered pace and momentum.

Both Thompson and Lawrence and Lorsch develop their analyses within an open-systems approach that regards the organization as an 'indeterminate' structure interdependent with its environment and facing the economic, informational, technological and social uncertainties which the latter presents. Yet, they maintain the initial logic of the systems framework in viewing the organization as a reactive or adaptive social unit which is largely determined by the character of the environment in which it functions. To a considerable extent, they continue in an analytical tradition that sees the organization as being largely, if not totally, a prisoner of the environment in which it is embedded. The emphasis lies in the reactive response that managers, and other organizational personnel, are forced to make both to immediate and wider shifts in its task and/or institutional setting, rather than contemplating the possibility that the former may be able and willing to shape their environments to a considerable extent. It is a view of the organization as a 'victim' of its environment, rather than as a 'creator' and manipulator of its task and institutional setting. This conception sets the theoretical tone for the development and application of the systems framework in organizational analysis. It also provides a point of attack for those who were highly critical of the over-deterministic logic of analysis that the latter relied on.

## ORGANIZATIONS AS NEGOTIATED ORDERS

In many respects, the core conceptualization of complex organizations offered by the negotiated order framework is the antithesis of that presented by the systems framework. While the latter stresses the supra-individual structural and institutional 'essence' of organization which imposes itself on social action, the former emphasizes the processual and interactional qualities of organizational phenomena which have to be constructed, reproduced or transformed through the intentional interventions of organizational members. Systems theory treats organizations as entities, things or objects which determine, to a considerable extent, the courses of action which people follow. As objective forces or structures, organizations are assumed to possess a developmental logic that necessarily imposes itself on individuals whatever their preferences and intentions. The negotiated order framework, on the other hand, treats organization as the temporary product or outcome of interactional processes between individuals and groups that is always open to revision and reformulation by them. It calls attention to the underlying fragility and impermanence of organizational structures, rather than seeing the latter as immutable features of the institutional landscape which change relatively slowly and only in response to the promptings of the external environment in which they take on functional significance and meaning.

The core assumptions that lie at the heart of the negotiated order framework in organizational analysis can be itemized in this way:

1. Organizations are social units that are created, sustained and transformed through social interaction; they have no separate existences as entities or structures independent of their grounding in social interaction.
2. As socially constructed and negotiated phenomena, organizations are most appropriately conceptualized as emerging out of the ongoing interaction of participants; they constitute temporary arrangements or patterns arising out of the social interaction undertaken by social actors which are always open to modification, revision and change through their interventions.
3. In so far as they are the products of negotiated interaction, then they have temporal limits in the sense that they will

be reviewed, re-evaluated, revised, revoked or renewed over time.

4. The organizational relationships and order arising out of this negotiating process have to be worked at; the organizational bases and forms produced and reproduced through interaction have to be continually reconstituted.

5. The more formalized and 'permanent' conventions, rules and relationships entailed in established structures set partial limits to and some direction for the process of negotiation; they provide the more stable elements of complex organizations as a general background against which foreground day-to-day negotiations can be set.

6. These, more formalized, organizational elements constitute a relatively fluid structure of power and control which constrains and facilitates political bargaining between organizational coalitions or 'stakeholders' over the allocation, distribution and utilization of scarce resources, as well as shaping the 'constituencies of interest' which crystallize around these bargaining relationships.

The negotiated order view suggests that the existence of organizations as coherent and sustainable social units is entirely dependent on their continuous reconstruction through social action; they reproduce and restructure themselves in and through the medium of social interaction. Rather than treat key features of organization – such as goals, structures, technologies, socialization mechanisms and control systems – as supra-individual or collective forces which impose themselves on social actors, the negotiated order framework is based on the belief that these factors only take on meaning and significance in so far as they are recognized and utilized by actors in the course of their negotiating activities. In short, this framework is based on the core presupposition that the organizational bases on which collective action is mobilized and the organizational mechanisms through which it is channelled and directed have to be continually reconstituted by means of negotiative processes engaged in by social actors:

there is no social order without negotiated order; that is negotiation is part and parcel of any social order. . . . Of course, not everything is either equally negotiable or – at any given time or period of time –

negotiable at all. . . . Rather than seeing a relatively inflexible structure with a limited and determinable list of structural properties, we have to conceive of a ward, hospital or any other institutions as *a structure in process.*[20]

This emphasis on 'structure in process' emerging from social interaction clearly indicates that social actors play a strategically pro-active and self-conscious role in shaping and reshaping organizational arrangements. As a result:

Negotiated order theory down-plays the notion of organizations as fixed, rather rigid systems which are highly constrained by strict rules, regulations, goals and hierarchical chains of command. Instead, it emphasizes the fluid, continuously emerging qualities of the organization, the changing web of interactions woven among its members, and it suggests that order is something at which the members of the organization must constantly work. Organizations are thus viewed as complex and highly fragile social constructions of reality which are subject to the numerous temporal, spatial, and situational events occurring both internally and externally.[21]

Thus, structural components such as divisions of labour, hierarchical authority, systems of rules and regulations, and control mechanisms emerge out of negotiative processes between individuals and groups or 'agencies' located within various arenas and levels of organizational life. While these features can assume a degree of fixity and facilitate a substantial degree of control over the direction, course and outcome of negotiation, they cannot be regarded as 'structural givens' which determine action processes. Structures have to be configured, confirmed and reconfirmed by the fundamental negotiating processes that give them 'organizational life' and meaning in the first place.

Consequently, the negotiated order framework also highlights the crucial explanatory role of such variables such as 'temporality, the situational context in which social action takes place, and the emergence of contingency arrangements'.[22] The grounds on which negotiation takes place, the situational conditions in which it proceeds and the specific outcomes that it produces are all substantially influenced by organizational 'life cycles' and the specific practices through which they are represented and implemented, such as timetables, calendars, periodic reviews and the work patterns arising out of routine operational tasks.

However, the working relationships between individuals and groups which are developed out of this temporally patterned sequence of negotiation and bargaining are prone to break down as a result of misunderstanding, over-specialization or conflict. As a result, they have to be recreated and re-established through interaction and through the development and institutionalization of certain mechanisms that sustain organizational order in the face of conflict and disorder. All organizations have 'generalized mandates' concerning their core values and cultures which specify broad objectives such as 'patient care' or 'customer service'. These are translated into operational rules and systems of a more formalized kind which provide a general background against which more informal, interactional processes can take place.

Yet, these more formalized and permanent features of organizations are relatively vague in the 'action recipes' which they establish. At the same time, they have to be confirmed through complex negotiating processes between organizational actors that inevitably modify and reshape the practical impact they exert on the courses of action which the latter actually follow. The operational effect of formal structures is highly dependent upon the selective judgements made by members as to the specific scripts or rules they follow and the use which they make of 'official' mandates to justify their action. Organizational structures are seen to be firmly embedded within a dense and intricate web of interaction which gives them 'life' and relevance for the negotiation of social order between individuals and groups with very different interests and interpretations of what 'ought to happen'.

The recognition of conflicting interests and values – and the very different action prescriptions arising from them – as integral features of the process through which organizational order is negotiated leads to a consideration of power relationships. Power is approached as a capacity to control the course of events and the actions of participants so that the negotiation process reflects the preferred outcomes of certain individuals and groups over others. Power relationships, based on this differentially distributed capacity to control the course and outcome of negotiation, are seen to be situationally specific and contingent upon the conditions prevailing within an organizational setting over a particular period of time. Rather than viewing power resources and relationships as definitive and fixed structural attributes determining action, negotiated order theorists see them as varying over time, place and issue – that is, as open to revision and reconstruction as and when organizational conditions require and/or permit. Any talk of an organization's 'power structure' is interpreted as a shorthand term for a particular patterning of negotiation outcomes which is always likely to be undermined by subsequent events. While power relationships will be subject to some degree of institutionalization through hierarchically based authority structures and the ideological support which they give to established systems of command and control, they will always be exposed to the corrosive influence of negotiating processes and the decaying effect which they exert on the political *status quo*. This recommends a view of organizational power structures as 'the present products of social processes of interpretation, negotiation, conflict and accommodation, among diverse sets of participants who possess distinctive conceptions of their interests within the organization, and different resources which can be deployed in pursuit of those interests'.[23]

This analytical framework defines the central task of organizational analysis in very different terms to that suggested by the systems approach. The latter focuses on the analysis of formal structures and the determining influence which they exercise over organizational behaviour. The former concentrates on the theoretical reconstruction of reciprocal processes of negotiation over time and the manner in which they lead to the fabrication of relationships and arrangements that simultaneously facilitate and constrain the creation of new 'organizational orders'.

The initial empirical sites for the application and development of the negotiated order framework tended to be organizational settings which were inherently 'disordered' and disorganized, such as hospitals, welfare agencies and professional organizations.[24] Over time, it has been extended to industrial, political and governmental organizations in which the degree of formal institutionalization and resulting constraint on negotiation processes is relatively more pronounced.[25]

The clearest articulation of the basic assumptions associated with the negotiated order framework in organizational analysis is to be discovered in the development of a 'social action' approach or frame of reference from the late 1960s/early 1970s onwards.[26] Supporters of this perspective set themselves apart, in theoretical terms, from the systems framework by arguing that organizational structures have no independent ontological status as objects or mechanisms apart from their formulation and use in social interaction. In turn, this directed the focus of analytical attention towards the 'theories' of organization held by members and the manner in which they informed the courses of action which they followed to modify, change or preserve existing arrangements. The meaning of the latter for organizational actors and the complex ways in which their interpretations fed into collective interventions in the course of events emerged as the focal point for the social action perspective. Rather than privilege – in terms of conceptualization, understanding and explanation – the structural dimensions of organizations and the environmental pressures or demands which bring them into existence, social action theorists called attention to the social, historical and cultural contexts in which 'organizational projects' were mobilized. It is this complex, dynamic interplay between contexts, projects and interventions which forms the intellectual rationale for the development of a social action approach based on fundamental domain assumptions about the nature of 'organizational order' articulated by the negotiated order framework.

In recent years, the influence of the negotiated order/social action perspective can be most clearly discerned in the work of these researchers and writers who have concentrated on ubiquitous processes associated with 'organizational politics' and their longer-term impact on policy formulation and implementation.[27] Within this area of interest, the major task has been to map the various ways in which particular individuals and groups or coalitions are able to control and manipulate 'critical' organizational resources – such as, technology, information, knowledge, skill and ideology – in such a way that they frame the agenda for strategic and routine decision-making. Both in relation to 'high' policy issues – concerned with matters of long-term investment, relocation and reorganization – and 'low level' tactical considerations – such as production modifications, rule changes and work rescheduling – the capacity to secure and retain control over resources which can be mobilized to structure the decision-making agenda is seen to be crucial.[28] Thus, the capacity to shape organizational ideology and culture in such a way that it 'organizes in' certain issues and 'organizes out' others is seen to be central to the preservation of existing power structures and patterns of reward. At a lower level, the ability to control and skilfully deploy 'areas of uncertainty' within the production process – for example, machine maintenance and repair[29] – where problems and their correction cannot be predicted and anticipated in advance (because of a lack of appropriate technical knowledge and expertise), can provide a very effective source of tactical leverage from which negotiating power is derived and deployed.

Those researchers who have concentrated on strategic decision-making within organizations and the power struggles between 'dominant coalitions' which crystallize around choices concerning long-term policy have tended to focus their attention on the 'mobilization of bias'.[30] The latter refers to the processes whereby top management and their advisers manipulate core values and beliefs in such a way that potentially threatening issues – threatening, that is, to their power and control – are 'filtered out' before they are defined and accepted as 'problems' or issues requiring attention from decision-takers. Others have directed their attention to the 'micro-politics' of everyday organizational life to achieve a better understanding of the negotiating processes through which routine organizational work can be performed.[31] These negotiating processes are seen to be particularly important within organizational settings consisting of a relatively high proportion of 'professional' or 'semi-professional' groups with differing, not to say conflicting, ideas as to what needs to be done and how it should be done. In this situation, effective negotiating processes and the relations between the various interest groups or coalitions which can contain and manage overt conflicts or latent tensions are crucial to the maintenance of organizational order and the securing of routine work performance. By regulating and managing conflicting claims over organizational resources and the manner in which they are to be used in organizational, work, negotiating processes facilitate the establishment and maintenance of relatively stable and enduring working relationships. But the latter are open to renegotiations and revision if circumstances change.

Both groups of researchers – whether their focus is on 'high' or 'low' politics – view organizations as 'organized anarchies' or 'loosely coupled' networks precariously held together by negotiating processes and the power relationships emerging out of them.[32] This stands in stark contrast to the model of organization conveyed by the systems framework in which the overriding emphasis is directed to formal structures subject to an impersonal logic of change and development that imposes itself on social actors. Within the negotiated order perspective, control and coherence, in so far as they can be accomplished, emerge out of accommodation, patterning and compromise continually engaged in by social actors as they assemble a viable 'organizational system' out of the multiplicity of resources, problems and values that collective action requires. The systems approach insists that order resides in a set of structural attributes, authorized and institutionalized through a logic of organizational change and development which operates 'behind the backs' of social actors who are more or less forced to adapt to its imperatives if they wish the organization to survive.

However, serious doubts have been expressed as to the ability or inclination of the negotiated order frame-work to provide adequate understanding and explanation of the enduring structures of power and control that shape the situational and organizational arenas in which 'order' is constructed and maintained.[33] As Day and Day put it:

Perhaps the most serious limitation of the theory of negotiated order is its overall failure to place specific negotiative process within their total contextual framework. This characteristic has served to restrict the theory's level of analysis primarily to micro and middle-range processes and, as a consequence, it is quite possible that we may be getting a distorted picture of the actual nature and scope of some of these negotiations. Thus, although proponents of the theory acknowledge that occurrences and circumstances external to an organization do in fact effect the negotiations, relationships and structures within it, they fail to demonstrate how these external forces are incorporated in the explanatory framework of their perspective. Or, in other words, how are these macrolevel issues accounted for by this perspective; how do we go about relating them to what occurs within the organization, and vice versa?[34]

This seems to suggest that negotiated order theorists recognize the problem of incorporating a macro-level or structural perspective within their overall approach, but find it difficult to achieve this more because their analytical focus is fixed on micro-level negotiating processes and the middle-range structures which they produce. In other words, their approach leads them to overemphasize the freedom which social actors have to choose and construct their organizational arrangements and to underemphasize the constraining influence of overarching structures of power and control ingrained within the institutional structure of the wider society. There is too much attention to 'structures in process' and not enough to the 'structuring of processes'.

It is this perceived conceptual lacuna within the negotiated order framework – its lack of attention to the institutional constraints in which 'organizational order' is negotiated – that provides the starting-point for the development of the power and domination framework.

### ORGANIZATIONS AS STRUCTURES OF POWER AND DOMINATION

Within the systems framework organizational structures are seen as 'transcendent' entities; that is, possessing an independent logic of their own that can be isolated and analyzed without reference to social actors and the shared meanings through which they frame on events. The negotiated order framework, on the other hand, sees structures as 'immanent'; that is, as continuously constructed and reconstructed out of the flow of social interaction and the shared meanings that emerge from these negotiating processes. The systems approach inclines towards a deterministic mode of explanation in which the logic of systems change and development – whether at the environmental or organizational level – forces itself on social actors in such a way that they have to adapt to its dictates if they are to survive and prosper. The negotiated order perspective is predisposed towards a voluntaristic form of analysis in which the choices and interventions of organizational actors – whether at the level of strategic choice over long-term policy or tactical choices at the level of work performance – construct the structural context in which they operate according to their, conflicting and contested, preferences.

The power framework attempts to overcome this polarization in preferred analytical logics – between structural or environmental determinism and organizational choice – by focusing on the more permanent configurations of power and domination which simultaneously constrain and enable the technical and political activities of social actors – whether these are constituted as individuals or as corporate groups. It suggests that organizations are most appropriately conceptualized as:

1. Instruments or mechanisms geared to the protection and advancement of dominant economic, political and social interests prevailing within the societies of which they are a part; in this respect, organizations are constituted by the macro-structures of power and control in which they are located.

2. The structural arrangements and managerial practices typical of formal or complex organizations are determined by these wider configurations of domination; the latter also control the extent to which organizations reproduce the

ideological and political constraints in which they are embedded.

3. Within the context of institutionalized constraints set by dominant groups, specific organizational actors – such as managers, professionals, technicians, skilled and unskilled workers, and clients/customers – struggle to control the ideas and techniques through which work is coordinated.

4. This struggle for control generates endemic conflicts of interests and values within and between organizational actors over the way in which work is to be structured and the benefits derived from productive activity are to be distributed.

5. The conflicts that are embedded in the very social structure and fabric of organizational life produce contradictions and tensions which have to be regulated by administrative technologies and managerial practices of various kinds if coordinated productive activity – geared to the interests of dominant groups – is to be sustained.

6. These regulative technologies and practices are partially successful but usually give rise to problems of their own in terms of establishing new sources of potential power and control that are fought over by contending groups.

7. This 'dialectic of control' – that is, the continually shifting balance of resources and power reproduced by the uneven struggle between dominant and subordinate groups to exercise some degree of control over the conditions through which organizational existence is secured – is the primary source of structural change within complex organizations; endemic conflict between contending power groups over the conditions through which the most significant features of organizational life are reproduced is the underlying force that drives transformations – of varying magnitudes and scales – in structures and practices.

The power framework begins from the proposition that organizations are brought into existence and sustained as viable social units by the wider totality of power structures and control relations in which they are embedded. Organizations constitute strategic social arenas or sites through which the economic, political and social structures characteristic of advanced capitalist societies can be effectively integrated and directed to the interests of dominant groups.[35] The major concern of the latter is to maintain their dominant position within the power structures of advanced capitalist societies and the economic, political and cultural advantages that flow from continued occupancy of 'commanding positions' within the former. Formal or complex organizations must be approached initially as the tools or mechanisms through which these dominant groups secure and maintain the conditions necessary for their social reproduction and survival over time. They constitute the strategic mechanisms through which dominant groups mobilize material, political and ideological resources in support of their continued occupancy of commanding positions within macro-level power structures and the effective control which this facilitates over organized action. As Salaman puts it: 'organizational structure – the design of work and control – can only be seen in terms of a general process of organizational control initiated by, and in the interests of, those who run or dominate the organization.'[36]

Macro-level power structures and the sectional interests which they reflect shape the context in which organizations operate. But they do not necessarily determine the fine detail of the structural forms which the latter adopt to achieve routine coordination and control. Rather, wider configurations of institutionalized power and domination frame the contextual or environmental constraints in which specific organizational forms and practices are developed and deployed. This is so to the extent that the latter embody 'taken-for-granted' assumptions about the priority to be assigned to certain interests over others; built into the design and operation of routine organizational structures and practices there is a recurring bias in favour of automatically privileging objectives such as 'rationality', 'profitability', 'effectiveness' and 'efficiency' over values such as 'equity', 'justice' and 'security'. Thus, the generally accepted principles and rationales on which organizations rely to calculate the most appropriate courses of action that they should follow are seen to be pervaded by sectional biases which parade as states of affairs to the benefit of everybody:

It is this process of unobtrusive control through the medium of a seemingly irresistible rationality and an unquestioned everyday logic-in-use that explains why it is that organizations are protected from a too precarious dependence on the individual perceptions of their members but rather develop what seems to be a facticity, experienced as external to the individual members. The seeming facticity, experienced as external and constraining, derives from the shared rationality and logic-in-use of the members. . . . Ideology functions as an overarching idea-system or symbol-system that provides a protective shield for a version of reality that would minimise the disturbing effects of reinterpretation and reconstruction. It provides a fundamental justification and legitimation for what it would have us believe is an *established order*. It thus provides a rationale for a particular form of selectivity and seeks to exclude others.[37]

In this way, dominant groups within organizations establish 'vocabularies of motive' and belief systems which routinely filter out the expression of interests and values which are potentially threatening to the *status quo*. The underlying premises on which organizational action is based are fixed in such a way that they subtly restrict the range of options considered and the decisions likely to flow from them.[38]

Yet, the underlying ideologies and rationales that inform the systems of calculation through which organizational decision-making and action are undertaken are not completely the preserve of dominant interests. Within the framework of institutional and ideological constraints established by the latter, organizations are 'contested terrains' in which various groups and coalitions struggle to impose their preferences on structural designs and administrative processes:

Organizational action is an indeterminate outcome of substantive struggles between different agencies: people who deploy different resources; people whose organizational identities will be shaped by the way in which disciplinary practices work through and on them, even in their use of such techniques; people who seek to control and decide the nature of organizational action and those many things to which they will routinely have recourse in their membership, work and struggles. Consequently, the interests of actors in organizations and the decisions that they make are necessarily contingent on various forms of organization calculation. . . . Contingency reigns, albeit within a hegemonic personal cast.[39]

While the institutionalized structures of power and domination created and maintained by ruling elites and classes within the political economies of advanced capitalism restrict the range of strategic and tactical options available to oppositional groups, the latter are able to mobilize behind collective projects which challenge, and potentially threaten, the overarching control enjoyed by the former. As such, organizations are strategic sites for the conduct of pervasive power struggles between opposing groups over the control structures and practices – and their supporting rationales – through which work is organized, and the distributional outcomes which these mechanisms produce.

In this sense, organizations are locales or arenas in which endemic conflicts over the distribution of power and the allocation of resources flowing from it are carried on; they constitute indispensable mechanisms for directing struggles over control of the institutional machinery and ideological systems through which societies are governed and the differentially distributed structure of material and cultural rewards which they legitimate. They are integral components of and vehicles for a continuous struggle for control which pervades the very social fabric and collective life of all advanced capitalist societies. Within the latter, the major contextual constraint that work organizations face is the need to increase operational efficiency as indicated by their performance as profit-generating units. This imperative engenders various types of demands and pressures on organizational actors to structure productive activity in such a way that the long-term economic interests of dominant groups in securing sustained profitability become the paramount constraint directing work performance and organization.[40] Hierarchical authority structures, disciplinary technologies, monitoring and control systems, and supervisory practices are all seen to be pervaded by the demand for sustained profitability and the constraints which this necessarily forces on subordinate groups. Thus, the struggle to control the organizational mechanisms through which work performance is structured in capitalist societies so that it generates a surplus appropriated by dominant groups is built into the social forms constitutive of material production within such societies.

The struggle to control the organizational structures and practices through which productive activity is coordinated routinely reproduces contradictions and tensions which have to be regulated and contained if profitability and capital accumulation are to be sustained. These contradictions, and the tensions which they generate, encourage the development of administrative and managerial practices aimed at coping with the instabilities and uncertainties necessarily reproduced by a system of production based on an exploitative relationship between dominant and subordinate groups:

In any exploitative mode of production the central problem for the dominant group is to extract effort from the subordinate group. . . . In any . . . mode of production dominant groups have a variety of means for seeking the compliance of subordinates. Each mode involves a contradictory relationship between dominant and subordinate groups in which elements of antagonism and cooperation are necessarily intertwined. In such a situation, the problem for dominant groups is to live with and manage the consequences of the various contradictions that operate within the labour process . . . and outside it. They will develop means of managing the labour process in the light of their specific circumstances. . . . Behaviour around the issue of control can be termed struggle. Struggles vary in their character and intensity, and have histories which shape subsequent developments. The outcome of action shapes the structure in which subsequent action takes place.[41]

However, the administrative technologies and managerial practices which dominant groups deploy and depend on to maintain their control within work organizations generate problems of their own. The central problem for dominant groups is to organize work performance in such a way that it secures a surplus which can be transformed into profits and the sustained capital accumulation which this facilitates. This necessarily means that subordinate groups will be exploited to the extent that a significant proportion of the surplus which they reproduce is appropriated by dominant groups and used for their own purposes. Consequently, capitalist production entails a dominant group of exploiters and a subordinate group of exploited locked into a contradictory relationship in which they need each other to exist, but where each threatens the other's survival. The tensions and conflicts resulting from this contradictory relationship have to be managed if production geared to profit and capital accumulation is to continue on a reasonably stable basis. But, the specific organizational structures and practices implemented to regulate conflict can cause serious difficulties in their own right. Dominant groups can disagree over the organizational and ideological means to be deployed to manage conflicts over control. Subordinate groups play a crucial role in accepting – however grudgingly – their own exploitation and can exert a considerable influence on the actual outcomes which administrative technologies realize. The implementation of the latter usually establishes new sources of actual or potential leverage within the work organization which can be utilized and exploited by subordinate groups for the realization of their preferences. New forms of conflict regulation and administrative control often produce unforeseen and unintended consequences which make the task of conflict management even more hazardous, and unpredictable in the outcomes which it achieves.

Thus, enshrined within all work organizations there lies a 'dialectic of control'; that is, a dynamic process of struggle between contending groups to secure and command the conditions through which collective action is made possible:

All strategies of control employed by superordinate individuals or groups call forth counter-strategies on the part of subordinates. . . . No matter how great the scope or intensity of control superordinates possess, since their power presumes the active compliance of others, these others can bring to bear strategies of their own, and apply specific types of sanctions. . . . All forms of rule have their 'openings' that can be utilized by those in subordinate positions to influence the activities of those who hold power over them. One consequence of this is that technologies of power – in other words, formalized procedures of rule – rarely if ever work with the 'fixity' which, on the face of things, they might seem to possess. The more a social system is one in which the control exercised by superordinates depends upon a considerable scope of power over subordinates, the more shifting and potentially volatile its organization is likely to be.[42]

This process of contest and struggle between different strategies of control, and the organizational practices which it creates, is a dynamic force in the sense that it inevitably produces changes in power relationships and the administrative structures which they sustain. In so far as power relationships consist of patterned inequalities in the distribution of resources and the unequal capacities or opportunities which they offer to transform social situations in the light of preferred outcomes, then struggles to control the organizational mechanisms through which domination is secured and subordination maintained will have a pervasive impact on the way in which the former are structured. In this respect, the 'dialectic of control' is the dynamic process which underlies the changing balance of power experienced in all complex organizations and the crucial effect which it has on the capacity to shape and reshape the structures and practices through which domination is simultaneously protected and challenged at the level of routine everyday life or at the level of strategic decision-making and corporate governance.

The power perspective on organizations has attracted considerable support and attention within the sociology of organizations over the last two decades or so. One might say that it has undergone a revival in so far as it entails rediscovering and retrieving the focus on the symbiotic relationship between domination, control and organization which was of such theoretical significance and political import for Marx and Weber.[43] While calling attention to the vital explanatory relevance of contextual or environmental factors in shaping and changing organizational structures and practices, it conceptualizes these in fundamentally different terms from those adopted by supporters of the systems approach. It rejects the limitations inherent in the latter's focus on 'neutral' or 'objective' situational contingencies such as size, markets, technologies or resource niches.[44] Instead, it concentrates on the institutionalized economic, political and social structures through which organizations are reproduced and transformed over time as mechanisms facilitating and directing the struggle to control the conditions under and through which collective action is made possible.

Within this general problematic, the major task that has been undertaken by researchers working within the power framework has been to develop a more realistic understanding of the complexities of control within capitalist work organizations and the various forms of conflict which their utilization has engendered. In particular, the specific ways in which the 'dialectic of control' operates within workplaces to produce changes in the patterns of conflict that emerge out of the struggle between dominant and subordinate groups, as well as the wider impact of these changing patterns of conflict on the control strategies followed by employers and managers, has constituted a major area of concern for researchers working within the power framework. This work brings a very different understanding to bear on industrial bureaucracy from that conveyed within the systems framework. Far from constituting neutral technical machines designed to secure organizational survival and effectiveness, bureaucratic structures and practices and redefined as tools serving the interests of dominant groups. But these tools are also seen as only partially successful in realizing their creators' objectives in that they inevitably leave openings and opportunities for control to be exploited by subordinate groups.[45]

Examples of this kind of work are to be found in the analyses provided by Salaman,[46] Edwards[47] and Storey.[48] All three have focused on the practical activities in which managers engage to secure effective control over the organizational mechanisms through which production is coordinated and controlled, as well as the modes of worker resistance that have formed around these control strategies. Each of them is theoretically committed to a view of organizations as structures of control which have to be understood in terms of the encompassing systems of institutionalized power and domination of which they are a part. At the same time, they maintain that operational control structures and practices cannot simply be 'read off' from these wider configurations of domination, in so far as they unavoidably become part and parcel of the everyday struggle to shape the administrative routines by which work behaviour is coordinated and regulated. The translation of a general control imperative into an operational reality is fraught with danger and the need for practical modification in specific circumstances.

The need to map the intricate processes whereby principles and policies of labour control enunciated by owners and senior managers are translated – as well as being diluted and transmuted in the process of implementation – into operational practices adopted by lower levels of the managerial hierarchy has assumed central significance for these researchers. Their work has shown that operational control practices display a wide variety of forms that often hold a very tenuous relationship to the strategic goals and constraints enunciated by dominant coalitions. Indeed, the struggle within the managerial hierarchy to design and implement 'effective' control policies and practices within work organizations has attained as much, if not more, explanatory significance than the broader conflicts occurring between dominant and subordinate groups over these issues. The complexities and variations which necessarily result from the attempt to translate general control imperatives into organizationally specific practices are seen to be compounded by political conflicts within the managerial hierarchy which unavoidably reinforce the inherent tendency towards differentiation and fragmentation.[49]

Indeed, it is this emerging emphasis on variation in control structures and heterogeneity in forms of workplace conflict and cooperation which has led some commentators to suggest that the power perspective has encouraged an over-deterministic view of the realities of organizational control in practice.[50] The overriding emphasis which the power view lays on the ideological structures through which worker consent is manufactured and the organizational mechanisms by which managerial domination is maintained has been seen to preclude a more subtle and sensitive appreciation of the complexities of workplace morality and its cultural context. Instead of treating the work organization as a 'black box' or a 'strategic site' in which contending class or group interests slug it out and rationally manipulate internal structures and practices according to their sectional interests,[51] a growing body of opinion has suggested that the explanatory significance of the organization as a cultural and symbolic reality needed to be given more focused attention. The power perspective has tended to use the concept of 'culture' in a reductionist fashion; that is, organizational values and symbols are treated as an ideological resource – admittedly a vital resource – to be mobilized in support of various kinds of economic and political interests. It is the legitimizing function of culture – that is, its role in justifying and normalizing sectional interests and power as 'collective goods' – which has been the major focus for the power perspective. But, the critics argue, this focus has tended to direct attention away from the creative and interpretive role of organizational culture and symbolism, and redirect it towards the political functions that the latter fulfil in legitimating or challenging institutionalized power structures. In other words, the critics maintain that the power framework has conceptualized and utilized culture and symbolism in a relatively crude and deterministic manner by tying the latter to economic and political concerns which assume overwhelming explanatory priority; that is, by treating culture as derivative of political economy.

This critical response has provided the opening for an approach to organizations which treats them as symbolic constructions which pervade the lived-experience of all organizational members.

ORGANIZATIONS AS SYMBOLIC CONSTRUCTIONS

The increasing visibility and popularity of a view of organizations as symbolic constructions and cultural orders may be seen as a manifestation of a growing unease with 'mainstream' approaches – irrespective of their commitment of a systems, negotiated order, or power perspective. Increasing unease and discontent with more conventional approaches which concentrate on the structural, environmental and material aspects of organizational life to the exclusion of cultural and symbolic processes – or the reduction of the latter to the explanatory status of derivative epiphenomena – has culminated in the emergence of a conception of organization as a manifestation of primary processes oriented to the meaningful creation and interpretation of collective life. As Turner has recently argued:

After a long pre-occupation with the problems of building more rational, efficient and computer-like organizations, students of administrative activities have recently become much more aware of other facets of human life which contribute to the functioning of organizations and which constitute the nature of social life as it is lived in organizational settings. This new awareness focuses attention upon the symbolic, the qualitative, the sensuous aspects of human relationships and upon the central place of these qualities in the operation of organizations.[52]

While a wide range of substantive interests – myth, ritual, history, narrative, style, etc. – can be discerned within this recent upsurge of interest in organizational culture and symbolism, a number of common underlying assumptions about the nature of organizations have emerged to form the basic conceptual building blocks for the development of a coherent analytical framework. These may be summarized in the following manner:

1. Organizations are cultural artefacts that are produced, reproduced and transformed through processes of symbolic construction, mediation and interpretation in which all members are routinely engaged; organizational reality is constructed, internalized, sustained and changed through processes of cultural creation and enactment.

2. Organizational cultures are constituted through the generation of values, ideologies, rituals and ceremonies that express and make sense of participation within a collective enterprise.

3. As shared constructions of collective values and symbols, organizational cultures are shaped by and articulated through modes of thinking and conduct which embody and represent the collective experiences and meanings entailed in organizational membership.
4. Organizational cultures simultaneously socialize individuals into institutional patterns of thinking and acting, and into alternative schemes of interpretation and 'sense making' that diverge from the former.
5. Organizational cultures, and the collective meanings which they frame, transmit and reframe schemes of interpretation; they are never uniform or monolithic in the messages they communicate and their implications for social action; they consist of multiple rationalities and realities that overlap, interpenetrate and contradict each other.
6. Organizational cultures simultaneously support and question dominant structures of meaning, power and control; they consist of loosely coupled systems of meaning and interpretation that can be accessed and mobilized by various groups for their own purposes within and outside the organizations.
7. The degree of effective control that managers can exert over the impact of symbolic creation, transmission and interpretation is inherently constrained by the complexity of these processes and by the fact that dominant cultures are usually internally contradictory; the 'recipes for action' which the latter convey need to be supplemented by auxiliary systems of meaning and action that dilute and fragment the behavioural injunctions that they entail.

The symbolic or cultural framework shifts the focus of attention away from 'organization' to 'organizing'; it suggests that the process of organizing is most appropriately conceptualized as the enactment of cultural development and transformation. Culture becomes the basic resource and process through which social action and interaction are continually constructed and reconstructed to form a shared 'organizational reality'. The technical, structural and material entities associated with the latter – such as production systems, authority hierarchies and control mechanisms – are redescribed and reinterpreted as products of cultural processes which have to be endowed with collective meaning and significance before they enter into the practices through which 'organizations' are created and sustained. Thus the 'subjective' – rather than the 'objective' – aspects of organizational reality become the central focus for analysis in so far as they call attention to the socially constructed frames of value and meaning through which coordinated social life becomes possible. The existence of organizations as institutionalized patterns of coordination and control is seen to be dependent upon their realization and affirmation through the shared frames of reference and stocks of knowledge by means of which actors create and enact a shared and coherent sense of their participation in a collective process of 'institution building'.

This fundamental process of cultural enactment and reaffirmation is dependent on and expressed through specific symbolic forms such as values, ideologies, rituals and ceremonies. These forms provide the shared means by which collective involvement and identity with the project of organizing and the fact of organization can be realized by individuals and groups implicated in institutionalized relationships. As a social expression of human consciousness and creation, complex organizations have to be sustained through generative processes that yield and shape meaningful interaction. Organizational structures and the shared reality that they represent only exist as patterns of symbolic relationships and meanings sustained through the constitutive processes of human interaction and the cultural forms by which they are expressed, such as language, symbols, myths and stories. The accomplishment of organization and the meaning of individual and collective participation in such a shared configuration of meaning and values can only be achieved through processes of cultural creation and enactment made possible through expressive forms.[53]

Consequently, the reality and significance of organizational membership can only be understood through an informed appreciation of the modes of thinking and action typically associated with the cultural and symbolic meanings that the former provides. Acceptance of and identity with 'the organization' necessarily entails socialization into and internalization of the core values and norms associated with membership so that the individual defines their own existence and worth in terms of these institutionalized histories and ideologies. Yet, the conferring and acceptance of collective identities through socialization and internalization is unlikely to be complete or simple. Organizational membership usually offers the prospect of more than one cultural identity and the forms of social conduct that it supports. Dominant cultures may frame symbolic creation and discourse but their acceptance by individuals – certainly above and beyond ritual obeisance and public display – is often partial and conditional upon the constraints in which they operate. At the same time, the dominant cultures supported and reinforced by management often contain contradictory messages as to what to believe and how to act. They have to be interpreted and reinterpreted in the course of social interaction so that they continue to convey the meanings which managers intend in such a way that they have a realistic prospect of being accepted and acted on. Thus, cultural production, and the collective identities that it bestows, is a crucial feature of the managerial work necessarily involved in creating and sustaining viable organizations.[54]

This entails a recognition of the fact that organizational cultures consist of and convey multiple rationalities and realities; they contain and transmit a diverse range of meanings and interpretations which often conflict with each other in regard to the messages they send and their implications for action.[55] While top management may attempt to impose an overarching rationality as a basis for thought and action, this is likely to require supplementary interpretation in practice and to generate alternative rationalities which conflict with – in terms of inherent meanings and imperatives for action – the injunctions which the former contains. Thus, officially recognized and supported cultures promulgated by organizational elites will have to be interpreted by operational managers in particular contexts where the general imperatives which the former contain will need to be made relevant to situational conditions and constraints. This process of symbolic mediation, negotiation and supplementation on the part of individual managers is likely to dilute and fragment – at least in a practical or operational sense – the cultural coherence and force of institutionalized norms and ideologies.

At the same time, dominant cultures are unavoidably in competition with 'unofficial' sub-cultures – such as those entailed in membership of departmental, professional, craft and political groups – which offer alternative sources of meaning and legitimation for action that depart from approved norms.

Any large-scale organization will contain competing, not to say conflicting, sources of cultural creation, enactment and mobilization which make the task of achieving effective cultural control and indoctrination even more fraught with uncertainty and ambiguity. Officially approved and supported ideologies associated with bureaucratic authority and careerism will play a pivotal role in containing potentially disruptive sub-cultures which corrode institutionalized structure of power and control.[56] But their practical impact in stabilizing and buttressing the organizational *status quo* is often uneven and unpredictable in its consequences.

As a result, the capacity of managers to exercise effective control over the processes of symbolic construction and communication in complex organizations is rather precarious and uncertain. By its very nature, cultural production and enactment is a slippery process which is inherently resistant to close monitoring and control by managers who may wish to restrict the range of meanings made available to organizational members so that it squares with prevailing definitions of the situation.[57] In addition, the management of meaning and the manufacture of consent are practised in social and organizational contexts configured through multiple rationalities and ideologies that defy easy corporation and absorption into officially sanctioned cultural narratives. While the latter often resonate with the values of technical rationality and instrumentalism as 'natural' or 'taken-for-granted' realities reasonably underpinning organized action, they require support and supplementation through symbols, myths and rituals which makes their status as an unquestioned and unquestionable legitimatory discourse even more visible and open to interruption. In other words, the reliance on and use of official ideologies by managers to legitimate sanctioned interpretations of organizational reality – such as technical efficiency, operational effectiveness, administrative rationality and economic viability – inevitably reveals their 'mundane' quality as contested and contestable definitions of the situation. Their 'sacred' quality – that is, their status and role as unchallengeable accounts of organizational order and the action imperatives that it entails – is unavoidably demystified in the very process of mobilizing them to legitimate preferred courses of action and to deny that aura of legitimacy to alternative action strategies.[58] As Pfeffer[59] has argued, technical rationality is the 'religion' of formal or complex organizations and managers are its high priests. But a conception of organizations as cultural artefacts and symbolic constructions soon reveals the ideological status and political function of this religion:

> The belief in the value of rational decision procedures and planning, coupled with the belief in their use as the foundation of organizational decision-making, provides a common ideology linking together members of a given organization and uniting participants of formal organizations. These ideologies help to hide the use of power and legitimate decision outcomes . . . rational decision procedures and planning are part of a ritualized ideology, used to legitimate and partially obscure the actual choice processes that are taking place.[60]

The major theme that had directed work undertaken within the cultural/symbolic framework has been the management of meaning and the various practices and devices – language, discourse, ritual, myth, narrative, etc. – through which cultural managers attempt to 'bring off' acceptable definitions of organizational reality as a basis for collective action.[61] They take their cue from Pfeffer's argument that:

> The task of those who wish to exercise power in organizations is to present the advocated decisions and activities in a meaningful and sensible way to the organizational participants, so that a social consensus, and social definitions around these activities and decisions, may be developed. Thus, political activity in organizations involves both labelling and sense-making, as well as the development of social consensus around the labels and definitions of the decisions and actions.[62]

It is in this context that Pettigrew defines the management

of meaning as entailing 'a process of symbol construction and use value designed both to create legitimacy for one's actions, ideas and demands, and to delegitimate the demands of one's opponents'.[63] He suggests that a focus on the practices through which legitimation and delegitimation are striven for – such as language, myth and ideologies – will lead researchers to concentrate on the complex interaction between 'front stage' decision-making and power and 'back stage' structures of domination and control.[64] The mobilization of cultural resources to construct and sustain unobtrusive ideologies of domination and control becomes a strategic issue within this research tradition in so far as it directs attention to the role of these 'hidden' or 'unobtrusive' processes in facilitating the manipulation of symbols and values to structure the decision-making agenda before actual decision-taking occurs.[65] This selectively filters out any recognition of problems or issues which would potentially threaten and undermine prevailing ideological interpretations which are enacted and supported by dominant groups.

A less dramatic, more mundane and everyday illustration of the deep involvement of managers in processes of cultural production and enactment can be seen in the contributions of Gowler and Legge,[66] and Mangham.[67] The former maintain that:

the fact that managers spend a great deal of time talking is more than a matter for passing comment, and not necessarily something to be deplored. This endless talk, especially the rhetoric, may be the way in which social control is maintained while, in situations of great uncertainty and complexity, managerial prerogatives are simultaneously accomplished and legitimated. This is not an inconsiderable achievement. Indeed, this may be what 'achievement' is really all about. . . . The preferred image of the natural order is produced by the rhetoric of bureaucratic control, which presents the proper access to and allocation of scarce resources as a 'neutral' technical business. But in order to accomplish this it simultaneously incorporates, through backgrounds, ambiguous and controversial moral-aesthetic meanings . . . the manager has to acquire the political ability to so manipulate his verbal and written outputs.[68]

Mangham's research provides a grounded illustration of the symbolic and cultural processes through which managerial control is legitimated, but within a context which clearly illuminates the inherently precarious nature of such an accomplishment and the conflict between competing rationales in which it is embroiled. His study and analysis of boardroom interaction between senior executives in a large engineering company indicates that organizations are created, maintained and transformed through the processes of meaning construction, negotiation and mediation in which managers are regularly involved:

the construction of meaning accomplished through the medium of language is *the* central feature of interaction and, thus, of the process of organizing. . . those features of the organization which are often taken by the members to be crucial for its survival . . . emerge not from outside but from within, from a process of definition, construction and improvisation. . . . Reality is socially constructed, whether or not a particular resource (material or otherwise) is valued is, ultimately, a matter of definition and the processes of definition are shot through with language. . . . What occurs in the boardroom of Friction Free Castings Ltd is a series of improvisations around power and status enacted by a number of performers.[69]

Within this process, Mangham argues, managers – particularly senior managers and executives – play a crucial role in reconciling divergent interests and interpretations through the construction and promulgation of 'narratives' that bring some sort of order and coherence to the chaos of conflicting voices that strive to shape and control the organizational agenda. Some of these narratives are relatively simple stories concerning recent organizational history and its significance for present troubles. Others are much more complex in terms of the mythological themes that they weave around past events and their ideological import for current organizational action. In both cases, the manager is caught within a creative process which will ultimately shape the courses of action which are actually followed and the way in which their longer-term consequences are interpreted and justified.

Yet, it is this very focus on the micro-processes through which organizational reality is defined and organizational order constructed which have led some commentators to question the inherent analytical and explanatory limitations of the cultural/symbolic approach.[70] They have questioned

whether a relatively narrow concentration on the minutia of
cultural production and enactment in organizations closes off
a sustainable interest in the wider structural context in which
these processes are located and take on broader collective
meaning and explanatory relevance. In particular, they have
argued that the cultural/symbolic framework entails a logic of
analysis which unavoidably directs attention away from the
extra-organizational structures of economic and political
power and domination in which ideological production and
identity work must be situated. By focusing on the status of
organizational participants and managers in particular as
creators of symbolic orders supporting and legitimating
shared meanings, cultural theorists seem to neglect the
encompassing societal structures in which these processes are
located. In their overwhelming desire to avoid reifying
organizational structures – that is, treating them as social
forms which constrain, if not determine, the process of
organizational construction – cultural theorists may be guilty
of underestimating the explanatory relevance of institutionalized forms which enter into the very process of cultural
production and enactment.

The tendency to believe that the symbolic approach may be
'soft on structure' – or at least on those macro-level structures
in which cultural processes producing and reproducing
'organization' have to be contextualized and ultimately
explained – has encouraged the development of an alternative
approach that attempts to overcome the theoretical separation or duality between 'structure' and 'process' that seems to
pervade organizational analysis. This analytical framework
treats organizations as 'social practices' which require simultaneous reference to structure both as a constraint on actions
and as a resource facilitating action that transforms established arrangements.

ORGANIZATIONS AS SOCIAL PRACTICES

Each of the frameworks reviewed in preceding sections of this
chapter tend to concentrate on either the 'structural' or
'processual' aspect of organization. The systems perspective

focuses on the formal organizational designs through which successful adaptation to environmental demands and pressures can be achieved. The negotiated order approach attempts to catch the intricate and subtle processes of 'give-and-take' between organizational actors through which more permanent arrangements are established and preserved over time. The power and domination view highlights the macro-level institutionalized structures of coordination and control which shape intra-organizational designs and practices. The symbolic perspective emphasizes the cultural processes that create and sustain a shared sense of organizational membership and identity, as well as focusing on the role they play in reproducing definitions of 'organizational reality' which are conducive to sectional interests.

The practice framework attempts to provide a definition of organization and conceptual resources for analyzing it which achieves a partial synthesis between the 'structural' focus of the systems and power perspectives and the 'processual' focus of the negotiated order and culture approaches. Conceptualizing and analyzing organizations as social practices entails the following assumptions:

1. Organizations are social practices geared to the assembly and integration of other social practices concerned with transforming the conditions – both material and ideal – under which collective action is made possible.

2. As practices geared to the assembly and integration of other practices, organizations are reproduced through the design and deployment of various administrative mechanisms by means of which managers attempt to realize effective regulation of and control over the performance of work.

3. These administrative mechanisms of assembly, integration and control embody structural resources – such as hierarchies, information systems and rules – and require processual facilitators – such as ideologies, coalitions and cultures – for their effective reproduction and implementation so that the conditions under which organized action becomes possible are established.

4. Both the structural resources and processual facilitators necessary for organizational assembly and control become

focal points for power struggles between contending groups
to gain access to the authoritative mechanisms – through
which 'organization' is accomplished – and the allocative
outcomes that they produce.
5. Power struggles to manage authoritative mechanisms and
the allocative outcomes that they produce form the
underlying dynamic for change and transformation in the
social practices through which organizations are created.
6. This conflict dynamic has to be analyzed in relation to the
strategic choices made by specifiable groups of social actors
and the decision-making practices through which they are
formulated and the action recipes through which they are
undertaken.
7. The modes of calculation, techniques for decision-making,
and means of action available to and utilized by organizational agents as a basis for intervening in the course of
events to maintain or change structures in their favour
becomes central to an understanding of power struggles
and the organizational outcomes they realize.

Within the practice framework, organizations are viewed as
administrative mechanisms containing authoritative and
allocative resources through which collective action can be
coordinated and mobilized in support of productive activity
which transforms the environmental conditions in which it is
undertaken. The administrative practices through which
organizing is accomplished provide a focus for struggle over
the political and economic resources that they contain and a
means for temporarily resolving this conflict in favour of
certain groups rather than others. This conflict to control the
practices by means of which organized action is made
possible is never completely regulated in favour of dominant
groups; it is always likely to slip the latter's grasp and to
produce movements for change and transformation which can
destabilize the *status quo* and threaten the interests which it
protects.

Consequently, the conceptual means by which social actors
come to an understanding of their own interests and the
strategies they pursue to realize the former are of central
importance for analyzing this conflict dynamic and the

change in organizational practices it can initiate. The modes of calculation and deliberation that social actors rely on to identify their preferred outcomes and the strategies in which they engage to realize the latter have a dramatic influence on the form and content of those administrative practices through which organization is achieved. Indeed, it is the 'logics of action' formulated and pursued by social actors as they struggle to shape the organizational practices through which collective projects are mobilized and coordinated which forms the empirical starting-point for the practice framework.

Acceptance of the practice view necessarily entails a rejection of the concept of organization as a unified entity, effectively controlled by a dominant agent (that is, employers/ managers), able to translate its preferences into outcomes in an unconstrained and unproblematic manner. Instead, it suggests that the organization is most appropriately concep- tualized as

a heterogeneous non-unitary, dispersed and fractured entity or social agency ... as the 'site' or locus of a combination of social mechanisms and calculating practices which are juxtaposed and articulated at that 'site' but where this combination is not analysed as a unity ... the notion of an (organization) is 'dispersed' through, or into, a series of pertinencies that inhere around that locus called the (organization). ... These can be formulated with respect to a range of different social and theoretical practices, positions and prob- lems ... there can be no overarchingly unambiguous or fully coherent 'meta-objective' for the (organization), but rather more a shifting series of conflicting, contradictory and contingent partial objectives organized with respect to particular knowledges and interests.[71]

Viewed in this light, management is seen as that agency which is concerned to reconcile conflicting conceptions and interests so that they can be shaped and directed towards the realization of coordinated work performance. This process of reconciliation and direction is dependent upon the ad- ministrative mechanisms and practices that are available to management in the light of the constraints and obstacles it perceives it is facing. Managerial control is now conceived as a series of practices pertaining to different sites or arenas, within and outside the enterprise, which can give rise to variable outcomes.[72] These practices will themselves embody conceptions of preferred interests and outcomes based on modes of deliberation and calculation prioritizing certain objectives and conditions over others. Both these dominant conceptions and the calculating practices through which they are formulated and pursued will be contested by other groups struggling to exert some influence, if not control, over the established mechanisms of assembly and implementation:

The different actors and sub-agencies will deploy different and perhaps even competing conceptual apparatuses of calculation and assessment . . . a more 'political' mechanism is required to offer the ground for a decision and an attempted reconciliation . . . such political mechanisms will fulfil the function of interrupting the diverse calculating practices operating within the entity of the [organization] . . . in order for a decision of some sort to emerge.[73]

In this way, the practice framework draws attention to the highly *diverse* administrative practices and mechanisms through which organizations are established and sustained, rather than similarities in formal structures emphasized by the systems perspective and some versions of the power approach. In consciously directing attention to the diversity of organizational practices rather than general or universal similarities in structural design and operation, the practice framework also requires a fundamental reworking of the concepts of 'interests' and 'strategies'. The latter are no longer conceived as the properties of particular individuals or subjects but as the products of the practices, mechanisms and processes circulating within the organization, as well as the constraints which their operation encounters. Subjective calculations and assessments are caught within the discursive practices through which they are articulated and emerge as constructs to be acted on by the various social actors through which the organization is constituted as a dispersed social agency:

The actions of social actors are critically dependent on the modes of assessment of their situation that they deploy in reaching decisions, and on the specific sets of social relations in which they are implicated . . . several distinct modes of assessment are employed by firms operating within a single national economy, to say nothing of differences between national economies themselves. There is no uniquely defined mode of assessment given by the assumption of rationality and by such rigours as the market place may impose.[74]

Thus, the forms of discourse available to and utilized by social actors – particularly managers – in assessing their organizational situation and deciding on some courses of action appropriate to that assessment is a central concern for the practice framework in its focus on the strategies through which organizations are constituted and the interests which they embody. The discursive practices through which social actors decide upon certain courses of action, the social conditions in which they are formulated and implemented, and the outcomes that they produce are all located within organizational arenas consisting of contradictory and conflicting discourses which cannot be captured by one overarching rationality or ideology. The actual courses of action followed by organizational actors will reflect the ambiguity which this multiplicity of circulating and competing discourses or rationalities generates.

The major substantive issue which has directed organizational research conducted within the practice framework is the ways in which social actors constitute their interests and pursue them within networks of negotiation, coalition and control so that they are translated into viable collective 'projects'.[75] Specific organizational practices and mechanisms such as recruitment, appraisal and promotion are analyzed within the modes of calculation informing such activities and the preferred outcomes which they entail. Thus, employment discrimination against black workers in work organizations is seen as the product of specific social practices, and the racial ideological systems through which they are legitimated, which 'close off' the organizational labour market to penetration by ethnic groups.[76] More often than not, these calculating practices and supporting ideologies are not explicitly formalized or standardized but have to be identified and analyzed through detailed study of the everyday routines through which organizational work is accomplished.

In a similar vein, the organizational practices which privilege certain conceptions of the economic imperatives that ought to inform productive activity and deny that status to alternative modes of economic calculation and control have to be set within rationalities geared to short-term profitability rather than long-term economic growth and stability.[77] The rationalities and practices associated with the imperative for economically acceptable short-term returns on capital employed are seen to distort manufacturing strategies in favour of policies which damage a firm's manufacturing base and the organizational disorder – in terms of threats to long-term economic viability and their social fall-out as indicated by rising unemployment and intensified conflict – which it produces.

In both cases – racial discrimination in employment practices or class domination in manufacturing practices – existing organizational practices have to be analyzed as the outcomes of particular modes of discourse which embody interests and strategies that are privileged by prevailing modes of calculation and forms of action. In turn, the latter have to be viewed against the wider structure of power relations in which they are rationalized as acceptable and 'natural' ways of proceeding. Yet, the translation of institutionalized power relations into viable collective projects enacted through organizational practices cannot be guaranteed in any direct and unproblematic fashion. Indeed, established power structures:

guarantee nothing, but only conditionally and contingently arrange a series of possibilities for disputation or action ... power becomes diffused or dispersed into and through the network of relationships operative within the [organization]. It is always partial, particular and dependent. It is more the effect of the practices and mechanisms of social interaction and the knowledge lodging within these, rather than something which has a definite 'place' where it is held and from which it is deployed ... it [control] is rather dispersed into the interstices of the economy and the organization. Hence, the concept of managerial control ... always implies a highly specific set of organizational principles and conditions, facing a series of changing constraints.[78]

This indicates that the relationship between macro-level structures of domination and intra-organizational politics is likely to be rather more complicated and indirect than suggested by some theorists working within the power framework.[79] It also implies that organizational practices will play a crucial role in mediating between the constraints embedded in macro-structures and the opportunities made available by micro-processes of political negotiation and control.[80] This suggests that the 'dialectic of control' between domination and negotiation may be better understood through a detailed appreciation of the specified organizational practices that facilitate reconciliation between conflicting interests and knowledges rather than subsumed within an overarching 'hegemonic ideology' or rationality.

## DEBATE AND DEVELOPMENT

Each of the analytical frameworks reviewed in this chapter focus on different problems as providing a basis for their conceptual development and deployment in empirical research on complex organizations. This range of problematics – that is, a framework of concepts directed to the elucidation of a core issue or problem – can be summarized as in Table 3.1.

*Table 3.1* Problematics in organizational analysis

| Framework | Problem focus |
| --- | --- |
| Systems | Adaptation |
| Negotiated order | Construction |
| Power and domination | Control |
| Cultural/ symbolic | Meaning |
| Practice | Assembly |

Systems theory is primarily concerned with the adaptation of internal organizational structures to a changing set of external environmental contingencies. In providing a better understanding of the complex processes through which organizational adaptation to environmental contingencies can be realized, systems theory aspires to give management a useful intellectual technology whereby it can match internal designs to external conditions in such a way that operational efficiency and strategic effectiveness are maximized.[81] By providing more systematic and valid knowledge on the general processes through which organizational adaptation is successfully realized, management will be in a better position to deal with the complexities and problems that they will encounter in gearing the organization's design to a changing pattern of external demands and pressures, and the uncertainty which these inevitably generate.

The negotiated order perspective begins its analysis 'one step back' from where systems theory starts. Rather than taking the existence of predetermined structures for granted, the former starts with the problem of how 'organization' is possible; that is, it probes the social processes through which organizational structures – and the shared sense of 'reality' that they convey – are constructed and maintained. It sees organizations as much more precarious and fragile collections of negotiated agreements and arrangements that are always open to renegotiation and reconstruction. It presumes that 'structure' is something that has to be continually worked at and reproduced through social interaction rather than treating it as a transcendent object or entity imposed on social actors by the environmental imperatives that they face.

The power and domination framework concentrates on the political and economic structures through which organizational control is accomplished and sustained. It begins from the presupposition that the most significant aspect of complex organizations is the mechanisms of control that are necessary to regulate endemic conflicts of interest and value between contending groups. These control mechanisms are viewed as reflections of a deeper structure of ideological domination and economic power that is embedded within the political economies of advanced capitalist societies. The latter establishes a set of parameters or constraints in which the struggle between dominant and subordinate groups to control the mechanisms through which profitable productive activity becomes organized is fought out. The ideological resources and processes through which this form of class-based organization is legitimated and accepted as 'natural' or 'inevitable' are also seen as a central interest for the power perspective. While the negotiated order approach interprets ideological production and mobilization in the context of intra-organizational interest group politics, the power framework analyzes the construction and promulgation of legitimatory rationales in relation to the structures of class domination and control that they articulate and protect.

The cultural/symbolic framework attempts to achieve a much more sensitive and subtle appreciation of the belief systems and ideologies that sustain a collective sense of organizational reality and identity. It rejects the rather crude 'reductionist' tendency evident within the power framework; that is, its predilection to reduce cultural and symbolic work to the underlying, more basic or fundamental, economic and political structures which it is presumed to serve. Instead, it strives to provide a more grounded analysis of the processes and practices of cultural production and enactment that makes the social existence and recognition of 'organization' a practical possibility.[82] Culture is what the organization is, rather than something it has.

The symbolic processes and cultural practices which make it possible for organizations to exist as viable social constructions reproduced through their members' modes of thinking and acting provides the analytical focus for this approach. In this respect, it sets itself apart from structural frameworks that tend to reify the organization as an objective entity that is produced and reproduced through a *sui generis* logic of institutional transformation which operates behind actors' backs and imposes itself on their collective understanding.[83] In its place, it offers a conception of organization and a form of discourse which highlight the descriptive and explanatory significance of symbolic creation and cultural enactment as constitutive processes of organizational existence.

Finally, the practice perspective focuses on the multiplicity of ways in which the dispersed social agencies and resources that feed into work organizations are assembled to form

The Sociology of Organizations

coherent and viable collectives. It calls attention to the practices or mechanisms through which this process of assembly is achieved and the, often conflicting, modes of calculation and deliberation that have to be reconciled if the former is to be realized. While accepting the importance of symbolic and cultural practices for the assembly of diverse resources and dispersed inputs into viable social units, it refuses to privilege these over the administrative and political mechanisms through which the latter is made possible. Indeed, it reinforces the explanatory significance of wider structures of economic and political power and the particular organizational practices through which they are mediated to direct and regulate collective action.

Broadly speaking, it is possible to see these perspectives as being located within a more general process of intellectual development characterized by an underlying dynamic of formulation, critique and reformulation. Systems theory became established as the intellectual orthodoxy in the 1950s and shaped the overall agenda to which alternative perspectives responded in a critical and creative fashion.[84] Yet, each of the perspectives have experienced their own internal difficulties when their core assumptions and concepts have been broadened out to incorporate a wider range of empirical phenomena. Thus, the extension of the conceptual core associated with systems theory to accommodate a more serious interest in dynamic processes of conflict and change has made that core more vulnerable to attack and erosion by those advocating a power view of organizations. Similar processes of elaboration and the difficulties it creates have been experienced by the other perspectives.

This overarching process of intellectual innovation and development will be discussed in greater detail in the following chapter which focuses on particular theory groups operating within the general frameworks outlined in this chapter and the research programmes they have initiated. However, it is possible to identify some overarching intellectual movements in organizational analysis occurring over the last twenty years or so in which the specific frameworks discussed in this chapter can be situated. The former are summarized in Table 3.2.

*Table 3.2* Intellectual shifts in organizational analysis

| From ⟶ | To |
|---|---|
| Organization theory from above | Organization theory from below |
| Regulative order | Struggle to control |
| Organizational constraint | Organizational constuction |
| Formal administrative structures | Political/cultural processes |
| Situational contingencies | Strategic choice |
| Environmental determinism | Environmental enactment |

The left-hand side of Table 3.2 summarizes the agenda for organizational analysis which the systems framework established by the end of the 1950s and which itself shaped a great deal of work undertaken in the 1960s. Essentially, it was an organization theory written from the point of view of an administrative or managerial elite whose major concern was to establish and maintain order. This was to be achieved through the organizational constraints imposed on behaviour by means of formalized planning and control systems directed by situational contingencies and the wider context of environmentally determined imperatives in which they originated. Over the last twenty years or so the intellectual hold this agenda has exerted on the study of organizations has been considerably loosened. It has been superseded by the formulation of an interrelated set of issues and approaches which characterize the sociological analysis of organizations in very different terms to that prevailing in the mid/late 1960s.

In place of the orthodox systems view, we have an organization theory which is increasingly written from the point of view of those who are subject to the power and control of dominant groups. The struggle to control the organizational mechanisms through which order is realized and contested has emerged as the central issue for this alternative agenda. Within this struggle for control, the social construction of organizational reality through the engagement in political and cultural processes that simultaneously support and challenge accepted definitions of the situation is seen as a primary point of reference. The strategic choices which inform the promulgation of dominant organizational ideologies, and their challenge by 'subversive' views that break with prevailing interpretations of the organizational *status quo*, take on particular explanatory significance within this wider intellectual movement.

As a result, the environment is no longer seen as an independent entity or process that imposes itself on organizational decision-makers and the structural designs which they implement. Now it is viewed as a resource to be enacted and manipulated by those who are in a position to control the cognitive practices through which it is configured as an interpreted reality to be acted on by dominant coalitions within the organization.

These wider shifts in intellectual orientation and emphasis are revealed and articulated through the research programmes that have been pursued by various groups of theorists operating within the frameworks outlined in this chapter and the research programmes which they have developed. They are reviewed and assessed in the next chapter.

REFERENCES

1. Bernstein, R.J., *Beyond Objectivism and Relativism* (Basil Blackwell, London, 1983), p. 225.
2. Hass, J.E. and Drabek, H., *Complex Organizations: A Sociological Reader* (Free Press, New York, 1978), p. 3.
3. Reed, M.I., *Redirections in Organisational Analysis* (Tavistock, London, 1985).
4. Blau, P., 'The Study of Formal Organizations' in Parsons. T. (ed.), *American Sociology* (Basic Books, New York, 1968), p. 54.
5. Elliott, D., 'The Organisation as System' in Salaman G. and Thompson, K. (eds), *Control and Ideology in Organisations* (Open University Press, Milton Keynes, 1980), pp. 85–104.
6. Donaldson, L., *In Defence of Organisation Theory: A Reply to*

*the Critics* (Cambridge University Press, Cambridge, 1985), pp. 22–6.

7. Inkeles, A., *What is Sociology?* (Prentice-Hall, Englewood Cliffs, NJ, 1964), pp. 34–5.

8. Parsons, T., 'Suggestions for a Sociological Approach to the Theory of Organisations I and II', *Administrative Science Quarterly*, vol. 1, 1956, pp. 63–85 and 225–39.

9. The concept of task environment is developed in more detail in Scott. W.R., *Organizations: Rational, Natural and Open Systems* (Prentice-Hall, Englewood Cliffs, NJ, second edition, 1981).

10. Selznick, P., *TVA and the Grass Roots* (University of California Press, Berkeley, 1949), p. 253.

11. *ibid.*, pp. 251–2.

12. This development is reviewed and assessed in Morgan, G., *Organizations in Society* (Macmillan, London, 1990) and Thompson, P. and McHugh, D., *Work Organisation: A Critical Introduction* (Macmillan, London, 1990).

13. The context between 'closed' and 'open' systems approaches and its implications are discussed in Silverman, D., *The Theory of Organisation* (Heinemann, London, 1970).

14. For an informative review of contingency theory see Burrell, G. and Morgan, G., *Sociological Paradigms and Organisational Analysis* (Heinemann, London, 1979).

15. Donaldson, L., *op. cit.* (1985), p. 30.

16. *ibid.*, p. 31

17. Thompson, J.D., *Organizations in Action* (McGraw-Hill, New York, 1967).

18. Lawrence, P.R. and Lorsch, J.W., *Organization and Environment* (Harvard University Press, Cambridge, Mass., 1967).

19. Thompson, J.D., *op. cit.* (1967), p. 10.

20. Strauss, A., *Negotiations: Varieties, Contexts, Processes and Social Order* (Jossey-Bass, San Francisco, 1978), pp. 250–8.

21. Day, R.A. and Day, J.V., 'A Review of the Current State of Negotiated Order Theory: An Appreciation and a Critique', *Sociological Quarterly*, vol. 18, winter 1977, pp. 126–42 (p. 132).

22. *ibid.*, p. 132.

23. Elger, A., 'Industrial Organizations: A Processual Perspective' in McKinley, J.B. (ed.), *Processing People: Cases in Organizational Behavior* (Holt Rinehart and Winston, New York, 1975), pp. 91–149 (p. 103).

24. For an early example of this work see Strauss. A., Schatzman,

L., Ehrlich, D., Bucher, R. and Sabshin, M., 'The Hospital in Modern Society' in Friedson, E. (ed.), *The Hospital in Modern Society* (Macmillan, New York, 1963).

25. Pfeffer, J., *Power in Organizations* (Pitman, Boston, 1981).
26. For reviews of this development see Silverman, D., *op. cit.* (1970); Burrell, G. and Morgan, G., *op. cit.* (1979); Reed, M.I., *op. cit.* (1985); Thompson and McHugh *op. cit.* (1990) and Weeks, D., 'Organisations: Interaction and Social Processes' in Salaman, G. and Thompson, K. (eds), *op. cit.* (1980), pp. 105–27.
27. Pettigrew, A., *The Politics of Organisational Decision-Making* (Tavistock, London, 1973) and *The Awakening Giant: Continuity and Change in ICI* (Basil Blackwell, Oxford, 1985).
28. Child, J., 'Organisation: A Choice for Man' in Child, J. (ed.), *Man and Organisation* (Allen and Unwin, London, 1973), pp. 234–55; Hickson, D.J., Butler, R.J., Cray, D., Mallory, G.R. and Wilson, D.C., *Top Decisions: Strategic Decision-Making in Organisations* (Basil Blackwell, Oxford, 1986).
29. Crozier, M., *The Bureaucratic Phenomenon* (Chicago University Press, Chicago, 1964).
30. Clegg, S., *Frameworks of Power* (Sage, London, 1989).
31. Edwards, P.K., *Conflict at Work: A Materialist Analysis of Workplace Relations* (Basil Blackwell, Oxford, 1986).
32. Weick, K. E., 'Sources of Order in Underorganized Systems: Themes in Recent Organizational Theory' in Lincoln, Y.S. (ed.), *Organizational Theory and Inquiry: The Paradigm Revolution* (Sage, Beverly Hills, 1985), pp. 106–36
33. On this point see Strauss, A., *op. cit.* (1978), pp. 247–62 and Donaldson, L., *op. cit.* (1985), pp. 107–13.
34. Day, R. and Day, J., *op. cit.* (1977), pp. 137–8.
35. For an elaboration of this view see Thompson, P. and McHugh, D., *op. cit.* (1990), pp. 40–5.
36. Salaman, G., 'Towards a Sociology of Organizational Structure' in Zay-Ferrell, M. and Aiken, M., *Complex Organizations: Critical Perspectives* (Scott, Foresman, Illinois, 1981), pp. 22–45 (p. 35).
37. Thompson, G., 'The Firm as a Dispersed Social Agency', *Economy and Society*, vol. II (I), 1982, pp. 233–50 (pp. 223–32).
38. For a further development of this point see Perrow, C., *Complex Organizations: A Critical Essay* (Random House, New York, third edition, 1986), pp. 128–31.
39. Clegg, S., *op. cit.* (1989), pp. 197–8.
40. Whitley, R., 'Organizational Control and the Problem of Order', *Social Science Information*, vol. 16 (2), 1977, pp. 169–89.

41. Edwards, P.K., *op. cit.* (1986), pp. 69–72.
42. Giddens, A., *The Nation-State and Violence* (Polity Press, Cambridge, 1985), pp. 10–11.
43. Perry, N., 'Recovery and Retrieval in Organizational Analysis', *Sociology*, vol. 13 (2), 1979, pp. 259–73.
44. This point is taken further in the following chapter.
45. The implications of this point for an understanding of the dynamics of organizational conflict are discussed in Thompson, P. and McHugh, D. *op. cit* (1990).
46. Salaman, G., *Work Organisations: Resistance and Control* (Longman, London, 1979); *Class and the Corporation* (Fontana, Glasgow, 1981).
47. Edwards, P.K., *op. cit.* (1988).
48. Storey, J., 'The Means of Management Control', *Sociology*, vol. 19 (2), 1985, pp. 193–211.
49. Hyman, R., 'Strategy or Structure?: Capital, Labour and Control', *Work, Employment and Society*, vol. 1 (I), 1987, pp. 25–55.
50. Reed, M., 'The Labour Process Perspective on Management Organization: A Critique and Reformulation', in Hassard, J. and Pym, D. (eds), *The Theory and Philosophy of Organizations: Critical Issues and New Perspectives* (Routledge, London, 1990), pp. 63–82.
51. Tomlinson, J., *Unequal Struggle: British Socialism and the Capitalist Enterprise* (Methuen, London, 1982).
52. Turner, B. (ed.), *Organizational Symbolism* (De Gruyter, Berlin, 1990), p. 1.
53. Smircich, L., 'Concepts of Culture in Organizational Analysis', *Administrative Science Quarterly*, vol. 28, 1983, pp. 339–58.
54. Reed, M., *The Sociology of Management* (Harvester Wheat-sheaf, Hemel Hempstead, 1989).
55. Bryman, A., 'Organisation Studies and the Concept of Rationality', *Journal of Management Studies*, vol. 21 (4), 1984, pp. 391–404; Brunnson, N., *The Organisation of Hypocrisy: Talk, Decisions and Actions in Organisations* (Wiley, Chichester, 1989).
56. Jackall, R., *Moral Mazes: The World of Corporate Managers* (Oxford University Press, Oxford, 1988).
57. Anthony, P.D., 'The Paradox of Management Culture', *Personnel Review*, vol. 19 (4), 1991, pp. 3–8; Axtell-Ray, C., 'Corporate Culture: The Last Frontier of Control', *Journal of Management Studies*, vol. 23 (3), 1986, pp. 287–98.
58. MacIntyre, A., *After Virtue: A Study in Moral Theory*

(Duckworth, London, 1981); Anthony, P.D., *The Foundation of Management* (Tavistock, London, 1986).

59. Pfeffer, J., *op. cit.* (1981).
60. *ibid.*, pp. 194–6.
61. Several of these studies are reviewed and assessed in Reed, M., *op. cit.* (1989), pp. 101–23.
62. Pfeffer, J., *op. cit.* (1981), p. 188.
63. Pettigrew, A., *op. cit.* (1985), pp. 44.
64. There is an obvious link here with the power perspective.
65. Legge, K., *Power, Innovation and Problem-Solving in Personnel Management* (McGraw-Hill, Maidenhead, 1978).
66. Gowler, D. and Legge, K., 'The Meaning of Management and The Management of Meaning: A View from Social Anthropology, in Earl, M.D. (ed.), *Perspectives on Management* (Oxford University Press, Oxford, 1983), pp. 197–233.
67. Mangham, I., *Power and Performance in Organizations: An Exploration of the Executive Process* (Blackwell, Oxford, 1986).
68. Gowler, D. and Legge, K., *op. cit.* (1983), pp. 229
69. Mangham, I., *op. cit.* (1986), pp. 82–104.
70. Thompson, P. and McHugh, D., *op. cit.* (1990).
71. Thompson, G., *op. cit.* (1982), pp. 235–7.
72. Johnston, L, 'Controlling Police Work: Problems of Organisational Reform in Large Public Bureaucracies', *Work, Employment and Society*, vol. 2 (1), 1988, pp. 51–70.
73. Thompson, G., *op. cit.* (1982), pp. 237–8.
74. Hindness, B., 'Rationality and the Characterization of Modern Society', in Whimster, S. and Lash, S. (eds), *Max Weber, Rationality and Modernity* (Allen and Unwin, London, 1987), pp. 137–53 (p. 147).
75. This research is reviewed in detail in Reed, M., *op. cit.* (1985), pp. 137–73.
76. Jenkins, R. and Parker, G., 'Organisational Politics and The Recruitment of Black Workers' in Lee, G. and Loveridge, R. (eds), *The Manufacture of Disadvantage* (Open University Press, Milton Keynes, 1987), pp. 58–70.
77. Higgins, W. and Clegg, S., 'Enterprise Calculation and Manufacturing Design', *Organization Studies*, vol. 9 (1), 1988, pp. 69–90.
78. Thompson, G., *op. cit.* (1982), pp. 244–5.
79. Burrell, G., 'Radical Organisation' in Dunkerley, D. and Salaman, G., *The International Yearbook of Organisation Studies, 1979* (Routledge, London, 1980).
80. This point is developed further in Chapters 4 and 6 of this book.

81. On this point see Donaldson, L., *op. cit.* (1985).
82. Turner, B., 'The Rise of Organizational Symbolism', in Hassard, J. and Pym, D. (eds), *op. cit.* (1990), pp. 83–96.
83. Silverman, D., *op. cit.* (1970).
84. Reed, M., *op. cit.* (1985), Chapter 6 of this book will develop this point further.

# / 4 /

# THEORY GROUPS AND
# RESEARCH PROGRAMMES

## INTRODUCTION

This chapter reviews and assesses the research programmes that have been carried through by various theory groups located within the broad analytical frameworks outlined in the previous chapter. A theory group is constituted by a number of people who share an agreed conception of 'organization' which is elaborated and developed through their collective participation in the wider social networks and debates that shape the academic structure of organizational analysis.[1] These networks and debates provide a relatively loose and dispersed pattern of interaction and interdependence between identifiable theory groups through which the production and evaluation of research programmes can be undertaken. However, organization theory lacks the theoretical order and methodological discipline imposed by the relatively tightly coupled inter-dependencies between theory groups found in the 'established sciences'. As Whitley has argued, organization theory is more like a 'fragmented adhocracy'; that is, a field of study characterized by

limited reputational control over intellectual goals and priorities, low degrees of coordination of research strategies and results around common theoretical purposes, and subject to the conflicting pressures of specificity and applicability on the one hand, and generality and academic respectability on the other.[2]

In this respect, organization theory can be seen as a field of study occupied and exploited by a number of, often overlapping, theory groups that have extremely porous boundaries and weak interdependencies between each other so that they form a loosely coupled network of intellectual activity. Thus, the academic organization of organization theory more closely resembles the Californian gold fields in the second half of the nineteenth century than the rationally structured and tightly controlled disciplinary regimes operative in twentieth-century natural sciences. The theoretical claims or territories staked out and defended by various groups are continually fought over within an intellectual power struggle subject to minimal external controls. The relatively strong disciplinary-based structures and controls over objectives and methodologies operative in the natural sciences are substantially diluted and weakened within the field of organizational studies. Intellectual plurality and organizational fluidity are inherent within the field of organizational studies.[3] Within the latter, theory groups mobilize resources in support of their research programmes without the institutionalized reputational and organizational controls dominant in the natural sciences.[4]

Research programmes consist of the shared problematics or puzzles worked through over time by theory groups by their collective engagement in cognitive and social practices aimed at deepening and advancing their preferred conceptions of 'organization' as a strategic social unit. Research programmes provide a minimum degree of shared theoretical identity and continuity within a highly fragmented and poorly institutionalized field of study. They consist of a central theoretical core which is protected and extended by a series of conceptual and methodological innovations aimed at enhancing the analytical power and empirical reach of the former. However, this, unavoidable, process of elaboration and extension always involves a degree of risk in so far as it can erode, if not undermine, the simplicity, clarity, coherence and certainty which the theoretical core provides.[5] The more conceptually refined and methodologically ambitious a programme becomes, the more the risk of exposing 'the core' to developments and findings that cannot easily be accommodated within its theoretical parameters.

A review of the research programmes worked through by identifiable theory groups will place us in a better position to understand the trajectories of intellectual change and development which have emerged in organization theory over the last twenty years or so. This is so to the extent that we will be better placed to appreciate more fully the interests informing the production and reception of research programmes and the debates between different lines of analysis which they have opened up between contending theory groups.[6]

Within each of the analytical frameworks outlined in the previous chapter, the research programmes undertaken by two constituent theory groups will be discussed. In the case of the systems framework, the work of the Aston group and the population ecology group will be reviewed. Within the negotiated order perspective, the contributions of the ethnomethodologists and the symbolic interactionists will be assessed. In the context of the power framework, the programmes initiated and developed by the labour process theory group and the poststructuralists will be explored. The work of the organizational symbolists and the institutional theorists will be discussed against the background of the cultural framework specified in the previous chapter. Finally, the work of the radical Weberians and managerial realists will be reviewed and assessed in relation to the practice framework.

Each of these theory groups develops a particular research programme by concentrating on and working through a specific problem or puzzle drawn from the wider analytical frameworks in which their work is located. The Aston researchers and population ecologists focus on the problem of organizational adaptation to various kinds of environmental forces or pressures. The ethnomethodologists and symbolic interactionists concern themselves with the production and reproduction of organizational order by actors through their engagement in various types of cognitive and social practices. The labour process and poststructuralist groups concentrate on the emergence of more sophisticated forms of organizational surveillance and control in advanced capitalist societies. Organizational symbolists and institutional theorists are interested in the construction and reconstruction of organizational reality through the deployment of highly diverse and sophisticated forms of myth, ritual and symbolism. Finally, the radical Weberians and managerial realists are concerned to formulate a more systematic understanding and explanation of the political and ideological practices through which 'organizations' are assembled and sustained as viable social collectivities. The interrelationships between analytical frameworks, theory groups and research programmes are summarized in Table 4.1. Each of the theory groups and their research programmes will be described and evaluated in turn. An overall assessment of the broader theoretical trends and intellectual trajectories which have emerged from their contributions will be provided in the concluding section of the chapter. This will establish the context in which the issues that have emerged to structure the contemporary research agenda in organizational analysis and their longer-term implications for future developments can be reviewed in subsequent chapters.

## THE ASTON GROUP

The Aston group published their first research paper in 1963.[7] This paper provided the outlines of the strategic direction which successive generations of Aston researchers would follow over the next twenty years.[8] Three themes emerged from this foundation paper: first, the need to overcome the theoretical and methodological polarization evident in organizational analysis at that time; second, the aspiration to develop a general theory of organization with broad comparative scope;[9] third, the provision of a conceptual framework and a research apparatus that would facilitate the development of a general theory.

The original Aston researchers contested that, even in the early 1960s, organization theory was in danger of polarizing between a formalist tradition focused on institutionalized managerial control systems to the virtual exclusion of actual behaviour and a behavioural tradition which committed the opposite sin of concentrating on group attitudes and behaviour to the virtual exclusion of structural and contextual constraints. In direct opposition to this polarizing tendency, the Aston researchers offered a conceptual framework and

*Table 4.1*  Frameworks, groups and programmes in organization
theory

| Analytical frameworks | Theory groups | Research programmes |
|---|---|---|
| Systems | Aston/population ecology | Organizational adaptation |
| Negotiated order | Symbolic interactionists, ethnomethodologists | Organizational order |
| Power | Labour process theorists, poststructuralists | Organizational control |
| Cultural | Organizational symbolists, institutional theorists | Organizational reality |
| Practice | Radical Weberians, managerial realists | Organizational assembly |

research technology which would integrate a concern with
structural constraints and group behaviour within a model of
the organization as an open system. At the same time, this
framework and its related methodology were seen to provide
the means through which 'systematic exploration of the
causal connections between contextual factors and certain
administrative systems rather than others, or certain group
and individual behaviours rather than others'[10] could be
carried through. In particular, the Aston researchers felt that
an excessive reliance on a unitary conception of bureaucratic
structure and a qualitatively based case study methodology
had prevented organizational analysis from developing firm
empirical generalizations located within an overarching
comparative analytical framework.

The continuation of the Weberian approach to bureaucratic
structure as a general concept based on unexplicated assumptions about human rationality and the continuing strength of
an in-depth, qualitatively based case study research strategy
had prevented organization theory from attaining recognition
as a generalizing discipline.[11] The latter could only be

achieved if bureaucracy was reconceptualized as a structural variable rather than an ideal type[12] and studied through the systematic application of a highly formalized, quantitatively based methodology. By reconceptualizing bureaucracy as a combination of distinct, but interrelated, dimensions or variables subject to statistical analysis, organizational theorists would be placed in a much better position to formulate a general theory of the 'machinery of government' in a wide range of organizational types and across a broad range of organizational contexts or settings.[13]

The theoretical approach and methodological strategy developed to achieve this task entailed three aspects. First, the broad acceptance of a systems view of complex organizations.[14] Second, the identification of three separate, but linked levels of analysis in the study of organizations; that is, the 'organization' proper, the group and the individual. Initially, the Aston researchers concentrated on the first of these levels. The prior identification of meaningful statistical relationships between environmental or contextual variables and internal structural variables would facilitate a better understanding of the external constraints within which group behaviour and individual attitudes develop.[15] Thus, the relationship between dimensions of formal organization structure and of organization context become the initial focal point for the Aston researchers because it was thought to establish the institutional framework in which behaviour was determined.

The third aspect of the Aston group's strategy was the research methodology on which they relied to identify meaningful statistical relationships between structural and contextual dimensions. This placed a very heavy emphasis on quantitative techniques in general and multivariate analysis in particular:

What most sociologists are engaged in is some form of multi-variate analysis, but at times it would be almost impossible to gather this . . . every sociologist who does empirical work is attempting to measure in the sense that s/he is assigning magnitudes to objects . . . measurement is central and where relationships between objects can be sensibly expressed in terms of numbers, much more powerful analytical operations may be performed. . . . Thus one begins with a particular theoretical position and is *inexorably* led to search for data in a highly formalistic and systematic way, while, it is hoped, the whole operation is open to inspection and replication.[16]

Appropriately armed with this methodology, the Aston group felt that organization theorists would be in a position to do something they had been unable to achieve in the past; that is, to construct profiles or taxonomies of formal organizational structure based on firm empirical foundations, rather than the a priori theorizing conducted by Weber and those who followed in his intellectual wake. In their first research paper, six primary dimensions of structure and eight contextual dimensions were itemized which would facilitate the operationalization of specified statistical relationships between variables within and between different levels of analysis. Later research statistically and conceptually rendered these down into three primary contextual dimensions which were seen to be systematically related to three primary structural dimensions in empirical studies initially carried out on forty-six work organizations in the Birmingham area.[17]

This research suggested that the three primary contextual variables – that is, size (number of employees and net assets), dependency (degree of external control) and technology (operational process and equipment layout) – were systematically related to or 'predicted' three structural variables: structuring of activities (extent of specialization, standardization and formalization) with size; concentration of authority (extent to which formal decision-making authority is centralized at the apex of the hierarchy) with dependency; and line control of workflow (impersonal or personalized workflow control) with technology. These relationships were explained in terms of a deterministic logic of analysis which suggested that the three contextual variables pushed organizations inexorably in the direction of more explicitly structured relationships.

Increased size generated a more standardized and formalized pattern of administrative control due to the 'need' to cope with the increased complexity that enlarged scale produces. Greater dependence on external organizations caused higher concentrations of decision-making authority at the top of the organizational hierarchy due to the 'pressure' for enhanced public accountability and control. More integrated production technologies forced organizations to move towards impersonal line-control systems because they 'demanded' more advanced administrative structures if they were to be operated efficiently and effectively. In each case there is a very strong presumption in favour of external or environmental pressures determining the structural response made by the organization. These external pressures generate appropriate internal responses due to the environmentally imposed requirement for operational efficiency and effectiveness as preconditions for organizational survival. An organizational dynamic pushing in the direction of greater bureaucratization along all three structural dimensions was explained in terms of the contextual or environmental pressures which brought it into existence and reinforced the internal adaptations it produced.

The Aston researchers were clear that their project dealt with

what is officially expected should be done and what is in practice allowed to be done; it does not include what is actually done, that is, *what really happens* in the sense of behaviour beyond that instituted in (formal) organisational forms.[18]

However, the logic of their position is that organizations, and by extension the behaviour and attitudes of groups and individuals within them, will *have* to adapt in particular ways to the contextual or environmental constraints which face them. Consequently, they assume that the *processes* of organizational government – that is, the actual decision-taking activities in which members are engaged and their impact on structural outcomes – are very severely constrained by the contextual and structural settings in which they occur. In other words, there is a considerable degree of environmental/structural determinism inherent in the explanatory logic underpinning the Aston research programme and the contribution that it makes to the further development of a systems-based approach in organizational analysis. It is also the case that the Aston group work with a conception of formal organization structure that privileges – in terms of understanding and explanation – a managerial view of the organization and the environmental pressures that it faces.[19] In this respect, the Aston approach suffers from a more serious case of 'contamination' by 'Weberian type' assumptions about a universal human rationality than its adherents suggest. It is guilty of assuming a trans-cultural, context-free bias in favour of an ahistorical, atemporal and value-free commitment to organizations as the primary institutional carriers of a 'means–ends' rationality similar to that promulgated by classical management theorists. Indeed, it may be the case that the Aston group have presented us with a more refined, methodologically speaking, theory of formal organization structure and design similar to that formulated by classical writers such as Fayol[20] and Brech.[21] The former have simply constructed a more sophisticated reinterpretation of the latter's prejudices in favour of a view of organizations as formal administrative structures determined by a universal institutional logic of rational control and operational effectiveness. While the classical writers locate the source or cause of this 'rational imperative' for control, efficiency and effectiveness in universal principles of organization, the Aston researchers trace its origins to the environmental contingencies that determine the structural mechanisms through which system survival and adaptability have to be secured.[22]

These organizational mechanisms will be subject to empirical variation in the particular institutional forms through which they are expressed. But this variation is itself accounted for in terms of environmental pressures which have to be placated in some way or other through appropriate managerial responses.

The Aston group focus on the problems of organizational response or adaptability from the point of view of a 'focal organization'; that is, a single entity faced with a specific profile of contextual constraints and the structural mechanisms which they demand for efficient and effective operation. Another group of researchers, the Population Ecology group, have concentrated on the process of 'environmental selection' of organizational forms of structures from the point of view of collections of organizations treated as common members of similar population categories. They have concentrated on the problem of selection of organizational forms from an inter-organizational, rather than an intra-organizational, perspective.

## POPULATION ECOLOGISTS

At first glance, it is the differences, rather than the similarities, between the work of the population ecologists and the Aston group which seem to stand out. The former are primarily concerned with environmental selection of organizational forms rather than structural adaptation to environmental contingencies. They concentrate on dynamic movements and related mechanisms of change at the level of total organizational populations rather than static snapshots of formal structures at selected points in time. Their primary unit of analysis is the 'population' and its environmental niche rather than the organizational unit and its task environment. The underlying objective of their work is to map and explain the interrelationships between generic organizational processes and the wider, macro-level social structures in which they unfold. They reject the idea of a latent or implicit logic of efficiency and effectiveness as a rationale for explaining the process of organizational adaptation which has been so prominent in systems-based contingency theory. Instead, they argue for selection processes that operate at the level of macro-level environments rather than at the level of immediate organizational domain or task environment (including factors such as size, markets, dependence and technology).[23]

Yet, underlying these substantial differences of focus and approach lie much more significant similarities in the way in which organizations and organizational change are theorized and the implications of these similarities for the type of analysis which the population ecologists recommend.

The theoretical contrast drawn between selection and adaptation is less pronounced than it seems at first sight. As Hannan and Freeman suggest: 'There is a subtle relation between adaptation and selection that depends usually on the choice of level of analysis ... processes involving selection can usually be recast at a higher level of analysis as adaptation processes.'[24] In other words, environmental selection of organizational structures for whole populations of organizations can be recast as a process on institutional adaptation to macro-level forces or demands. Adaptative learning for single organizational units or organizational sets usually consists of selection between various structural forms. In both cases, the weight of analysis lies on 'external constraints that limit prospects for autonomous action'.[25] Thus, the Population Ecology and Aston groups jointly gear their theories to the presumed determining force of environmental necessity as an explanation for structural change. This is true at the level of the individual organizational unit and at the level of large numbers of organizations occupying similar environmental niches and the forms they select.

This shared concern with environmental necessity also reinforces the deterministic thrust of the underlying logic of analysis on which both groups rely. While Hannan and Freeman[26] rightly point out that all sociological explanation is to some degree or another deterministic in the sense that it deals with *constrained* action, they underestimate the strong determinism inherent in their preferred conceptualization of organizational units or sets as structures subject to environmental imprinting. As Morgan argues:

The naturalistic metaphor which is at the heart of population ecology is fundamentally flawed for the simple reason that people can reflect on their own behaviour and change it. Indeed, social behaviour is in a continuous process of construction and interpretation. . . . The population ecologists, in their eagerness to emphasize competition and the market, neglect this. They ignore the way in which people within organizations will seek to shape the environment.[27]

The shared deterministic predilections of the Population Ecology and Aston groups highlights a third area of agreement; their joint commitment to a systems model of organization and all that entails in terms of an explanatory bias in favour of structural analysis and a corresponding neglect of action processes. Both groups are committed to a view of organizations as goal-directed, boundary-maintaining activity systems dependent on the maintenance of certain structural regularities which secure long-term stability and survival.[28] This focus on structural regularities which exert a deterministic impact on organizational behaviour substantially downgrades the influence of actors' interventions on organizational outcomes. As Hannan and Freeman put it:

> Of course, individual actions do matter for organizations, but they matter more to the subunits in which the individuals work than to the organization as a whole. And they matter more to that organization than they do to the population of organizations. From the perspective of explaining variability in the organizational world, the motivations and preferences of particular actors do not matter very much.[29]

This viewpoint is significant in two respects: first, it presumes a conceptualization of the 'organizational world' that can be formulated and advanced without recourse to social action: second, it polarizes an individualist, not to say reductionist, interpretation of social reality with a collectivist outlook that favours a conception of the social world as consisting of groups or institutions that behave according to their own developmental logic. In neither case, is there any room for collective actors whose social existence and relevance is dependent on an identifiable decision-making machinery or process, but whose actions and institutional impact cannot be reduced to individual motivations or preferences.[30] Consequently, population ecologists and the Aston group are unwilling or unable to overcome the traditional dualism between environmental/structural determinism and strategic/group choice that has bedevilled organizational analysis. Instead, they advocate a view of organizations and organizational change which privileges, both in terms of definitions and explanations, environmental forces over social choices.

The research conducted by the population ecologists 'seeks to understand how social conditions affect the rates at which organizations change *forms* and the rates at which forms die out ... an ecology of organizations also emphasizes the dynamics that take place within organizational populations'.[31] Rather than take the single unit or focal organization as their basic unit of analysis, the population ecologists are concerned with large numbers or sets of organizations which share a common environmental niche and the resources it contains. Over the long term, those forms or structures which survive within a population do so because their niche has selected them out as being most successful in the endemic struggle to secure and retain those resources that guarantee organization survival. Any understanding of these processes must access, theoretically and empirically, the wider institutional contexts or macro-structures – such as the state, industrial sectors and class structures – in which populations are located. Understanding the dynamics of structural change at the interorganizational level requires an analytical framework and a research methodology that explains *generic* organizational processes and their embeddedness within the institutional processes and structures which operate at the societal level.

Consequently, the nature and distribution of material and social resources within organizations' environments – rather than internal leadership, decision-making processes or managerial strategy – is regarded as the primary factor explaining the direction and content of organizational change by the population ecologists. Instead of conceptualizing their environment from the point of view of internal decision-makers, the population ecologists view the environment as consisting of large-scale concentrations or clustering of resources (that is, 'niches') which select those organizational terms through which organizational survival is secured.

This process of interorganizational change in organizational forms within populations dependent on a shared environmental niche is explained in terms of a three-stage model consisting of 'variation', 'selection' and 'retention'.[32] Underpinning this three-stage model is the key assumption that environmental pressures make competition for scarce resources the central mobilizing force in organizational change. The model itself sets out to explain how organizational forms or structures are established, survive and become diffused throughout a population or, conversely, fail to become established and die out.

Variation in organizational forms across organizational populations within and between industrial or political sectors is taken as a given or 'natural' feature of all environments; it is assumed that there must be inherent structural variation across environmental niches if externally directed change is to occur. This automatically downgrades the explanatory significance of decision-makers exercising 'strategic choice' over organizational change and the forms that it produces. The former are regarded as being largely in the grip of larger macro-level environmental forces over which they have little or no influence, much less control. Variation in organizational forms is conceptualized as resulting from changes in ecological circumstances rather than strategically focused social action.

Selection refers to those structures which are positively selected by the environment due to the fact that they match the requirements of the latter in terms of providing relatively superior effectiveness in task performance and the longer-term viability that it promotes. Thus, effective organizational forms are selected out by the environment because they secure a better share of the limited resources that the niche makes available and put them to better use than do competitor structures.

Retention highlights those mechanisms which preserve initially selected forms or structures so that they gradually become widely diffused throughout the population as a whole. Appropriate material and social technologies that facilitate the retention of effective forms will ensure that they are preserved, reproduced and duplicated by sufficient numbers of organizations so that they become institutionalized as established ways of organizing across the total population. These retentive mechanisms reinforce, and are reinforced by, the very strong inertial forces operating in all organizations; that is, their inbuilt 'conservative' tendency to resist externally imposed internal changes, which seriously destabilizes established patterns. Organizations evolve new structures at a slower rate than the environment because they 'respond relatively slowly to the occurrence of threats and opportunities in their environments'.[33] If organizational forms are defined in terms of four core characteristics – stated goals, authority structures, core technology and marketing strategy – then, the rate at which they, individually and collectively, respond to environmental pressure is likely to be relatively slow and to entail a significant degree of protection for well-established mechanisms for organizing collective behaviour.[34]

This kind of analysis suggests that the formation of new types of organizations with novel organizational forms is crucial to the process of increasing diversity in organizational populations. As Hannan and Freeman argue:

> the dynamics of diversity depend mainly on the rate at which new and diverse organizations are created and then at which organizations of various types disappear. The formation of new kinds of organizations is central to the process of increasing diversity in the world of organizations. If the rates of founding and fundamental structural change became zero, organizational diversity would only decline over time as the various forms of organizations constrain the dynamics of diversity and the speed of organizational evolution.[35]

They have conducted empirical research on this issue in relation to three sectors or population types – trade unions, newspapers and semi-conductor companies. What this empirical research has revealed is that as the numbers of organizations occupying a particular niche increases – that is, as its density increases – then those organizational forms which will be most successful in meeting the intensified competition for resources are those that stress continuity and stability over innovation and novelty. In the long run, organizational effectiveness and survival seems to be primarily dependent on the selection and retention of structures that favour a longer-term assessment of the increased competition that higher density creates.

This review of the work of the Aston and Population Ecology groups reveals three major characteristics. First, that they are concerned with the processes through which environments select and organizations adapt structures that secure long-term survival. Second, that they both stress the importance of environmental determinism over the impact of the strategic choices made by powerful social actors within organizations or the wider contexts in which they operate. Third, they share an explanatory commitment to a view of organizational change that emphasizes the operation of a 'systems logic' which works its way through behind the backs of social actors. In other words, both groups share an allegiance to a perspective that minimizes, to the point of extinction, the role that individuals and groups play in shaping the organizational and environmental constraints to which their actions are subjected.

The contribution of the symbolic interactionists and ethnomethodologists considered in the following section is located at the opposite end of this theoretical spectrum; that is, it stresses the explanatory centrality of actors' choices and minimizes the continuing force of environmental or structural constraints. Social action moves from the margins to the core of organizational analysis.

### SYMBOLIC INTERACTIONISTS

The research programme undertaken by the symbolic interactionists and ethnomethodologists stands in sharp contrast to that pursued by the Aston group and the Population Ecologists. The former focus on the patterns and structures that emerge out of the interactional processes and accounting practices in which members are routinely involved. Instead of viewing structures or forms as entities that are externally imposed on organizational actors, interactionists and ethnomethodologists direct attention to the socially constructed nature of organizational order and the creative processes through which it is established. Within this latter perspective, 'organization' is articulated as a much more transient and fragile ordering of the ebb and flow of interactional processes and the group networks arising out of them. Beneath the official veneer of permanence and stability entailed in and represented by formal structures and control systems, there lies a chaotic underlay of negotiation, localized knowledge and 'rules in use' which make 'organization' possible. In this sense, symbolic interactionists and ethnomethodologists attempt to penetrate the 'inner logic' of organizational order and the everyday practices through which it is expressed and continued as a living process. It is organizational living, rather than organizational machinery, which lies at the core of the research programme undertaken by the two groups reviewed in this section and the one that follows.[36]

In focusing on the negotiation of organizational order, the symbolic interactionists have developed a research programme which has its roots in work carried out on asylums,[37] business firms[38] and hospitals[39] in the late 1950s and early 1960s. This earlier phase indicated that the more formalized aspects of organizational life – goals, hierarchies, rules, roles, divisions of labour and control systems – are always breaking down in the sense that the coherent vision of structural order which they represent merely provides a highly schematic and partial set of guidelines as to how individual and collective action should be undertaken.[40] Official goals and formal structures only have significance for social action if they become embedded in negotiating processes that establish the working agreements through which 'things get done'. Indeed, the former may be viewed as an outcome of the latter in so far as they embody earlier agreements which have emerged out of previous phases of negotiation that have temporarily attained the status of institutionalized understandings as to 'how to get on'. Formal structures and control systems are now simply seen as the officially designated and codified agreements arising out of complex negotiating processes between organizational actors. They lose their status as ontologically privileged aspects of organizational reality and their aura of legitimacy as 'naturally' authorized systems of government and control. Formal organization is regarded as a shorthand representation of and justification for agreements worked through by actors continually engaged in renegotiating and reworking the constantly shifting foundations of organizational order. It is denied explanatory status as an independent entity or force that programmes organizational behaviour and is transformed into one symbolic representation amongst many others of the struggle to impose shared meaning on a recalcitrant and messy social reality. The bases of collective action in complex organizations have to be continually reconstituted through negotiating processes which display certain general patterns or configurations but are operationally contingent upon their location in specific organizational settings:

Rules and roles are always breaking down – and when they do not, they do not miraculously remain intact without some effort, including negotiating effort, to maintain them . . . when individuals or groups of organizations of any size work together 'to get things done', then agreement is required about such matters as what, how, when, where and how much.[41]

This original work and approach was developed further in the 1960s and 1970s through a series of case studies on 'people processing' organizations employing relatively high proportions of professional or semi-professional workers.[42] The majority of the organizational sites in which this research was conducted dealt with people and their problems, as defined and legitimated by various social control agencies, as their raw material and deployed a range of social technologies and cognitive practices to process these human needs. Prime examples were prisons, hospitals, social work and welfare agencies, and educational institutions.[43] In turn, this empirical work encouraged a deepening interest in the dynamics of professional power in human service organizations, and their impact on general access to and control over the processing practices and techniques which the latter depend on to handle human and social problems.[44]

The research carried out by this group on people processing agencies confirmed and re-enforced the original perception of organizational goals and structures as highly ambiguous components of a social order that has to be 'made and remade' by all members. Formal organization functions as a symbolic resource or reference point which members routinely deploy and articulate to secure their own preferences and interpretations over a series of interactional encounters within the spatial and temporal limits laid down by organizational timetables. Doctors and nurses draw on vaguely phrased institutional objectives and relatively open-ended rules when they negotiate over how a patient is to be treated and where that patient is to be placed. Social work managers and case-work personnel selectively mobilize administrative regulations and therapeutic practices when they negotiate over whether a 'child at risk' should be placed in care and under what conditions. Prison warders and inmates bargain over the application of general rules and regulations to specific situations by drawing on a complementary understanding of what needs to be done to maintain order from conflicting, but overlapping, sub-cultures through which official goals are related to operational circumstances. In each case, the nature, scope and outcome of negotiated interactions within and between professionals and non-professionals is highlighted and their impact on the somewhat more permanent features of formal organization more clearly documented and specified.

In this way, the research conducted by the symbolic interactionists has revealed the subtle and complex negotiating processes through which social order is created and sustained in the midst of constant and destabilizing organizational change. At the same time, it has begun to turn its attention to the social conflicts which shape the course and outcome of symbolically mediated negotiation and their location within wider structures of power and control beyond a particular organizational locale or setting. It is at this point that a more focused appreciation of the institutionalization of 'professional power' within modern societies and its broader implications for participation in organizational decision-making enters the analysis.

Within the work of the symbolic interactionists there is growing recognition of the way in which the negotiation of everyday organizational life is structured by power relations that are located both at the level of the individual organization and the wider political economy in which it is situated.[45] Earlier work focused on the way in which the organization's division of labour – its mechanisms of differentially distributing access to and control over resources such as time, space and knowledge – and inequalities in the distribution of professional power between various occupational groups shaped the internal negotiating process.[46] Later work on the institutionalization of professional power within modern societies and its implications for organizational work suggested that the more specific and localized negotiating patterns emerging between interest groups at the intra-organizational level needed to be contextualized within the macro-level power struggles taking place at the interorganizational level.

One of the clearest expressions of this later development is Friedson's analysis of professional power in modern medicine and its impact on health care delivery systems and practices in America.[47] His analysis suggests that the organizational capacity of the medical profession to exert effective monopoly control over the services that it provides places poorly organized groups, such as clients, in a very weak position *vis-à-vis* their bargaining power. The medical division of labour in modern health care systems, he suggests, becomes subordinated to the interests of doctors. However, interprofessional power, and its organizational dynamics, are crucial in this context in so far as doctors are placed in a position to attack and destroy 'interlopers' and the potential threat that they pose to monopoly control over service delivery:

It is possible to reserve the term 'profession' for that form of occupational organization which has at once gained for its members a labour monopoly and a place in the division of labour that is free of the authority of others over their work. Work, as such, and the skills it entails, while not irrelevant, are not the focus for discrimination so much as the organized place of an occupation in the labour market and in a division of labour. . . . When an occupation gains effective organization, therefore, it can raise powerful barriers against the process of rationalization which management has been fairly free to advance in the case of those less-than professionally organized technical workers.[48]

Friedson is particularly interested in the interorganizational power mobilized by doctors in relation to other professions and political agencies such as the state, as well as regulatory bodies of various kinds, as a strategy for securing and maintaining their dominant position within the medical division of labour. In turn, this has provided them with a very effective power base at the intraorganizational level:

Most of medicine's control has not been exercised directly in negotiation with clients or employers, but rather indirectly, through licensing, registering and certifying legislation that establishes constraining limits around what can be negotiated among workers with managers in concrete settings.[49]

This interorganizational focus on professional power and its role in constraining intra-organizational negotiation indicates that the symbolic interactionists have taken the admonishments of their critics seriously and have attempted to develop their approach so that it is better equipped to deal with 'the hard realities of power and politics and the influence they exert upon the negotiative process'.[50] However, the explanatory price which may have been incurred in this shift of focus towards macro-level power structures and their role in shaping intra-organizational politics has been a weakening interest in the micro-level negotiative interactions which create and sustain the texture of organizing everyday life.

This latter theme – the accounting practices through which everyday life is ordered in organizational settings – is the central point of reference for the research programme undertaken by the ethnomethodologists. Rather than sacrifice the integrity of actors' reasoning processes and practices on the altar of institutional analysis, the ethnomethodologists have maintained a very strict and rigorous concern with the description and understanding of everyday encounters and the practices through which they attain the status of ordered situations. While initially developed and received as a logical extension of the symbolic interactionist approach, the work of the ethnomethodologists came to be seen as entailing a 'radical subjectivism' that rejected many of the key assumptions underpinning the former's focus and application.[51]

## ETHNOMETHODOLOGISTS

The central problem directing the work of the ethnomethodologists is to provide a more grounded and rigorous understanding of the shared schemes of reference and accounting practices through which organizational members construct and comprehend the social orders of which they are a part.[52] This demands a very strict focus on the everyday 'practical reasoning' in which members are routinely engaged and its role in sustaining shared definitions of organizational reality. It is the 'sense of organization' underlying and informing social interaction in the organizational setting which provides the major point of reference for ethnomethodological research in this area. The latter indicates that the methods and techniques of practical reasoning relied on by members to establish and maintain a shared sense of organizational order exhibit certain stable properties which are repeatedly used in a range of situations.[53] As a study of the methods through which actors make sense out of their organizational involvements, ethnomethodological research suggests that the former collectively share certain basic common-sense schemes of typification and accounting practices of which they may be formally unaware. In this respect, ethnomethodologists have been less interested in the subjective interpretations of organizational life formulated by members for their own sake and much more interested in the underlying, even universal, patterns or properties that they reveal. They are more interested in the formal accounting methods and procedures which inform organizational behaviour and less concerned with the substantive meanings which they entail.[54]

While ethnomethodologists see symbolic interactionism as playing a useful role in challenging and undermining the coherence and value of structural or environmental determinism in organizational analysis, they are intent on creating a much more radical rupture or break with mainstream or orthodox approaches.[55] This is so to the extent that they demand a much more detailed and systematic exploration of the cognitive structures that undergird social interaction, while firmly rejecting the importation and imposition of 'alien' theoretical abstractions such as 'formal organisation'.[56] Consequently, ethnomethodologists are determined that their brand of organizational research will remain true to the 'perspective of the actor' in that it will be restricted to a detailed description and analysis of the schemes of interpretation and accounting methods that actors rely on to generate shared definitions of organizational reality.[57]

This research programme and its underlying rationale have been pursued in empirical studies of police-keeping routines on 'Skid Row';[58] law enforcement agencies concerned with the regulation and control of juvenile delinquency;[59] the everyday operation of 'plea-bargaining procedures and practices in American courts;[60] the dynamics of people processing methods in public welfare agencies;[61] and an exposé of the implicit selection methods and techniques relied upon by large-scale public and private sector bureaucracies in Britain.[62]

A more in-depth exploration of two of these studies – Bittner's study of the peace-keeping practices relied on by policemen and Cicourel's study of juvenile law enforcement agencies will be useful in illustrating the general character of the research programme followed by the ethnomethodologists and its wider implications for our understanding of complex organizations.

Bittner's study of police peace-keeping practices follows on from his earlier theoretical paper outlining an ethnomethodological reading of the concept of organization.[63] The latter provided a critique of structuralist interpretations of the concept of organization which privilege managerial accounting practices and misleadingly invest them with a veneer of universal rationality and objectivity. In their place, he offers a reading which systematically explores the unexplicated common-sense meanings and methods which actors rely on to construct and sustain a shared sense of organizational structure. This requires the researcher to uncover the various ways in which members invoke and use the concept of 'formal organization' as 'a generalized formula to which all sorts of problems can be brought for solution'.[64] He concludes that:

formal organizational designs are schemes of interpretation that competent and entitled users can invoke in yet unknown ways whenever it suits their purposes. The varieties of ways in which the scheme can be invoked for information, direction, justification and so on, without incurring the risk of sanction, constitutes the scheme's methodical use.[65]

Bittner's research on the practices through which 'beat-cops' maintain order on 'Skid Row' exemplifies this reading. It highlights the way in which the policemen's sense of appropriate behaviour when dealing with minor criminals is shaped by a conception of 'normal' police work and its problematic relationship to legal formality. Rather than follow a strict interpretation of what the law requires, patrolmen acquire a first-hand knowledge of 'Skid Row' subculture and the operational practices that are required to keep the peace without overloading the official judicial process. While the operational decisions of patrolmen seem *ad hoc* and arbitrary, Bittner argues that they are informed by a detailed background knowledge of petty crime in poorer areas and the general categorizations which this provides for dealing with particular circumstances. Thus, the major problem for patrolmen is to match the resources which the law and formal police procedures make available to the situational exigencies which he/she is faced with on an everyday basis. The peace-keeping role of policemen and women in these areas is seen to be shaped by three main considerations: the need to acquire a rich body of concrete knowledge appropriate to the maintenance of control in an area in which petty crime is a constant reality; the problem of deciding when inhabitants of such an area require the full force of the law in relation to their perceived threat to maintaining the peace; finally, the overriding organizational imperative to minimize pressure on formal mechanisms of legal enforcement so that they can continue to function at an acceptable level of operational adequacy. In short, to prevent an organizational paralysis in law enforcement agencies brought on by operational overload and administrative chaos.

Considered in these terms, the police force can be interpreted as an organizational setting in which individual members use and manipulate formal organization in such a way that it corresponds to the operational requirements of keeping the peace in an area which is always likely to pose a threat to social order and organizational effectiveness. Rules and regulations have to be translated into common-sense frames of reference and practices – that is, 'rules-in-use' – through which the contradictory demands of legal formality and organizational work are kept in some kind of rough and ready balance.

Cicourel's research is directed to the decision-making processes and practices followed by juvenile law enforcement agents in two Californian cities. It unearths the organizational processes and procedures through which individuals are labelled as 'delinquents' and the formal justification which this categorization provides for various forms of treatment and punishment. Cicourel exposes how the official records and statistics kept by law enforcement agencies such as courts, probation departments and police forces present

.ı idealizations' of the complex organizational process-
chat is involved in attributing 'delinquent behaviour' to
.dividual action. How these agencies transform individual
conduct into organizationally acceptable examples of 'delinquency' which are then used to legitimate the decisions on
which action is taken concerning how such individuals
should be processed is the central theme of Cicourel's
research.

His research indicates that at each stage of the 'processing
system' – arrest, arraignment, trial – members of the
appropriate agencies such as probation officers, policemen,
court officials, rely on general interpretive schema and
accounting methods through which the available 'facts' are
constructed and construed to legitimate reasonable inferences
as to motive, intentions, character and behaviour. Bureaucratically defined versions of deviance are generated and
justified as representing an 'objective' account of what
actually happened and the manner in which that conduct
should be treated. The formalized system of categories which
officials rely on to locate and interpret various forms of
behaviour have to be understood in terms of the accounting
practices that the latter rely on to make 'defendable decisions'
and the legal action which they warrant.

The coding techniques that officials depend on to generate
acceptable and defendable definitions of delinquency –
reports, statistics, assessments – can only be understood,
Cicourel argues, in terms of an insider's knowledge of
background expectancies and the sense of order and control
which they permit. Statistical evidence is often assembled in
such a way that it automatically supports official decisions
and the 'conventional' assumptions on which they reside;
that delinquency is a function of a disorganized environment
of broken homes in which the jurisdiction of legal agencies is
required to 'normalize' deviant behaviour. In turn, these
organizationally specific typifications and classifications are
seen to derive from the larger communities in which they
take on meaning. Cities are partitioned by prevailing norms
and values into 'difficult areas' in which delinquency is much
more likely to occur. Organizationally processed definitions
and decisions then create 'managed accounts' of deviancy to

fit in with these socially established and sanctioned norms. The practical reasoning in which agency officials are engaged is seen to reflect more general attitudes about how 'delinquency' should be defined and the kind of treatment that it requires legitimated. However, it is in this very area – that is, the intermeshing of organizational processing and institutionally sanctioned and supported action – that ethnomethodology seems to be at its weakest. Cicourel concludes that:

my accounts represent a view of how delinquent types are produced by assuming 'inside' knowledge, the routine social meanings employed by law-enforcement personnel in face-to-face encounters and the more managed language of the official report ... the researcher must untangle the use of language categories reflecting everyday organizational theories and practices, together with the features of legality and justice or procedural due process.[66]

Yet, he gives relatively little emphasis to the way in which these officially sanctioned definitions of 'delinquency', and their location in institutionalized structures of power and authority, impact on organizational decision-making. He is documenting a process of bureaucratic handling, and the practical reasoning which underpins it, without any systematic reference to the wider systems of social control and political domination in which they both have to be located and interpreted. His research provides an insight into the 'micro-politics' of organizational categorization and treatment bereft of any sustained analysis of the institutionalized structures of class control and domination in which they take on meaning and significance for organizational behaviour. In short, there seems to be a distinctive lack of any coherently developed 'institutional vision' on the part of those who have advanced the ethnomethodological research programme in the study of organizations. The subtle processes through which the construction and maintenance of organizational order is shaped by these broader structures seems to be a significant omission in the collective research work pursued by the ethnomethodologists. It is at this point that the projects undertaken by those who support a view of organizations as instruments or tools of sectional domination and control enter the story.

## LABOUR PROCESS THEORISTS

Labour process researchers have attempted to develop a more systematic and empirically sensitive understanding of the various strategies through which management strive to control the organization of productive activity in capitalist societies. While a wide range of interests encompassing the deskilling implications of new technology, gender relations and inequalities in the workplace, and forms of worker participation, can be discerned in the research undertaken by this group, the core of their research programme consists of a series of historically informed empirical studies focused on managerial control strategies and practices in work organizations.[67] Over a period of more than two decades following the publication of Braverman's pioneering book in 1974,[68] members of this group have attempted to construct and articulate a general theoretical perspective on organizations which explains the complex interaction between intra-organizational control practices and the wider structures of class power and domination in which they are utilized. Thus, the processes and structures through which employers and managers realized a variable degree of control over workplace behaviour emerged as the central question driving the efforts of this group to provide an integrated theoretical framework for explaining the characteristics and dynamics of work organizations and employment systems in advanced capitalist societies.[69]

Most of the empirical research undertaken by the labour process group is concerned with long-run historical transformations in the organizational forms through which capitalist employers and their managers have struggled to secure effective control over productive activity geared to the generation of surplus value and its appropriation in the form of profits.[70] This historical research has been complemented by a series of in-depth case studies of managerial control strategies and techniques in a range of profit and non-profit organizations which reveal the fine detail of the struggles that crystallize around the processes owners and managers depend on to secure worker compliance.[71] Taken together, these studies indicate that control over workplace relations is a 'contested terrain' in which power struggles over the mechanisms through which work behaviour becomes structured is the central dynamic underlying the long-term transformation of productive organization in advanced capitalist societies.

This 'contested terrain' is explored and analyzed in relation to three key concepts: the labour process; managerial control strategies; and forms of worker resistance. The labour process within capitalist economies consists of those materials and activities through which commodities and services are produced and offered for profitable sale on the market. Under capitalism, it necessarily entails an antagonistic relationship between the interests of owners and managers on the one hand and workers on the other. The behaviour of the former is driven by the imperative to extract maximum surplus value and the sustained capital accumulation which this facilitates. The latter are motivated by a desire to maximize their economic returns from gainful employment while minimizing the expenditure of effort and commitment that they have to provide to earn their wages. Profitable production within capitalist economies necessitates 'adequate mechanisms' for directing, supervising, evaluating, disciplining and rewarding labour.[72] In this way, the labour process under capitalism establishes a series of mechanisms through which the productive *potential* of wage labour can be translated into *actual performance* at such a level that profitable production can be routinely achieved within a conflictual relationship between two class groupings and their various representatives in the workplace. Within the labour process under capitalist production relations, managers employ a series of structured control systems and operational practices as a means of organizing productive activity in line with the requirement for sustained capital accumulation. Consequently, there is a 'general control imperative' that constrains all managers in capitalist economies, in that they are unable to rely on market mechanisms alone to achieve effective discipline within the work organization. They must have a range of organizational mechanisms available to them through which work performance can be regulated and controlled in such a way that profitable production can be guaranteed. However, the manner in which this general demand for overall control of the labour process works its way through into particular control practices engaged in by managers within specific organizational locales – what Edwards calls 'detailed control' – is open to a considerable degree of variation and diversity.[73]

There is no direct or causal link between the general control imperative and workplace practices; the relationship between overall shifts in the structure of economic organization within capitalist societies and the control strategies and practices followed by managers in work organizations is mediated and filtered by a complex series of cultural, political and historical circumstances which shape organizational forms in particular ways. In turn, internal political processes within management play an important role in filtering and assessing the specific control implications of general environmental developments for their organization.[74]

Labour process researchers have suggested that any control system can be conceptualized in terms of three interrelated mechanisms and the specific practices associated within them:[75] first, a directive mechanism specifying the nature, timing and sequencing of work task performance; second, an evaluative mechanism for monitoring and correcting work performance when it falls short of pre-set targets; third, a disciplinary mechanism eliciting compliance with the manager's direction of the labour process. More sophisticated control mechanisms and practices have been identified by Littler relating to the technical division of labour within the workplace, the structure of bureaucratic control within the administrative organization and the regulative systems operating within the employment relationship.[76]

These control mechanisms are seen to regulate conflict and to generate novel forms of worker resistance within the work organization. This is so to the extent that they are premised on the simultaneous search for two contradictory objectives – more effective forms of surveillance and discipline combined with higher levels of commitment and initiative. As Hyman puts it:

the function of labour control involves *both* the direction, surveillance and discipline of subordinates whose enthusiastic commitment to corporate objectives cannot be taken for granted; and the mobilization of the discretion, initiative and diligence which coercive supervision, far from guaranteeing, is likely to destroy.... Shifting fashions in labour management stem from this inherent contradiction: solutions to the problem of discipline aggravate the problem of consent and vice versa.[77]

Viewed in this light, managerial control strategies and practices, whatever their particular logic and form, will inevitably generate worker resistance and resultant conflict to the extent that they are geared to contradictory policy objectives that are very difficult, if not impossible, to integrate within a coherent organizational framework. Worker recalcitrance and resistance is built into the control process within capitalist work organizations in so far as it has to accommodate tensions and conflicts which cannot be solved by any single management strategy. As Edwards argues, the underlying logic of the control process in capitalist work organizations is the management of conflicting pressures for discipline and commitment that are integral to and recurrent features of the wider economic system in which they operate:

Struggles between workers and employers derive their character from the capital–labour relation within the mode of production ... struggles are active and creative, in several senses. They represent the working through of structural influences, they mediate effects from outside the capital–labour relation, and they have a dynamic and history – indeed, a logic – of their own; as they develop, they create understandings of how work shall be performed ... in any workplace there are norms as to what is usual conduct. Struggles produce and reproduce these norms, and in so doing they develop logics of their own such that two identical workplaces might take an increasingly divergent path from a common starting point.[78]

This suggests that while broad patterns of worker resistance and systems of conflict regulation have to be understood and explained within the structural constraints imposed by a general control imperative necessary to sustain capital accumulation, the forms that conflict will assume within particular work organizations are open to a wide range of negotiated variation and diversity.[79] Thus, industrial conflict has to be understood as the outcome of a complex interaction between macro-level structural constraints and local negotiations that follow separate, if not divergent, logics of institutionalization. The former press in the direction of tighter, more integrated, control and discipline; the latter demands a more pragmatic, and hence 'messy', accommodation to organizational realities.

The major debate which has emerged within the research programme followed by the labour process researchers relates to the identification and explanation of long-run trends in control strategies and their implications for patterns of accommodation and resistance within work organizations.

Work carried out during the earlier phases of the labour process group's research programme anticipated an inexorable movement towards more direct forms of control. Within the latter, technological rationalization and bureaucratic centralization combined to form control regimes centred on work intensification and worker subordination through coercive, not to say authoritarian, compliance structures and reward systems geared to the internal fragmentation and social isolation of individual workers. Underlying developments within the capitalist labour process were assumed to press in the direction of a control apparatus which eliminates the uncertainty in the expenditure of labour and ensures the continuous realization of profit. This is achieved by implementing a fully mechanized technology and imposing an administrative system that degrades work into a set of mindless routines and fragments shop-floor life. Braverman's[80] original analysis suggests that Taylorism, considered as a managerial control strategy and practice, realizes the 'real subordination' of labour to the structural imperatives of monopoly capitalism in three respects. First, it makes the labour process completely independent of workers' skills and autonomy. Second, it achieves the complete divorce of mental and manual labour by separating conception from execution and centralizing the former in the hands of management. Third, it progressively strips all remnants of knowledge and residues of skill from individual workers so that management secures effective control of every step of the production process.

However, later phases of the research programme carried forward by the labour process group have substantially moved away from this earlier formulation and rejected the unilinear interpretation of long-term trends in organizational control regimes under advanced capitalism that it entailed. More recent analyses have indicated that employers and managers have a range of control options available to them which cannot be reduced to the structural imperatives embedded in monopoly capitalism. As Littler argues, 'the linkage between the logic of capital accumulation and transformations in the labour process is an indirect and varying one.'[81] This implies that the organization of the production process in advanced capitalist societies depends on a range of economic, administrative, ideological and cultural resources which are assembled in different ways by different managements to form reasonably coherent control regimes appropriate to their operating circumstances.[82]

Consequently, more recent research on the dynamics of organizational control within the labour process group has focused on the ideological and cultural practices in which managers engage to secure the commitment of workers to corporate goals and their translation into profitable production activities.[83] This work anticipates a trend towards more differentiated and flexible control regimes in which worker commitment is harnessed to production through the deployment of a strategy based on 'responsible autonomy' rather than 'direct control'. The former requires the application of practices and techniques more usually associated with professional forms of work organization in which workers, either individually or in groups, are encouraged to identify with organizational goals and to internalize a normative involvement in their task performance. A number of human resource development practices and planned internal labour market systems have been introduced into the larger corporations in their quest to secure and sustain effective worker commitment.[84] In turn, this has encouraged the development of a more internally differentiated labour force in which a highly skilled and rewarded 'core' of employees is subjected to a control regime of 'responsible autonomy', while an unskilled and poorly rewarded 'periphery' is exposed to the coercive practices inherent in 'direct control'.[85] 'Attitudinal restructuring' through cultural indoctrination and control, rather than crude economic compulsion begins to emerge as a central feature of managerial control strategies under advanced capitalism.

The overall effect of these developments has been to question, if not undermine, the analytical coherence and explanatory utility of the concept of 'control strategy'.[86] The latter seems to dissolve into a plethora of practices or techniques which can be assembled in a wide variety of different ways depending on the operational contingencies which a particular management faces. In short, labour process theory seems to 'degenerate' into contingency theory. Yet, many continue to advocate retention of the concept of control strategy, while theoretically relocating it within a more sophisticated analysis of generic processes of surveillance and resistance which function both within the production system and other arenas of organized life in modern capitalist societies.[87] This has provided a theme through which the work of the labour process group links up with that undertaken by the poststructuralists.

### POSTSTRUCTURALISTS

The work of the poststructuralists considerably broadens and extends the research agenda for analyzing the structure and dynamics of organizational control in modern societies. Their research has been concentrated on the strategic role which the human sciences and related professional groups have played in constituting organizational members as 'governable persons' who are subjected to much more subtle and indirect forms of ideological and cultural control that those envisaged by the majority of labour process researchers.[88] In addition, the poststructuralists reject the structural or class determinism which they see as being inherent within the labour process approach and argue the case for a perspective on the dynamics of organizational control that gives explanatory priority to:

a disparate series of practices based on notions of the measurability of normality and deviance. The task of measuring is the province of the expert who is simultaneously endowed with the power of defining the normal and treating the deviant to bring it back to the norm. Thus power and knowledge go together; they are working simultaneously through practices on the bodies of people to make them 'normal'.[89]

In this sense, the poststructuralists are primarily concerned with the way in which 'normal' organizational subjectivity and homogenized collective identities are constructed. They see the latter as emerging from a series of discursive practices and social technologies which derive from the knowledge and power made available by specialized social scientific fields and techniques from the middle of the eighteenth century onwards. Within the poststructuralist approach,

the meanings of and membership within the categories of discursive practice will be constant sites of struggle over power, as identity is posited, resisted and fought over in its attachment to the subjectivity by which individuality is constructed. Identity is never regarded as being given by nature; individuality is never seen as being fixed in its expression.[90]

Several members of the labour process group have signalled a growing interest in the organizational practices through which individuals are constituted as 'subjects' with normal 'identities' appropriate to the constraints embodied in the formal positions that they occupy within the organization's authority structure.[91] At the same time, they have called attention to the need to appreciate the various ways in which members resist the normalized identities which the organization attempts to bestow and strive to construct alternative subjectivities that question the internalized discipline which 'official' discourse imposes.

The key figure in this research group and programme is the French philosopher and historian, Michel Foucault.[92] His work on the historical development and organizational implementation of various forms of control practices and regimes in 'total institutions' such as prisons and asylums – that is, carceral institutions which remove individuals from normal society[93] – has provided an inspiration for subsequent research that has focused on similar processes in economic and administrative organizations. In this respect, Foucault's research on the practices and techniques through which modern organizations discipline and control subject populations in such a way that they internalize formalized administrative norms is seen to complement Weber's analysis of the long-term process of bureaucratic rationalization as the hallmark of modernity.[94] Thus, O'Neill has argued that:

certain developments in Foucault's studies of the disciplinary society may complement Weber's formal analysis of the modern bureaucratic state and economy . . . Foucault is able to go beyond Weber's legal–rational concept of legitimacy to capture the medicalization of power and the therapeutic mode of the legitimation function in the modern state . . . his studies of the prison, hospital and school go beyond Weber in grounding the legal–rational accounting process in techniques for the administration of corporeal, attitudinal and behavioural discipline. Foucault thereby complements Weber's formal rational concept of bureaucracy and legal domination with a physiology of bureaucracy and power which is the definitive feature of the disciplinary society.[95]

O'Neil suggests that the major significance of Foucault's work in this context lies in his detailed exploration of the practices through which the internalization of self-discipline and control is routinely achieved in prisons, hospitals and schools. The latter, O'Neill argues, can be seen as a form of discipline and control which underwrites the more formalized control mechanisms operative in capitalist enterprises and the modern state apparatus – those organizational sites on which Weber concentrated in his research. In both cases – that is, in relating to formal organization and disciplinary practices – technical experts play a crucial role in developing theories and technologies of control aimed at identifying and treating 'deviant behaviour' in such a way that the established norms and routines of 'normal society' can be protected. Disciplining organizations, such as hospitals, prisons, asylums and schools, are now seen as sites or fields in which the practices of recording, observing, monitoring and evaluating the attitudes and behaviour of large populations (in order to administer them through therapeutic regimes of one sort or another) become central to an understanding of organizational surveillance and control in modern societies.

Foucault himself focused on four interrelated organizational practices or techniques for achieving effective surveillance over and control of subject populations which were derived, to a considerable extent, from the discursive formations constructed by the applied social sciences (such as criminology and social work) from the late eighteenth century onwards: first, the division, distribution and arrangement of bodies into administrative categories and spatial locations; second, a detailed prescription of daily activities through supervisory techniques of various kinds; third, the division of 'organizational time' into periods during which specific activities take place; finally, an administrative infrastructure of information gathering, storage and control that systematically links the arranged bodies and their respective activities.[96]

The starting-point for the practice of organizational surveillance and control is the spatial allocation of individual bodies within semi-enclosed domains as typified in prisons, asylums, military barracks, hospitals and schools. It is then continued through a series of techniques which are dedicated to ensuring that detailed control over everyday behaviour is realized: timetables, division of work tasks, classification of inmates into generalized administrative categories based on gender, age, ability, and their location within a formal status hierarchy. These techniques are overlain by a general infrastructure of administrative control based on three major mechanisms: continuous observation of inmates through architectural and organizational designs based on hierarchical principles; normative codes and ideologies which lay down standards of proper behaviour and a calibrated system of coercive sanctions to deal with deviance from the norm; finally, assessment procedures which monitor the progress of individuals during their institutional careers. In Foucault's view, this constitutes a generic form of disciplinary power characteristic of modern society that is economical and unobtrusive in its functioning, and is directed to the crucial problem of transforming potentially recalcitrant human agents into docile and obedient subjects.[97] Foucault's analysis of the role of modern organizations as disciplinary technologies is reflected in the recent work of more mainstream organizational researchers such as Blau[98] and Perrow.[99] Both of these researchers have developed an interest in the more unobtrusive and indirect control processes integral to the operation of modern organizations and the way in which they interface with more formal mechanisms of surveillance directed to gathering information about and supervising subject populations. Thus, Perrow argues that unobtrusive control – that is, control over the cognitive premises and social norms underlying action – is more economical and effective than direct bureaucratic discipline, but more difficult to achieve and sustain. The former is more effective in the sense that the inmate or subordinate internalizes the attitudinal and behavioural norms that the organization requires. It is more economical in the sense that voluntary compliance is secured without the high expenditure of energy and effort associated with more coercive forms of supervisory control. Yet, it is more difficult to sustain over long periods of time and across geographically dispersed organizational sites. Unobtrusive control through normalization and indoctrination requires a relatively complex and sophisticated administrative and therapeutic apparatus to maintain the collective moral or ideological order from which the 'correct' cognitive categories and premises will be drawn to establish the basis for individual conduct. Consequently, it is more expensive in terms of resource allocation and utilization than simpler and more direct forms of surveillance and control, but more reliable and lasting from the point of view of those 'in power'.[100]

Foucault's approach has been extended from its original application in carceral or total institutions to the analysis of surveillance and control in capitalist enterprises and administrative organizations concerned with political management and military power.[101] Burrell has argued that:

the prison is only the extreme form of what Foucault calls disciplinary power, for its boundaries extend well beyond the walls of the penitentiary. Within the whole range of organizations found in contemporary society, one finds not a plurality of power but *a unified power field* encapsulated within the bureaucratic, military and administrative apparatus. . . . Disciplinary power is invested in, transmitted by and reproduced through all human beings in their day-to-day existence. It is discrete, regular, generalized and uninterrupted. It does not come from outside the organization but it is built into the very process of education, therapy, house building and manufacture. . . . According to Foucault, since all of us belong to organizations and all organizations are alike and take the prison as their model, we are all imprisoned within a field of bio-power even as we sit alone.[102]

However, it is this inbuilt tendency towards a form of 'backdoor' structural determinism that has provided the focal point for critiques of the poststructuralist analysis of organizational surveillance and control in modern societies. Burrell's assumption that the prison or, more generally, carceral institutions, provide a template or paradigm case against which all other types of organizations can be analyzed has been criticized on several grounds. In addition, the suggestion that there is 'a unified power field' inherent within bureaucratic organizations is also open to doubt.

  First, Foucault's analysis may drastically overestimate the reach and effectiveness of disciplinary power in carceral institutions and more particularly those organizations in which the degree of 'enclosure' or sequestration and control is much more limited, for all sorts of reasons, than within the former. Second, it seriously underestimates the significance of inmate or subordinate resistance and its powerful impact on the long-term development of control mechanisms and practices in complex organizations of all types. Third, it singularly fails to recognize the inbuilt contradictions of different control strategies and the circuits through which they pass because of its theoretical – that is, explanatory – commitment to a conception of 'power' as a protean force which is everywhere and nowhere. Giddens provides an exemplary summary of these criticisms:

There is no need to accept the whole sweep of Foucault's arguments to acknowledge that 'disciplinary power' becomes associated with a range of organizations involved in regularizing activities in time–

space. . . . We may regard disciplinary power as a sub-type of administrative power in general. It is administrative power that derives from disciplinary procedures, from the use of regularized supervision, in order either to inculcate or to attempt to maintain certain traits of behaviour in those subject to it. . . . But Foucault is mistaken insofar as he regards 'maximized' disciplinary power of this sort as expressing the *general nature* of administrative power within the modern state. Prisons, asylums and other locales in which individuals are kept entirely sequestered from the outside . . . have to be regarded as having *special* characteristics that separate them off rather distinctively from other modern organizations . . . the imposition of disciplinary power outside contexts of enforced sequestration tends to be blunted by the very real and consequential countervailing power which those subject to it can, and do, develop.[103]

If Giddens' strictures are taken seriously, then we need to attend much more closely, and with a much less deterministic sweep, to the ways in which cultural manipulation and control has to be 'worked at' within complex organizations. We also need to attend to the power struggles which coalesce around the processes and mechanisms associated with cultural or symbolic work. It is the latter concern and approach which has characterized the research of the organizational symbolists and institutional theorists in contemporary organizational analysis.

## ORGANIZATIONAL SYMBOLISTS

The research of the organizational symbolists has been directed to achieving a better understanding of the cultural and linguistic processes through which organizations are reproduced as shared systems of meaning and structural forms.[104] Symbolic discourses and orders are regarded as cultural and linguistic creations which ambiguously represent a multiplicity of disparate meanings which can be assembled in different ways to represent and project different 'images' of the organization. By its very nature, the concept of symbol is ambiguous and diffuse, facilitating many different 'readings' of organizational reality and the multiplicity of 'identities' which it bestows on groups and individuals. Symbolic creation and exchange within organizations is reflected in and through many different modes of representations such as architectural design, physical ecology, interior decor, modes of dress, interaction rituals and ceremonial procedure. Organizational histories, myths, rituals and narratives constitute and make 'real' what is taken for granted as the 'objective' reality of organizational life.

The organizational symbolists set out to question and undermine taken-for-granted assumptions about an objectified organizational reality and to reveal the highly subjective and selective processes through which the latter is constructed and sustained as the dominant representation of 'what is going on'. In this way, their work displays a great deal of sensitivity to the politics of organizational symbolism; that is, to the sectional interests and values that inform and underpin processes of cultural reproduction and enactment. This locks them into a concern with organizational history – with the processes through which 'the past has been mapped into or stored in the present'.[105] Consequently, the cultural tensions and struggles that occur before established organizational forms become institutionalized has emerged as one of the central themes of their research programme. This signifies a radical break with functionalist conceptions of organizational culture which emphasize the integrative and coordinating role of symbolic work.[106] In sharp contrast, organizational symbolists have stressed the fragmenting and conflict-generating aspects of symbolic work in complex organizations. The latter is seen to produce competing definitions of organizational reality which inevitably subvert any notion of an overarching, all-embracing symbolic narrative and cultural order that unifies and integrates a multiplicity of meanings into a single voice:

Complex organizations contain conflicting values, perceptions and interests. Just as the value of an overarching culture is more informative about a society on a small, remote Pacific island than about a society such as the United States, so it may be more useful for understanding smaller, more homogeneous organizations ... than for the analysis of large, complex organizations where the regulation of conflict is a more pragmatic course than the limitation of its roots. . . . If culture is seen as a powerful integrating force in complex organizations, viewing it as glue is apt to lead to understatement of the autonomy of the parts and thus to understatement of the causal roles they play. It also encourages overstatement of the integrating and understatement of the disintegrating forces, and it may produce less dynamic models than warranted.[107]

It is the inherently dynamic quality of organizational culture – its innate capacity to remake organizational reality and to carry the new practices and forms that this remaking process throws up – which has emerged as a major research interest for the organizational symbolists. Within the research undertaken by the latter, two interrelated concerns have been evident: first, the significance of organizational culture as an epistemological device and normative framework that shapes the cognitive processes through which individuals make sense of their organizational experiences; second, the role of organizational culture as a political weapon within power struggles to control organizational decision-making and the outcomes it produces. The former stress the relevance of organizational culture for an understanding of socialization processes and communication practices in organizations. The latter calls attention to the mobilization of symbolic resources in support of particular political projects so that they are legitimated as acceptable policies that the organization ought to follow.[108]

Schein's[109] work on organizational culture and its role in facilitating and/or blocking structural change in organizations is representative of the 'cognitive approach'. He defines culture as:

a pattern of basic assumptions – invented, discovered or developed by a given group as it learns to cope with its problems of external adaptation or internal integration – that has worked well enough to be considered valid and, therefore, to be taught to new members as the correct way to perceive, think and feel in relation to those problems.[110]

While the emphasis of his analysis lies in the integrative aspects of organizational culture – the way in which basic assumptions and values shape cognitive premises so that they accord with accepted definitions of organizational reality – he also shows that the meanings which they convey are open to multiple interpretations that often contradict each other. Consequently, a considerable degree of confusion, not to say conflict, is built into the patterns of basic assumptions on which organizational behaviour is based. Management can never be sure that their message is getting across because new members are socialized into a range of cognitive assumptions and behavioural patterns that permit, indeed encourage, continual re-evaluation of established norms and the symbolic commitments that they entail.

Pettigrew's[111] work on changing corporate cultures and structures is indicative of the 'political approach' to the analysis of organizational symbolism and culture. For him, organizational cultures provides:

> a continuing sense of what reality is all about in order to be acted upon. Culture is the system of such publicly and collectively accepted meanings operating for a given group at a given time. This system of terms, forms, categories and images interprets a people's own situation to themselves. . . . In a competitive situation there is clearly a point where ideas for change become unsupportable, and the issue becomes not one of mobilizing power for the pre-existing idea but seeing how the idea can be modified and connected to rising values and environmental priorities, so its power requirements can be assembled. Metaphors and myths help to simplify – to give meaning to – complex issues that evoke concern. Myths also serve to legitimate the present in terms of a perhaps glorious past, and to explain away the pressures for change which may exist from the discrepancies between what is happening and what ought to be happening. In these various ways, it may be possible for interest groups to justify continuity in the face of change, and change in the face of attempts to preserve continuity.[112]

Thus, Pettigrew is advocating that the analysis of structural change in large-scale, complex organizations must be focused on the use of culture as a symbolic resource that is mobilized and manipulated by interest groups engaged in a struggle for power to control the agenda for decision-making and the long-term strategies for organizational change and development which that agenda legitimates. Consequently, corporate culture is regarded as a plural and collective phenomenon operating at different levels within an organization in such a way that it simplifies and attributes shared meaning to organizational issues. This process of simplification and interpretation is inherently political in so far as it privileges certain visions of the past, present and future over others. But it is always contested by alternative metaphors and myths which undermine and challenge the organizational *status quo* – particularly at a time when change within the wider environment seems to question established definitions of organizational reality and the images and practices they embody.

However, it is the institutional aspects of cultural socialization and ideological transformation which often seem to be neglected in the ethnographic focus of the organizational symbolists and their detailed anthropological explorations of competing and conflicting workplace sub-cultures. The research of the organizational symbolists has been primarily directed at achieving a better understanding of the 'localized' cultural processes that shape changing systems of meaning and structural forms at the level of individual organizations. The work undertaken by the institutionalists has been more systematically concerned with the wider societal contexts in which organizational myths and ideologies are constructed and sustained.

## INSTITUTIONALISTS

The major issue which has directed the work of institutional theorists within organizational analysis has been the strategic role played by institutional norms and values in shaping organizational structures. What Scott[113] has identified as the complex interaction between 'institutional logics' (systems of social beliefs and socially organized practices associated with specific functional areas such as the economy, law, education, etc.) and organizational designs (the patterns of relationships through which collective action becomes structured) has emerged as the central problematic directing their research. In particular, the significance and force of the cultural 'messages' transmitted by distinctive institutional systems (such as the family, the state, the economy and the educational system) for organizational structures has attracted their attention.

Much of the latter has been focused on the institutional norms and conditions which gave rise to such rationalized formal structures as the dominant organizational systems in modern societies.[114] Rather than emphasize the role of market economies and centralized states in facilitating the emergence and eventual dominance of rational bureaucracy, the institutionalists have stressed the explanatory significance of 'institutionalized myths' which make formal organization easier to create and more necessary to sustain over the long term:

In modern societies, the myths generating formal organizational structure have two key properties. First, they are rationalized as impersonal prescriptions that identify various social purposes as technical ones and specify, in a rulelike way, the appropriate means to pursue these technical purposes rationally. Second, they are highly institutionalized and thus in some measure beyond the discretion of any individual participant or organization. They must, therefore, be taken for granted as legitimate, apart from evaluations of their impact on work outcomes.[115]

As such the growth and diffusion of these institutionalized myths make it possible for formal organizations and their directing elites to occupy domains of work activity and to define the latter in ways that are supportive of their political interests and ideological values. Meyer and Rowan analyze this process through which institutionalized myths create and sustain organizational forms which occupy and control operational domains as one of 'institutional isomorphism':

organizations are structured by phenomena in their environment and tend to become isomorphic with them ... organizations structurally reflect socially constructed reality ... institutional theories, in their extreme form, define organizations as dramatic enactments of the rationalized myths pervading modern societies, rather than as involved in exchange – no matter how complex – with their environments[116]

This form of analysis suggests that organizations adopt structural forms that are externally legitimated in terms of collectively valued purposes and norms, rather than in terms of environmentally mediated demands for technical efficiency and operational effectiveness as emphasized by the Aston researchers and the Population Ecology group. Organizational

survival and effectiveness depends less on efficient coordination and control of productive activities and more on the
capacity to become isomorphic with the dominant social
norms and interests constituting an institutional setting
within which longer-term viability has to be secured.[117]
Indeed, the research carried out by the institutionalists
indicates that the requirements of technical or instrumental
rationality and the norms of institutional legitimacy may
often conflict with each other; the need to maintain activity
that has ritual and ceremonial meaning – that is, which
legitimates an organization's existence and resource claims –
may often run counter to a means/ends calculus based on
narrow measures of operational efficiency:

Ceremonial activity is significant in relation to categorial rule, not
in its concrete effects. A sick worker must be treated by a doctor
using accepted medical procedures; whether the worker is treated
effectively is less important. A bus company must service required
routes whether or not there are many passengers. A university must
maintain appropriate departments independently of the departments'
enrolments. Activity, that is, has ritual significance: it maintains
appearances and validates an organization.[118]

In this respect, the institutionalists have highlighted the
problem that all organizations face in coping with, if not
resolving, the inconsistencies which established institutional
norms as goals generate. Organizational elites often find
themselves in a situation where they have to secure external
support from incompatible segments of their institutional
environments. Managers have to accommodate a range of
competing, not to say conflicting, rationalities and somehow
achieve a workable *modus vivendi* between operational
efficiency and institutional viability. School managers, when
designing the content and delivery of curricula, have to
negotiate between government directives and pressure group
demands from teachers and parents. Professions have to
achieve some workable accommodation between an internalized ethical code and imposed organizational requirements. The contradictions between generalized mandates and
everyday routines, and the uncertainties that they produce,
must be squared in some way or another. The development

and diffusion of formal organization is seen primarily as a product of the quest for legitimacy and the practical support which flows from this, as opposed to the emphasis on 'objective' environmental imperatives and their automatic translation into appropriate organizational action.

Considered in these terms, the institutionalists give clear expression of, and support to, Ahrne's arguments that the growth of organizations and their power to shape the environments in which they operate has to be understood through an analysis of the interaction between 'inner structuration' and constraining institutionalized orders:

Organizing is a struggle for control and order in confrontation with a recalcitrant environment. . . . Organizing is a method of making human activities permanent in order to increase control over uncertain environments. . . . Organizing occurs as responses to uncertain environments. It is a struggle against hostile surroundings. . . . Through its hierarchy, its rule, and its artifacts and symbols, an organization becomes an extraindividual entity. . . . Organizations are, to a large extent, engaged in activities whose aim is to influence and control the nearest environment without including it in the organization.[119]

This leads Ahrne to suggest that institutional settings may be most appropriately thought of as a social landscape in which collective actors (i.e. organizations) struggle to increase their control by manipulating their material and ideological resources. These social or institutional landscapes are not coherent units in the sense of possessing a clear analytical identity and structure. They are more usefully conceptualized as consisting of multiple, overlapping and intersecting power networks in which organizational action has to be understood as the outcome of a complex interaction between 'internal' patterning processes and 'external' institutionalized orders. Modern social landscapes consist of diverse institutional processes and structures which are assembled and developed by organizations to provide a very loose form of structuring and control. In this way, organizing creates a temporary permanency which eliminates some uncertainty through the limited rational control and coordination that it provides:

In the metaphorical language of landscapes, organizing may be likened to gardening, to cultivation and arrangement of the soil for the plants to grow in a controlled way. Gardening also presupposes constructing shelters against undesired influences from the environing landscape in the form of rain, wind, sunshine or insects. It also involves regulating nature through water and nutrient supplies. Gardening is a constant struggle to manipulate and control the environment. In the same manner, organizations establish their own domains within different kinds of social landscape.[120]

Within this type of framework, the processes whereby organizations achieve some degree of isomorphism with their institutional environments – that is, their structures come to imitate, resemble and perhaps even incorporate selected aspects of their cultural and political settings – can be analyzed as consisting of complex combinations of external constraint, strategic choice and habituated routine. In attempting to secure and develop an institutional domain and base which will provide legitimation and material support for their activities, organizations must achieve a loose coupling between their internal work patterns and external institutionalized rules and norms. They must lock into institutional myths through ceremonial rules and rituals of production and administration in such a way that their claims to operate as rational and efficient social units can be externally legitimated. At the same time, they must achieve room for manoeuvre within their respective institutional environments by ensuring the development of internal work routines that cope with operational difficulties and crises in such a way that they can be shielded from excessive external monitoring and verification. A careful balancing act between external coupling and internal decoupling within an institutional setting that has to be placated to some degree by internalized rules, rituals and norms that minimally satisfy the requirements of socially established myths and cultural values, stands at the heart of successful organizational management from an institutional perspective.

The work of the organizational symbolists and institutional theorists has clearly enhanced our understanding of the cultural processes through which organizational reality is socially constructed and institutionally sustained in a sometimes hostile and often threatening environment. However, in concentrating so much of their attention on the cultural processes through which some kind of ontological security (at both the individual and collective level) and institutional legitimacy are secured, they may be guilty of underestimating the explanatory significance of the material and political structures that shape these processes and the organizational outcomes they produce. In short, they may neglect the force of the wider political economy in which organizations have to assemble collective activities into coherent and sustainable orders. It is this theme, the theme of organizational assembly and its location within political/economic power structures which shape the managerial practices through which the former is achieved, that has provided the focal point for the work of the radical Weberians and managerial realists considered in the following sections.

## RADICAL WEBERIANS

This group of researchers tend to draw on Weber's 'political' analysis of bureaucratic organization as an instrument of domination and control within a continuing power struggle to secure finite resources rather than his 'technical' interpretation of bureaucracy as a neutral tool of rational administration.[121] Consequently, they tend to emphasize the role of organizational rationality in securing effective administrative control over and coordination of members and clients, as opposed to its technical function in achieving integrated formal structures that are well adapted to environmental conditions. Whereas the former view tends to stress the significance of rationality as an ideological weapon and administrative mechanism for disciplining and managing subject populations, the latter approach highlights its contributions to the construction and implementation of organizational designs which facilitate operational efficiency and longer-term effectiveness. As McNeil argues:

For Weber, the rationalities, or modes of calculation, of managerial elites were the main mechanisms shaping the actual use of power. . . . The emphasis on the role of administrative rationalities does not exclude the influence of objective market, political, or strictly technical production factors on the systems of control that emerge. It simply stresses that administrative rationalities are decisive in determining how elites translate potential power into the actual exercise of power. . . . Weber argued that this makes modes of calculation key mechanisms in determining how managers will use the power they can mobilize, because such rationalities do provide a means of assessing the meaning of events.[122]

This focus on the administrative rationalities and related organizational mechanisms through which managerial elites attempt to secure effective control over their employees and extend this domination within the institutional settings in which they operate is expressed in the work of radical Weberians such as Perrow,[123] Salaman,[124] Mouzelis[125] and Clegg.[126] In their different ways, each of these researchers has analyzed the administrative rationalities and control mechanisms deployed by managers in their attempt to achieve effective discipline over subject populations in relation to the pressures and demands emerging within their organizations' political economies, as well as the highly problematic translation of these structural constraints into appropriate operational practices. Thus, the political economies which complex organizations inhabit is conceptualized as consisting of interrelated structures of economic power and networks of political relationships which generate pressures and demands for profit maximization within a competitive market and administrative effectiveness within a state-regulated socio-legal order.

Within the pattern of structural constraints established by particular political economies – whether at the level of national political economies or sectoral political economies configured at the level of particular industries – complex organizations are most appropriately regarded as 'locales' or 'arenas' in which different agents are engaged in a struggle to impose their conception of the decision rules or modes of calculation which 'ought' to inform collective action. The latter established the strategic mechanisms through which perceived structural constraints will be translated into accepted rationales mobilizing and legitimating certain forms of action rather than others. It is management's job to ensure, as far as possible, that they determine the rationalities, or 'rules of the game', which will structure organizational action and legitimate the consequences which flow from these decision mechanisms. As Clegg puts it:

To achieve strategic agency requires a disciplining of the discretion of other agencies: at best, from the strategist's point of view, such other agencies will become merely authoritative relays, extensions of strategic agency.... The articulation of interests by strategic agencies is thus the medium and outcome of unique positioning over the discretion of others' positioning in the organization field. It must be reproduced in order for existing structures of power to be reproduced ... organizational locales will more likely to be loci of multivalent powers than monadic sites of total control: contested terrains rather than total institutions.[127]

Considered in this light, access to and control over the rationalities or 'rules of the game' which structure the terrain on which conflict is engaged in, and decision-making agendas set, becomes a central concern for researchers working within this approach. However, their interest in the particular organizational mechanisms and practices that managers rely on in their attempt to realize effective administrative domination and control is always located within a wider appreciation of the institutionalized structures of economic and political power that contextualize and shape managerial behaviour. The political economy of organizational action does not determine managerial control mechanisms and practices, but it is certainly assumed that it sets the parameters within which the latter are deployed and the results they are expected to produce.

## MANAGERIAL REALISTS

This group of researchers have concentrated more on the detailed practices through which managers achieve effective organizational assembly and control. They have shifted the focus of their attention away from the macro-structures in which organizational assembly is attempted – economies, states, classes and regimes – towards the meso-level or middle-range sectors – industries, domains and markets – in which a more refined exploration of managerial practices can be undertaken. But they are at one with the radical Weberians in accepting the basic proposition that managers are unavoidably involved in a struggle for control over the administrative mechanisms and procedures through which 'organization' is realized. In this respect, both groups are united in a theoretical commitment to a conception of organization as a structured process or practice in which administrative power and environmental constraints are inextricably entwined. They reject the view that the efficiency or effectiveness of organization designs and managerial practices can be assessed independently of their location and interpretation within dominant ideologies and the legitimacy which the latter establish for certain interests within the political struggle to capture and occupy 'contested terrains'. They regard the politics of organizational design and the technical considerations encountered within decision-making processes over organizational structure as inseparable features of managerial practices geared to the assembly of collective action into viable institutional forms.

The theoretical roots of an approach to the study of managerial behaviour and organization grounded in a full-blooded political realism can be traced back to a series of case studies conducted in the 1950s and 1960s on the way in which internal interest group conflict within management shaped decision-making processes and outcomes concerning organizational redesign. During the 1970s and 1980s this work was developed and extended to incorporate a much more sophisticated understanding of the complex inter-penetration of internal managerial control struggles on the one hand and external transformations of institutional sectors or domains on the other. Within this second phase of research, prominent contributions have been made by Clark and Starkey,[128] Whittington[129] and Mills and Murgatroyd.[130] While there are significant differences of theoretical detail between the analyses articulated by these researchers, they share a common project establishing clearer linkages between sectoral developments and the politics of managerial action. They attempt this by focusing on the managerial practices through which institutional transformations are translated into coherent 'packages' of rules and mechanisms facilitating the re-assembly of activities into new organizational forms more appropriate to radically different sectoral conditions.

Clark and Starkey define 'sectors' as domains consisting of 'relatively similar enterprises which are in competition with one another, whilst also sharing similar requirements for state support and similar needs for technological evolvement'.[131] They also maintain that 'sectors develop institutions, languages and recipes which are distinctive and consequential. These cognitive and organizational features differ for the same sector between societies.'[132] Thus, their approach is based on the assumption that long-term changes in the conditions prevailing within any sector – markets, technologies, designs, etc. – will present problems to existing organizational designs. Managers will have to secure transitions in their internal structures to deal with these changed circumstances.

However, these organizational transitions will have to be mediated, if they are to succeed, through new sets of rules and mechanisms organized in loose, ambiguous, unformalized sets in which the 'power plays' of the major actors involved will have a dominating influence on their actual configuration and the structural repertoires which it facilitates. Consequently, their analysis of transitions in organizational forms within changing sectoral conditions attempts to link internal and external contexts through an unravelling of the highly complex political processes by which managers strive to realize a shift in the mechanisms and practices through which activities become structured. These new forms of structuration then provide the internal context in which subsequent phases of design transition, triggered by external changes in sectoral conditions, have to be engaged in – that is, they simultaneously enable and constrain the strategies of the major actors striving to come to terms with recalcitrant domains.

Whittington is concerned to provide a comprehensive explanation of the interaction between social structures and strategic choices in complex organizations and the manner in which it shapes the long-term development of structural forms. He rejects the environmental determinism that has plagued the work of the Aston group and the population ecologists, but is also wary of the excessive emphasis on subjective meaning and interpretation symptomatic of the work of action theorists such as symbolic interactionists and ethnomethodologists. Instead, he maintains that:

social structure grants certain actors the external power necessary to agency – control over both material resources and the labour of other actors. In this respect, the capitalist enterprise, combining labour and capital, potentially constitutes a particularly important instrument for agency. But capitalist structures alone rarely dictate how these corporate powers are actually used: the plural and contradictory nature of the social structure embodied within the firm precludes unambiguous determinism and allows sufficient autonomy for individual actors to choose which powers to use and how.[133]

Taking this as his starting-point, Whittington offers an analysis of the strategic choices followed by a number of companies operating in a recessionary economic environment in which market constraints were especially tight and restrictive. This analysis, he contends, must account for the structural resources which actors draw on and deploy to empower them as agents and the impact of the exercise of that agency on resulting organizational forms. The practices and mechanisms through which structural resources are mobilized by agents have to be understood both in relation to institutionalized systems of power and control, as well as the political strategies and tactics which actors rely on in various decision-making 'arenas'. Institutional analysis reveals the historically sedimented structures which agents draw on to enact their environments, while political analysis facilitates a more sophisticated and penetrating exploration of their actual strategies and tactics:

research into corporate strategic choices should proceed from two directions. Fundamental is an analysis of strategic conduct – an attempt to understand how the decision-makers see the world and what they seek from it. However, this understanding must be tempered by a more detached institutional analysis. Institutional analysis should be directed at amplifying actors' own accounts by establishing the structures upon which their actions both depended and worked.[134]

Consequently, Whittington sees strategic choice and the organizational forms which it generates as the outcome of a complex interaction between managerial politics and institutionalized constraints. These are brought together in the rules and resources which agents draw on in the social practices that reproduce social structures and the 'powers' that they make available to agents.

A similar approach is evident in Mills and Murgatroyd's development of the concept of 'rules' as a basis for understanding organizational action. They argue that: 'Rules, in the broadest sense, are outline steps for the conduct of action, and, depending upon combinations of circumstances and actors, those steps will be experienced as controlling, guiding and/or defining.'[135]

This basic conception of organizational rules as outline steps which guide action is then developed in such a way that it synthesizes both the enabling and constraining aspects of rule-governed conduct – that is, the inescapable fact that rules are created by actors but that they simultaneously constrain the action alternatives available to them over a series of decision-making situations. This development of the rule concept is itself theoretically grounded in a model of the organization as an interrelated network of social practices through which a wide multiplicity of activities are assembled to form institutionalized frameworks or patterns of collective action sustained over time and place by a matrix of rules. In this sense, the rule concept performs a linking function in that it connects forms of action to structural features by focusing on the diverse social practices through which actors construct rule matrices that shape their interaction and the institutionalized forms which it reproduces.

They deploy this approach in the analysis of a wide range of organizational processes such as socialization, institutional change, conflict management and the strategies of environmental positioning followed by senior managers in different kinds of markets. In all of these areas, Mills and Murgatroyd conclude:

whether at the level of seeking to understand the social mechanisms of control over the power and influence of organizations (as in the case of IBM) or the action of an individual in being negativistic towards some sub-group within the organization, rules have utility and value. . . . When an individual acts, he or she does so in terms of a rule matrix which is *in part* formed by the rules of the organization as formally established and informally communicated – that is, their understanding of the imperatives of co-ordination. However, their actions are also informed in part of their own judgements, experiences and rules (especially at moments of truth) and it is through an understanding of these two sets of rules working and acting concurrently (and sometimes in opposition) that we can develop an understanding of organizational action.[136]

## TRENDS AND TRAJECTORIES

This chapter has provided a detailed exposition and assessment of the research programmes undertaken by loosely coupled theory groups working within the broad theoretical parameters laid down by the analytical frameworks outlined in the previous chapter. It is now necessary to review and assess the underlying theoretical trends which emerge from the analysis conducted over these two chapters and the longer-term intellectual trajectories that they have followed. An interest in trends indicates a concern with the general theoretical movements in organizational analysis revealed by the discussion provided in the last two chapters. A focus on trajectories implies an interest in the broad intellectual paths which these trends have followed and their potential, if necessarily uncertain, long-term direction.

A number of interrelated trends can be identified as emerging from the review of analytical frameworks and theory groups' research programmes conducted in this and the previous chapter. First, the shift away from deterministic forms of explanation and towards explanatory logics which emphasize the crucial importance of human agency in shaping organizational structures and practices.[137] The former can be framed in a variety of ways – environmental determinism, structural determinism or cultural determinism – but they all share a commitment to the fundamental belief that 'explanation' consists in demonstrating how objective externalities programme actors' decisions and the courses of action which flow from them.[138] The inherent limitations and inadequacies of this view have been revealed by a growing recognition of the fact that human agents both individually and collectively enact social and organizational structures by engaging in forms of reasoning and action which transform the conditions under which they act. Structures or environments do not determine action because they are the creations of the actors themselves – even if the former invariably escape from the latter's control. Thus, the increasing visibility of and support for action-oriented frameworks and programmes in organizational analysis, as documented by Donaldson,[139] Whittington[140] and Clegg,[141] indicates the strength and impact of a deeper intellectual movement away from determinism and towards explanatory logics grounded in a model of organization as a construct or process reproducing structural forms. The ontological status of 'organization' as enacted process, rather than imposed structure, has emerged as a central strand of thinking in contemporary organizational analysis.

A second strand of development can be identified in the refocusing of attention on the problem of control, in contrast to a previous intellectual fixation with the problem of order. A sustained interest in the dynamics of control within and between complex organizations – a theme explored in greater detail in the following chapter – symbolizes a break with the age-old problematic of securing and maintaining social order in the face of deep-seated tensions and conflicts which are deemed to threaten the institutional *status quo*. Indeed, within the problematic of control, 'organizations' are redefined as power containers supporting institutionalized structures of dominations and regulation, rather than functional units buttressing the established order, the legitimacy of which can be automatically taken for granted. Thus, Weber's attempt to theoretically and empirically unravel the organizational mechanisms through which legitimacy is won and lost in modern societies finds a strong contemporary resonance in current research on the 'dialectic of control' in a wide range of organizational settings.

A refocusing of attention on the dynamics of control has also given encouragement and support to perspectives and programmes geared to the analysis of change and transformation in organizational forms. This stands in sharp contrast to the previous concentration on organizations as relatively fixed and permanent features of the institutional landscape. Change, and the inevitable uncertainty and instability that it generates, is now seen as an integral component of complex organization, rather than being approached as a residual or temporary condition within an inexorable long-term movement towards a relatively fixed and stable equilibrium.

The shift away from order and permanence towards control and change has also favoured a reorientation of theoretical development in which the politics of organization, rather than the technicalities of formal structural design, now play a strategic explanatory role. This burgeoning interest in the politics of organizational change and development has revealed the debilitating limitations of approaches that account for structural forms in terms of a 'logic of effectiveness'. Within the latter, a rational appreciation of technical constraints is presumed to exclude, or certainly marginalize, any attempt to relate organizational designs to the intra- and interorganizational power networks in which they take on meaning and significance. A myopic focus on transitions in organizational designs as the direct outcome of rational decision-making processes fixed on technical issues has been superseded by approaches that strive to link the 'design capacities' which authority and status come to legitimize with external networks of knowledge and power.[142]

Finally, the cumulative impact of these trends has been one that has undermined the aspiration to produce and police a narrow, discipline-bound conception of organizational analysis as an applied policy science primarily oriented to the administrative needs of managerial elites.[143] In its place, a much more open, not to say eclectic, conception of organizational analysis has gained considerable ground in recent years. In other words, a view of organizational analysis as a constituent field or area within the social sciences and sharing the latter's commitment to constructing and assessing explanations of organizational phenomena that are of interest to a wide range of groups and audiences within advanced and developing societies.[144] This, more 'open', view of organizational analysis has reinforced a reawakened interest in the general intellectual resources which the social sciences and the humanities can make available to students of organization who are grappling with problems which can no longer be contained and explored within the narrow confines of established theoretical categories.[145]

Each of the above trends can be located within broader intellectual trajectories and the overall directions in which the latter seem to be pressing.

The shift from determinism to voluntarism has been located within a sustained search for a general theory of action that can integrate a concern with structural constraint and human agency within one conceptual framework. While a number of alternative candidates have been paraded in recent years,[146] the most influential development in this domain has been Giddens' attempt to construct a theory of structuration which will synthesize institutional analysis of structural forms with strategic analysis of social action.[147] Thus, the theory of structuration is invoked and deployed by a growing number of organizational theorists reviewed in the last two chapters in their attempt to develop explanatory logics encompassing both the enabling or empowering aspects of 'structure', as well as its constraining or limiting influence.

The movement from order to control has strengthened the move towards a more well-developed institutional focus in organizational analysis. The latter is intended to provide a more systematic and coherent explanation of the inter-penetration of organizational forms and institutional con-figurations by exploring the processes through which 'internal' practices are embedded in and reproduce 'external' structures. Thus, the way in which organizationally specific administrative practices of coordination and control are based on institutionalized structures of power and domination operative in the wider society emerges as a strategic theme in contemporary analysis.

The reorientation towards change and instability, rather than permanence and equilibrium, has provided additional support for the development of a much more sensitive and sophisticated appreciation of organization theory's history and the changing set of practices which it has legitimated. As Thompson and McHugh argue:

Organisational theory and practice can only be understood as something in process, otherwise the search for general propositions and instant prescriptions becomes disconnected from reality as it has done in conventional ahistorical approaches. . . . This means locating organisational processes within their structural setting, examining their interaction with economic forces, political cultures and communities.[148]

The recognition of the need for a more self-reflexive understanding of the strategic role of 'politics' in shaping theoretical agendas and practical decision-making processes has helped sustain the momentum towards a much more pervasive intellectual pluralism in organizational studies over the last two decades or so.[149] Consequently, students of organization are now much more attuned to the range of theoretical and methodological options available to them and the need to display greater awareness of the inherent partiality and limitations of preferred choices.

Finally, the waning of disciplinary aspirations and waxing of multi- or interdisciplinary predilections has produced a field of study that is much more fragmented into competing, if not conflicting, theoretical frameworks and the conceptual languages which they promote. Indeed, some commentators have argued that the only way out of this 'tower of bable' is to reinstate a once dominant positivist epistemology and functionalist theory as the only acceptable intellectual basis on which 'proper' organizational analysis can be conducted.[150] Others have maintained that the process of fragmentation has gone so far that particular theory groups are hermetically sealed into their preferred frameworks or paradigms, unable to communicate, much less agree, with each other.[151]

Neither of the above strategies of long-term intellectual development seem particularly attractive and alternative ways of initiating and sustaining dialogue have been proposed.[152] Nevertheless, the highly fragmented nature of organizational analysis as a field of study occupied by

*Table 4.2* Trends and trajectories in contemporary organization theory

| Trends | | Trajectories |
| --- | --- | --- |
| Determinism ⟶ voluntarism | | Structuration |
| Order ⟶ control | | Institutionalism |
| Permanence ⟶ change | | Historicism |
| Technique ⟶ politics | | Pluralism |
| Discipline ⟶ field | | Fragmentation |

contending frameworks, programmes and groups is a reality which has to be addressed in any assessment of its current condition and future prospects. The trends and trajectories discussed in this section are summarized in Table 4.2.

## CONCLUSION

The last two chapters have provided a detailed exposition and assessment of the major analytical frameworks and research programmes developed and undertaken in organizational analysis over the last twenty years or so. This review and evaluation of the most significant theoretical movements of recent years has been set within an appreciation of the wider historical setting and intellectual context in which the former need to be located as provided in the first two chapters of this book.

The following two chapters move on to a more focused consideration of the issues that are currently shaping the research agenda in contemporary organizational analysis and their implications for longer-term prospects within the field. The analysis which they will provide needs to be set against the more recent background elaborated over the last two chapters.

REFERENCES

1. Mullins, N.C., *Theories and Theory Groups in Contemporary American Sociology* (Harper and Row, New York, 1973).
2. Whitley, R.D., 'The Management Sciences and Management Skills', *Organisation Studies*, vol. 9 (1), 1988, pp. 47–68 (p. 65); also see Whitley, R.D., 'The Fragmented State of Management Studies', *Journal of Management Studies*, vol. 21 (3), 1984, pp. 331–48.
3. Perry, N., 'Putting Theory in its Place: The Social Organization of Organizational Theorizing' in Reed, M. and Hughes, D. (eds), *Rethinking Organization: New Directions in Organization Theory and Analysis* (Sage, London, 1992), pp. 85–101.
4. Brown, C., 'Organisation and Science Studies' in Reed, M. and Hughes, D., *op. cit.* (1992), pp. 67–84.
5. Lakatos, I., 'Falsification and the Methodology of Scientific Research programmes' in Lakatos, I. and Musgrave, A. (eds), *Criticism and the Growth of Knowledge* (Cambridge University Press, Cambridge, 1970), pp. 91–196. This is obviously a very loose reworking of Lakatos's conception of research programmes.
6. Perry, N., *op. cit.* (1991).
7. Pugh, D. S., Hickson, D.J., Hinings, C.R., MacDonald, K. M., Turner, C. and Lupton, T., 'A Conceptual Scheme for Organisational Analysis', *Administrative Science Quarterly*, vol. 8 (3), 1963, pp. 289–315.
8. Pugh, D.S. and Hickson, D.J., *Organizational Structure in its Context: The Aston Programme I* (Saxon House, Farnborough, 1976).
9. Pugh, D.S., 'The Aston Research Programme' in Bryman, A. (ed.), *Doing Research in Organizations* (Routledge, London, 1988), pp. 123–35.
10. Pugh, D.S. *et al.*, *op. cit.* (1963), p. 291.
11. Pugh, D.S., 'Modern Organization Theory', *Psychological Bulletin*, vol. 66 (4), 1966, pp. 235–51.
12. The concept of ideal type and its methodological implications are explained in Albrow, M., *Bureaucracy* (Macmillan, London, 1970).
13. Pugh, D.S. and Hickson, D.J., *op. cit.* (1976), p. 185.
14. See previous chapter.
15. Pugh, D.S. and Payne, R.L. (eds), *Organizational Behaviour in its Context: The Aston Programme III* (Saxon House, Farnborough, 1978).

16. Hinings, R., Hickson, D.S. and Pugh, D., 'An Approach to the Study of Bureaucracy', *Sociology*, vol. 1, 1967, pp. 61–72 (p. 64).
17. Pugh, D.S., Hickson, D.J., Hinings, C.R. and Turner, C., 'Dimensions of Organization Structure', *Administrative Science Quarterly*, vol. 13 (1), 1968, pp. 65–105 and 'The Context of Organization Structures', *Administrative Science Quarterly*, vol. 14 (1), 1969, pp. 91–114.
18. Pugh, D.S. and Hickson, D., *op. cit.* (1968), p. 69.
19. Whitley, R., 'Concepts of Organizational Power in the Study of Organizations', *Personnel Review*, vol. 6 (1), 1977, pp. 54–9.
20. Fayol, H., *General and Industrial Management* (Pitman, London, 1949).
21. Brech, E.F.L., *Organization: The Framework of Management* (Longman Green, London, 1957).
22. Child, J., 'Organization: A Choice for Man' in Child, J. (ed.), *Man and Organization*, (Allen and Unwin, London 1973), pp. 234–57.
23. Hannan, M. T. and Freeman, J.H., *Organizational Ecology* (Harvard University Press, Cambridge, Mass., 1989).
24. *ibid.*, p. 13.
25. Aldrich, H. and Pfeffer, P., 'Environments of organizations', in Inkeles, A. (ed.), *Annual Review of Sociology*, vol. 2, 1976, pp. 97–105.
26. Hannan, M.T. and Freeman, J.H., *op. cit.* (1989), pp. 40–1.
27. Morgan, G., *Organizations in Society* (Macmillan, London, 1990), pp. 166–8.
28. Aldrich, H., *Organizations and Environments* (Prentice-Hall, Englewood Cliffs, NJ, 1979).
29. Hannan, M.T. and Freeman, J.H., *op. cit.* (1989), p. 60.
30. Hindess, B., 'Classes, Collectivities and Corporate Actors' in Clegg, S.R. (ed.), *Organizational Theory and Class Analysis: New Approaches and New Issues* (De Gruyter, Berlin, 1989), pp. 159–70.
31. Hannan, M.T. and Freeman, J.T., *op. cit.* (1989), p. 7.
32. Aldrich, H., *op. cit.* (1979).
33. Hannan, M.T. and Freeman, J.T., *op. cit.* (1989), p. 70. For a systems-based perspective which examines the issue of environmental resource dependencies and their implications for the interorganizational *politics* in more detail, see Pfeffer, J. and Salancik, G.R., *The External Control of Organizations: A Resource Dependency Approach* (Harper and Row, New York, 1978).

34. *ibid.*, pp. 79–84.
35. *ibid.*, p. 201.
36. Ahrne, G., *Agency and Organization: Toward an Organizational Theory of Society* (Sage, London, 1990).
37. Goffman, E., *Asylums* (Penguin, Harmondsworth, 1959).
38. Dalton, M., *Men Who Manage* (Wiley and Son, New York, 1959).
39. Strauss, A., Schatzman, L., Ehrlich, D., Bucher, R. and Sabshin, M., 'The Hospital and its Negotiated Order' in Friedson, E. (ed.), *The Hospital in Modern Society* (Macmillan, New York, 1963).
40. Strauss, A., *Negotiations* (Wiley and Son, New York, 1978).
41. *ibid.*, p. ix.
42. Etzioni, A. (ed.), *The Semi Professions and their Organization* (Free Press, New York, 1969).
43. McKinlay, J. B. (ed.), *Processing People: Cases in Organizational Behaviour* (Holt, Rinehart and Winston, New York, 1975).
44. Abbott, A., *The System of Professions* (Chicago University Press, Chicago, 1988). The theme of professional power is explored in greater detail in the following chapter.
45. Day, R.A. and Day, J.V., 'A Review of the Current State of Negotiated Order Theory: An Appreciation and Critique', *Sociological Quarterly*, Vol. 18, Winter 1977, pp. 126–42; Strauss, A., *op. cit.* (1978).
46. See Day, R.A. and Day, J.V., *op. cit.* (1977).
47. Friedson, E., *Professional Powers* (University of Chicago Press, Chicago, 1986).
48. Friedson, E., 'The Future of Professionalization' in Stacey, M., Reid, M., Heath, C. and Digwell, R., *Health and the Divison of Labour* (Croom Helm, London, 1977), pp. 14–40 (pp. 23–4).
49. *ibid.*, p. 23.
50. Day, R.A., and Day, J.V., *op. cit.* (1977), p. 136.
51. Attwell, P., 'Ethnomethodology since Garfinkel', *Theory and Society*, vol. 1 (1), 1974, pp. 179–210; Reed, M., *Redirections in Organisational Analysis* (Tavistock, London, 1985).
52. Turner, R., *Ethnomethodology* (Penguin, Harmondsworth, 1974); Silverman, D., 'Accounts of Organizations: Organizational Structure in the Accounting Process' in McKinlay, J.B., *op. cit.* (1975), pp. 269–302; Hassard, J., 'Ethnomethdology and Organisational Research' in Hassard, J. and Pym, D. (eds), *The Theory and Philosophy of Organisations* (Routledge, London, 1990), pp. 97–108.

53. Garfinkel, H., *Studies in Ethnomethodology* (Prentice-Hall, Englewood Cliffs, NJ, 1967); Heritage, J., 'Ethnomethodology' in Giddens, A. and Turner, J. (eds), *Social Theory Today* (Polity Press, Cambridge, 1987), pp. 224–72.
54. Coulter, D., 'Decontextualized Meanings: Current Approaches to Verstehende Investigations', *Sociological Review*, vol. 19, 1971, pp. 301–23.
55. Filmer, D., Phillipson, M., Silverman, D. and Walsh, D., *New Directions in Sociological Theory* (Macmillan, London, 1972).
56. Bittner, E., 'The Concept of Organization' in Salaman, G. and Thompson, K., *People and Organizations* (eds) (Open University Press, Milton Keynes, 1973), pp. 264–76.
57. Lassman, P., 'Phenomenological Perspectives in Sociology' in Rex, J. (ed.), *Approaches to Sociology* (Routledge, London, 1974); Jehenson, R., 'A Phenomenological Approach to the Study of Formal Organizations' in Psthas, G. (ed.), *Phenomenological Sociology* (Wiley, New York, 1973), pp. 219–47.
58. Bittner, E., 'The Police on Skid Row' in Salaman, G. and Thompson, K. (eds), *op. cit.* (1973), pp. 331–45.
59. Cicourel, A.Y., *The Social Organization of Juvenile Justice* (Heinemann, London, 1976).
60. Sudnow, D., 'Normal Crimes: Sociological Features of the Penal Code in a Public Defender Office' in Salaman, G. and Thompson, K. (eds), *op. cit.* (1973), pp. 346–57.
61. Zimmerman, D., 'The Practicalities of Rule Use' in Salaman, G. and Thompson, K. (eds), *op. cit.* (1973), pp. 250–63.
62. Silverman, D. and Jones, J., *Organisational Work: The Language of Grading and the Grading of Language* (Macmillan, London, 1976).
63. Bittner, E., *op. cit.* (1973).
64. *ibid.*, p. 272.
65. *ibid.*, p. 272.
66. Cicourel, A.Y., *op. cit.* (1976), p. 122
67. Thompson, P., *The Nature of Work: An Introduction to Debates on the Labour Process* (Macmillan, London, second edition, 1989); Knights, D. and Willmott, H. (eds), *Labour Process Theory* (Macmillan, London, 1990).
68. Braverman, H., *Labour and Monopoly Capital: The Degradation of Work in the Twentieth Century* (Monthly Review Press, New York, 1974).
69. For research incorporating non-capitalist societies see Burawoy, M., *The Politics of Production* (Verso, London, 1985).
70. Edwards, R., *Contested Terrain* (Heinemann, London, 1979);

Friedman, A., *Industry and Labour: Class Struggle at Work and Monopoly Capitalism* (Macmillan, London, 1977); Littler, C., *The Development of the Labour Process in Capitalist Societies* (Heinemann, London, 1982). Also see Chapter 1 of this book.

71. For a review of this work see Reed, M., *The Sociology of Management* (Harvester Wheatsheaf, Hemel Hempstead, 1989), chapter 2; Littler, C., 'The Labour Process Debate: A Theoretical Review' in Knights, D. and Willmott, H. (eds), *op. cit.* (1990), pp. 46–94.

72. Thompson, P., *op. cit.* (1989), p. 234.

73. Edwards, P.K., *Conflict at Work: A Materialist Analysis of Workplace Relations* (Basil Blackwell, Oxford, 1986).

74. Hyman, R., 'Strategy or Structure?: Capital, Labour and Control', *Work, Employment and Society*, vol. 1 (1), 1981, pp. 25–55.

75. Edwards, R., *op. cit.* (1979).

76. Littler, C., *op. cit.* (1990).

77. Hyman, R., *op. cit.* (1987), p. 41.

78. Edwards, P.K., 'Understanding Conflict in the Labour Process: The Logic and Autonomy of Struggle' in Knights, D. and Willmott, H. (eds), *op. cit.* (1990), pp. 125–52.

79. In this respect, there is some degree of theoretical convergence between negotiated order theory and labour process theory around the negotiated nature of organizational control systems.

80. Braverman, H., *op. cit.* (1974).

81. Littler, C., *op. cit.* (1982), p. 34.

82. Friedman, A., 'Managerial Strategies, Activities, Techniques and Technology: Towards Complex Theory of the Labour Process' in Knights, D. and Willmott, H. (eds), *op. cit.* (1990), pp. 177–208.

83. Burawoy, M., *op. cit.* (1985); Salaman, G., *Working* (Tavistock, London, 1988).

84. Storey, J., *New Perspectives in Human Resource Management* (Routledge, London, 1989).

85. Francis, A., *New Technology at Work* (Oxford University Press, Oxford, 1986).

86. Rose, M. and Jones, B., 'Managerial Strategy and Trade Union Response in Work Re-organisation Schemes at Establishment Level' in Knights, D., Willmott, H. and Collinson, D., *Job Redesign: Critical Perspectives on the Labour Process* (Gower, Aldershot, 1985).

87. Knights, D., 'Subjectivity, Power and the Labour Process', in Knights, D. and Willmott, H. (eds), *op. cit.* (1990), pp. 297–335.

88. This theme is pursued at greater length in the next chapter.
89. Morgan, G., *op. cit.* (1990), p. 100.
90. Clegg, S., *Frameworks of Power* (Sage, London, 1989), p. 151.
91. Knights, D. and Willmott, H. (eds), *op. cit.* (1990).
92. Foucault, M., *Discipline and Punish: The Birth of the Prison* (Penguin, Harmondsworth, 1979).
93. Goffman, E., *op. cit.* (1959).
94. O'Neill, J., 'The Disciplinary Society', *British Journal of Sociology*, vol. 37 (1), 1986, pp. 42–60.
95. *ibid.*, pp. 42–5.
96. Cousins, M. and Hussain, A., *Michel Foucault* (Macmillan, London, 1984).
97. Dreyfus, H.L. and Rainbow, P., *Michel Foucault: Beyond Structuralism and Hermeneutics* (Harvester Wheatsheaf, Hemel Hempstead, 1982).
98. Blau, P. and Schoenherr, R.A., *The Structure of Organizations* (New York, Basic Books, 1971).
99. Perrow, C. *Complex Organizations: A Critical Essay* (Random House, New York, third edition, 1986).
100. Perrow, C., *op. cit.* (1986), p. 129.
101. Dandeker, C., *Surveillance, Power and Modernity* (Polity Press, Cambridge, 1990).
102. Burrell, G., 'Modernism, Postmodernism and Organizational Analysis 2: The Contribution of Michel Foucault', *Organization Studies*, vol. 9 (2), 1988, pp. 221–35 (pp. 227–8).
103. Giddens, A., *The Nation State and Violence* (Polity Press, Cambridge, 1985), pp. 183–6.
104. Turner, B., *Organizational Symbolism* (De Gruyter, Berlin, 1989); 'The Rise of Organizational Symbolism' in Hassard, J. and Pym, D. (eds), *op. cit.* (1990), pp. 83–96.
105. Nord, W., 'Can Organizational Culture be Managed?' in Frost, P.J., Moore, L.F., Louis, M.R., Lundberg, C.C. and Martin, J. (eds), *Organizational Culture* (Sage, New York, 1985), pp. 187–96 (p. 191).
106. Allaire, Y. and Firsirotui, M., 'Theories of Organizational Culture', *Organization Studies*, vol. 5 (3), 1984, pp. 192–226.
107. Nord, W., *op. cit.* (1985), p. 195.
108. Smircich, L., 'Concepts of Culture and Organisational Analysis', *Administrative Science Quarterly*, vol. 28, 1983, pp. 339–58.
109. Schein, E., *Organizational Culture and Leadership* (Jossey Bass, San Francisco, 1985).
110. *ibid.*, p. 9.

111. Pettigrew, A., *The Awakening Giant: Continuity and Change at ICI* (Blackwell, Oxford, 1985).

112. *ibid.*, pp. 44–5.

113. Scott, W.R., 'The Adolescence of Institutional Theory', *Administrative Science Quarterly*, vol. 32, 1987, pp. 493–511.

114. Meyer, J. M. and Rowan, B., 'Institutionalized Organizations: Formal Structures as Myth and Ceremony' in Zey-Ferrell, M. and Aiken, M. (eds), *Complex Organizations: Critical Perspectives* (Scott, Foresman and Company, Dallas, 1981, pp. 303–22.

115. *ibid.*, p. 306.

116. *ibid.*, pp. 310–11.

117. Di Maggio, P.J. and Powell, W.W., 'The Iron Cage Revisited: Institutional Isomorphism and Collective Rationality in Organizational Fields', *American Sociological Review*, vol. 48, 1983, pp. 147–60.

118. Meyer, J.M. and Rowan, B., *op. cit.* (1981), p. 315.

119. Ahrne, G., *op. cit.* (1990), pp. 36–9.

120. *ibid.*, p. 37.

121. Beetham, D., *Max Weber and The Theory of Modern Politics* (Cambridge University Press, Cambridge, second edition, 1985); *Bureaucracy* (Open University Press, Milton Keynes, 1987).

122. McNeil, K., 'Understanding Organizational Power: Building on the Weberian Legacy' in Zey-Ferrell, M. and Aiken, M. (eds), *op. cit.* (1981), pp. 46–68 (pp. 53–4).

123. Perrow, C., *op. cit.* (1986).

124. Salaman, G., *Work Organizations, Resistance and Control* (Longman, London, 1979); *Class and the Corporation* (Fontana, Glasgow, 1981).

125. Mouzelis, N., *Organization and Bureaucracy* (Routledge, London, second edition, 1975).

126. Clegg, S., *Power, Rule and Domination* (Routledge, London, 1978); *Modern Organizations: Organization Studies in the Post Modern World* (Sage, London, 1990).

127. Clegg, S., *op. cit.* (1989), pp. 199–200.

128. Clark, P. and Starkey, K., *Organization Transitions and Innovation Design* (Pitman, London, 1988).

129. Whittington, R., *Corporate Strategies in Recession and Recovery: Social Structure and Strategic Choice* (Unwin Hyman, London, 1989).

130. Mills, A.J. and Murgatroyd, S.J., *Organizational Rules* (Open University Press, Milton Keynes, 1990).

131. Clark, P. and Starkey, K., *op. cit.* (1988), p. 16.

132. *ibid.*, p. 16. On the 'organization-in-sector' approach see Child,

J., 'On Organizations in their Sectors', *Organization Studies*, vol. 9 (1), 1988, pp. 13–18. The application of this approach is most clearly illustrated in Smith, C., Child, J. and Rowlinson, M., *Reshaping Work: The Cadbury Experience* (Cambridge University Press, Cambridge, 1990).

133. Whittington, R., *op. cit.* (1989), p. 77.
134. *ibid.*, p. 118.
135. Mills, A.J. and Murgatroyd, S.J., *op. cit.* (1990), p. 30.
136. *ibid.*, p. 191.
137. Reed, M., 'The Problem of Human Agency in Organizational Analysis', *Organization Studies*, vol. 9 (1), 1988, pp. 33–46.
138. Whittington, R., 'Structure and Theories of Strategic Choice', *Journal of Management Studies*, vol. 25 (6), 1988, pp. 521–36.
139. Donaldson, *In Defence of Organizational Theory* (Cambridge University Press: Cambridge, 1985).
140. Whittington, R., *op. cit.* (1989).
141. Clegg, S., *op. cit.* (1990).
142. Clark, P. and Starkey, K., *op. cit.* (1988).
143. Reed, M., 'Deciphering Donaldson and Defending Organisation Theory', *Australian Journal of Management*, vol. 14 (2), 1989, pp. 255–61.
144. Reed, M., 'Scripting Scenarios for a New Organisation Theory and Practice', *Work, Employment and Society*, vol. 5 (1), 1991, pp. 119–32.
145. This point is developed further in the next chapter.
146. Outhwaite, W., *New Philosophies of Social Science: Realism, Hermeneutics and Critical Theory* (Macmillan, London, 1987).
147. Bryant, C.G. and Jarry, D., *Giddens' Theory of Structuration: A Critical Appreciation* (Routledge, London, 1991).
148. Thompson, P. and McHugh, D., *Work Organizations: A Critical Introduction* (Macmillan, London, 1990), p. 32.
149. Reed, M., *op. cit.* (1985).
150. Donaldson, L., *op. cit.* (1985).
151. Burrell, G. and Morgan, G., *Sociological Paradigms and Organizational Analysis* (Heinemann, 1979).
152. This point is taken up in Chapter 6.

/ 5 /

# CURRENT ISSUES

## INTRODUCTION

The analysis developed in the previous two chapters has indicated that the current state of play in organizational analysis is very different from that prevailing in the later 1960s. This is so in a number of different, but interrelated, respects. First, the field is much more pluralistic, not to say fragmented, in terms of the substantially extended range of theoretical and methodological options available to students of organization. Second, the agenda to which these options can be applied is now much wider in the sense that it encompasses issues which cannot be contained within – or indeed comprehended within – the formal organizational designs programme at the heart of the systems approach. Third, the sociology of organizations is now exposed to, even embraces, a much more innovative and challenging set of intellectual influences which form the focus for current debates in socio-political theory.[1] Fourth, a growing number of practitioners are increasingly sensitive to, and appreciative of, the historical traditions and institutional contexts in which present concerns have to be located and interpreted. Fifth, there is now much greater awareness of the need to combine a concern with structural constraint and social agency within theoretical perspectives and research methodologies geared to the dialectical interplay between institutional configurations and strategic conduct. Finally, the substantive issues which have emerged to structure the research agenda for contemporary organizational analysis signify a rediscovery and retrieval of the perennial themes which have shaped the field's intellectual development for more than a century – but within a theoretical vocabulary that enriches and extends the intellectual inheritance which the latter bequeaths. These themes can be adumbrated in the following terms. A revived interest in the historical dynamics of organizational surveillance and control, and their implications for the practices through which 'organizational identities or subjectivities' are moulded and sustained, stands at the core of the research agenda in contemporary organizational analysis. This concern is reinforced by a renewed interest in the strategic role of professional expertise and power in structuring the organizational forms through which rationalization is extended and embedded in modern societies. The sustained momentum towards more rationalized systems of organizational coordination and control leads to a focus on the politics of organizational change and development as it impacts on the socio-economic and cultural divisions which continue to shape the allocation and authorization of collective power.[2] In turn, the complexities of the interaction between professional power and organizational governance raises the underlying question of the competing and conflicting ideological rationales which inform current organizational practice and their role in shaping decision-making processes.[3]

Finally, more recent debate concerning the meaning and significance of 'rationality' in complex organizations raises some crucial questions about the latter as carriers of a modernizing process which sweeps away the constraining influence of traditional values and ideologies.[4] This debate about the nature and import of organizational rationality also relates to the rise of what have been labelled 'postmodern' forms of organization.[5] The latter are seen as signifying the dynamics of a logic of institutional development which slows and then reverses the trend towards extreme differentiation and specialization which is characteristic of modernization.[6]

Taken together, these central issues – surveillance and control, professional power, the politics of organizational design, organizational rationality and the putative emergence of postmodern organizational forms – create a revitalized agenda for contemporary organizational analysis. This agenda resonates with the original concerns of the field's founding fathers – as discussed in Chapters 1 and 2 – but in a new theoretical idiom that speaks to current controversies over the present condition of and future prospects for such a vital social institution as complex organization. Each of these issues will be discussed in turn before turning to a broader assessment of their significance for lines of debate beginning to open up between new approaches and research programmes.

## SURVEILLANCE AND CONTROL

Control has emerged as *the* strategic issue in previous discussion. However, more recent work in this area has encouraged a much wider and sophisticated view of surveillance and control in complex organizations. This is so to the extent that recent analysis has displayed much greater sensitivity to the historical context in which different forms of control develop and their implications for the construction and maintenance of 'normal' organizational identities. It has also incorporated a far wider range of organizational sites or settings in which control strategies and mechanisms have been studied beyond the traditional confines of business firms or governmental bureaucracies.[7] The cumulative impact of these developments in the more recent analysis of organizational surveillance and control has been to generate a research agenda and a set of theoretical approaches which focus on the strategic role of administrative power in linking central authorities, bureaucracies and subject populations within modern societies. Thus, the surveillance and control capacities generated and deployed by modern organizations have crystallized into a major research theme in contemporary organizational analysis which has its intellectual roots in the 'theories of modernity' reviewed and assessed in Chapter 1 of this book. As Dandeker notes:

as surveillance involves a deliberate attempt to monitor and/or supervise objects or persons, it is to be found in its *most developed form* in formal organizations which possess an explicitly stated goal(s), together with a formal administrative structure for achieving these goals, including arrangements for maintaining the boundaries and passages between the organization and outsiders . . . modernity comprises an age of bureaucratic organizations. This is one indication of the long-term process of the rationalization of social action observed by Weber.[8]

Building on Giddens' analysis of complex organizations as administrative mechanisms geared to the maintenance and reproduction of systems of institutionalized power (as reviewed in Chapter 1 of this book), Dandeker offers a threefold classification of the activities associated with organizational surveillance. First, information collection, storage and retrieval; second, direct and indirect methods of supervising people or objects; third, the use of information coordination and control to monitor the behaviour of subject populations in order to secure their compliance on a routine basis.[9] It is the enduring and mutually reinforcing link between these three interrelated sets of activities or practices over time which establishes the administrative apparatus through which power relationships are institutionalized within modern societies to form relatively stable structures of rule and domination. Modern organizations are the quintessential mechanisms for securing effective surveillance and control in highly differentiated societies.

Yet, this administrative apparatus should not be considered as providing a totally efficient and effective basis for securing power and domination within complex organizations or the wider societies which they help to sustain and reproduce over time. As Giddens reminds us:

No matter how complete the power of one individual or group might be over others, resources are always available whereby subordinates can reciprocally influence power holders. The dialectic of control in modern organizations assumes various forms, but mostly these are associated closely with the time-space zoning of the organization. The setting of interaction and their relation to timetables, allows various forms of concealment which 'balance off' other forms of exposure. Even in the 'open' setting of direct supervision there are circumstances in which individuals can escape the supervisory gaze.[10]

What this suggests is that the capacity of organizations to

structure and control time/space allocation and utilization in line with formal commands is inherently limited by the 'areas of uncertainty', and hence autonomy, which they open up and make available for subordinates to exploit for their own purposes.[11] As devices for mobilizing administrative resources for the purpose of facilitating routine control and stable power relationships, complex organizations have certain in-built limitations and contradictions which constrain their capacity to promote 'normal' identities and to secure the behavioural patterns associated with them. Consequently, both superordinates and subordinates are necessarily involved in various 'trade offs' between control and autonomy; the former have to accept that any formalized surveillance system is necessarily incomplete and will require supplementation, while the latter – either individually or collectively – are only too willing and able to exploit the opportunities that 'gaps' in the surveillance system provide for concealment, subversion and avoidance. In this respect, the surveillance and control capacities of modern organizations are highly variable and relatively unstable both in relation to their ability to secure compliance on a routine basis and their effectiveness in socializing members into normalized identities. Nevertheless, they provide a control capacity which is far more effective in securing a degree of order and stability in highly complex societies than cruder forms of surveillance based on direct coercion and physical constraint.

Dandeker argues that the long-term historical development of surveillance capacities and the maximization of their control potential within formal organizations can be understood in terms of shifts in the power relations between dominant groups, subordinate populations and administrative personnel entailing four interrelated processes. First, a sustained transition from personal to impersonal control 'and the increasing significance of formal–legal regulations as the basis on which rule is exercised and legitimated in organizations'.[12] Second, a shift from personal, indirect and relatively diffuse systems of disciplinary control to bureaucratized systems of surveillance and domination. Third, the growth of much more complex, intensive and intrusive forms of information collection, storage, retrieval and manipulation concerning both the internal and external conditions of formal organizations. Finally, the development of extended managerial hierarchies and differentiated occupational structures subjected to processes of professionalization in which various groups struggle to secure and retain control over disputed areas of knowledge and expertise and the power which they can generate.[13] Taken as an institutional package, Dandeker concludes that the cumulative impact of these four linked processes of change in organizational surveillance and control has been to produce modern societies which 'are now in large part under fairly dense networks of surveillance'.[14] At the centre of these networks, lie the organizationally based administrative practices and informational systems through which effective surveillance over and control of large populations is regularly achieved.

In this way, Dandeker's analysis extends and reinforces Giddens' argument that modern organizations are the strategic mechanisms or devices for securing the reproduction and/or transformation of the core institutional structures – the capitalist enterprise, the bureaucratic state, a professionalized/expert division of labour and industrialized military power – constitutive of modernity:

The modern world is the world of organizations. Why should that be? At the most general level, the ubiquity of organizations is bound up with the significance of historicity within the culture of modernity. Historicity means using history to make history. The social world is not taken as given, but as intrinsically malleable in respect of the accumulation of knowledge about that world. When this outlook is regularized as a discursively available foundation of system reproduction, we have the core of an 'organizational culture'. A modern organization is a social system in which information is regularly used, and its discursive articulation carefully coded, so as to maximize control of system reproduction.[15]

Such a sustained analytical focus on the organizational practices through which the reflexive monitoring of system reproduction and/or transformation are secured in modern societies implies a shift of concern away from organizations as predominantly economic units and towards – one is almost tempted to say back to – their strategic administrative role in facilitating the intensification of surveillance and control as the *crucial* aspect of modernization. Thus, more recent work on the long-term historical development of the organizational practices and mechanisms through which an intensification of surveillance and control has been realized in modern societies has documented the strategic role of the former in developing and assembling the informational and supervisory systems by means of which reflexive monitoring of social action can be routinely performed.

One area in which this focus has proved to be particularly fruitful is in relation to the historical development of accounting principles and practices as they have facilitated an intensification of surveillance and control within modern societies.[16] Another area where this approach has been usefully deployed is in relation to the growth and diffusion of personnel management procedures and practices in entailing the development of a more sophisticated bureaucratic apparatus through which 'organizational history' – collating and integrating institutional and personal data and histories – can be accumulated and compiled for control purposes.[17] Research in both of these areas has moved away from a largely 'technical' assessment of their contribution to operational efficiency and effectiveness. It has concentrated instead on their often interlinked administrative functions in facilitating predictive control over the economic and human resources through and over which routine organizational surveillance is secured.

Thus, the development and diffusion of modern cost accounting methods is seen to be critical in establishing a mode of organizational governance over subject populations based on objective calculability and rational control. Within the latter, organizational members and clients could be treated as resources or objects subject to the same 'cost benefit' logic of efficiency and effectiveness as applied to non-human resources such as capital, land and machinery. This 'cost benefit' logic provides a quantitatively based mode of calculative rationality and administrative control in which human beings are made subject to the same 'calculus of expectations' as that applied to other resources. In turn, this permits the formulation, codification and continual up-dating of performance standards and norms against which individual behaviour can be monitored. Any deviation from these 'objective norms' can then be identified, investigated and subsequently subjected to remedial treatment of one form or another. In principle, at least, modern cost accounting principles and methods provided a crucial component in the ever-expanding armoury of administrative controls through which individual and collective behaviour can be subordinated to the tyranny of normalized standards which are legitimated through the values and practices of objective science. Organizational history becomes a repository of financial information and techniques through which future organizational development is routinely managed and controlled.

In the personnel field, recent research has detected a degree of disillusionment with relatively coercive control practices relating to work performance intensification. Currently, there is a corresponding enthusiasm for more sophisticated, culturally based control processes geared to effective socialization and personal development.[18] A shift towards the latter is seen to be expressed in the growing support given to recruitment, selection and appraisal techniques which aspire to provide effective 'attitudinal restructuring' and behavioural control through the manipulation of normative orientations which facilitate the development of cultural identities appropriate to senior management-determined corporate goals and policies.[19] At a more broadly based level of analysis, the ideology and rhetoric of 'human resource management', rather than the more traditional appellation of personnel management which came into vogue in the 1980s, can be interpreted as a symbolic representation of the perceived need for a strong corporate culture in which individuals are 'subject to unobtrusive collective controls on attitudes and behaviour'.[20]

However, this shift from 'control-by-repression' to 'control-by-seduction' merely serves to highlight the historical role which personnel management practices have played in attempting to mediate between the contradictory demands for compliance and cooperation within work organizations, in which the efficient utilization of and control over 'human resources' is the overriding priority.[21] Whatever set of control techniques or practices may be fashionable for a period of time, and the particular characteristics of the ideological/political context in which they receive legitimatory support, the long-term historical development of personnel management can be interpreted as entailing the growth of an informational and supervisory apparatus which *attempts* to secure a disciplined and integrated labour force.

In each case – that is, in relation to the growth and diffusion of modern accountancy and personnel practices – the expansion of particular areas of 'expertise', and the contribution which they make to enhancing the overall surveillance and control capacities of modern organizations in government, business and welfare, has to be related to the power struggles between different groups to establish effective monopoly control over specified domains of organizational practice and their primary status in contributing to organizational success. In short, the intensification of organizational surveillance and control capacity inherent within the process of modernization has to be related to the issue of professional power.

### PROFESSIONAL POWER

As Scott has argued, professional groups are the 'great rationalisers' of the twentieth century.[22] They have played a pivotal role in shaping the institutional structures and organizational forms which have developed in modern industrialized societies. Either in alliance with or engaged in conflict against state policy and the legal/administrative framework through which it has been implemented, professional groups and coalitions have provided the normative and cognitive resources and administrative programmes which have structured the organizational practices through which 'modernization' has been carried through.[23] While there has been a tendency to assume that professionalization and bureaucratization are antithetical processes,[24] recent research and analysis has been much more sensitive to the way in which the expansion of professional power and authority has promoted the advance of more sophisticated forms of organizational surveillance and control:

> although bureaucratic discipline is a functional requirement of all complex, industrial societies, with the continuing advance of modern technology it is increasingly subordinated to expertise and professional knowledge ... professionalization is understood as a component part of the broader process of bureaucratization.[25]

Dandeker's comment highlights the complex organizational processes through which bureaucratization, rationalization and professionalization interact to form the core institutional configurations characteristic of modernity. Bureaucratization signifies a sustained move towards impersonal forms of administration based on the diffusion of more elaborate information control systems and their deployment through the application of expert knowledge and skill associated with professionalization. In this way, the professionalization of work and the development of a more highly differentiated occupational division of labour within modern societies are seen to be intimately tied to the enhancement of organizational surveillance and control capacities through successive waves of bureaucratization. Rather than seeing bureaucratization and professionalization as opposed trajectories of institutional development and organizational change within modern societies, they are now seen as having an elective affinity with each other. This is the case in so far as they jointly promote and reinforce a long-term trend towards more rationalized – that is abstract, codified and integrated – systems of surveillance and control.

The particular ways in which bureaucratization and professionalization interact to advance the cause of organizational rationalization can be understood at a number of different levels of analysis: first, in relation to intra-organizational conflict and its impact on operational control systems; second, in regard of interorganizational relations and processes that shape the relative power and privileges of different professional groups within the socio-political and economic order; and third, in regard to the overall impact of changing professional powers and ideologies on the structures of domination and control which determine the distribution of allocative and authoritative resources[26] within modern societies. Underpinning research carried on at each of these levels, a generic conceptualization of 'profession' and 'professionalization' has begun to emerge. This conceptualization stresses the contested collective capacity to achieve and sustain monopoly control over a specific body of knowledge and related technical expertise which bear upon a defined territory or object domain as the central feature of the professionalization process. Hence, the 'credentialization' of an occupational group through formal training and qualifications and demonstrated competence in task performance are crucial to its success in establishing 'professional' status.[27] Thus, the ability of an occupational group to establish, protect and extend an effective 'jurisdictional claim' over an identifiable area of task-based expertise relevant to organizational performance is seen to be crucial in determining its success in achieving professional status and power within the expert divisions of labour which are characteristic of modern societies:

A jurisdictional claim made before the public is generally a claim for the *legitimate control of a particular kind of work*. This control means first and foremost a right to perform the work as a professional sees fit. Along with the right to perform the work as it wishes, a profession normally also claims rights to exclude other workers as deemed necessary, to dominate public definitions of the tasks concerned, and indeed to impose professional definitions of the tasks on competing professions. Public jurisdiction, in short, is a claim of both social and cultural authority.[28]

This view suggests that effective professional power and authority is based on abstract or expert knowledge which is mobilized and institutionalized through various forms of cognitive, ideological and organizational control strategies which establish 'the profession's' claim to monopolize defined areas of work. However, this claim to 'knowledge–power' is always likely to be contested, to varying degrees, by other groups which aspire to assert their crucial contribution to organizational performance and societal well-being. These jurisdictional conflicts and their impact on occupational power structures and class systems within modern societies are often seen in their most visible or direct form at the intra-organizational level. This is most obviously seen in the power struggles between different occupational groups to establish the pre-eminence of their expertise and its strategic contribution to organizational success. However, their pervasive influence on interorganizational networks of power and control, and their role in shaping and being shaped by, institutionalized patterns of societal-level resource allocation and authorization should not be forgotten. The struggle to establish and defend effective professional power bases stands at the core of institutionalization processes and organizational redesign programmes in modern societies.

At each of these levels of analysis – intra-organizational, interorganizational and societal – the contested capacity of particular occupational groups to expand their cognitive dominion by mobilizing abstract knowledge to annex new areas of 'organizational work' emerges as the key political process facilitating the advance of professional control and power. By establishing, defending and expanding their particular jurisdictional claims over defined areas of organizational work, professional groups – sometimes with state support, sometimes without it – construct systems of occupational monopolization, closure and control that usually push in the direction of bureaucratic rationalization and the expanded surveillance capacities which it generates:

the phenomena of credentialed exclusion, experts and professionals are based on the more general process of formal rationalization. . . . The later phase of formal rationalization, in which bureaucratization was more advanced, drew [the early professions] into bureaucratic organizations and created new professions which were born into bureaucracy. . . . Groups of credentialed experts differ from the autonomous liberal professions in the early phase of formal rationalization in that they have increasingly come under bureaucratic control as the process of formal rationalization has resulted in specific resources which the credentialed mobilize and in opportunities which they seize in the structure or system of closure and power of which they are a part.[29]

The implication of this analysis is that the 'organizational professions' – as opposed to the 'liberal' professions – will become increasingly prominent, not to say dominant, within modern societies because they possess the expert power necessary to facilitate the expansion of organizational surveillance and control capacities on which the maintenance of socio-political order within the latter increasingly depends.[30] While the 'organizational professions' are dependent on their employment within formal bureaucracies and state support to a much greater degree than the relatively autonomous, liberal professions,[31] they also provide a very powerful social force pressing in the direction of 'rationalized power practices' and the calculated control over social behaviour which they make possible.[32]

Consequently, a model and ideology of professionalism based on a relatively autonomous relationship between individual client and independent practitioner (accredited and supported by an appropriate professional body) gives way to a strategy and form of professionalization in which various occupational groups have conducted a 'Faustian pact' with bureaucratic organization within the centralized state apparatus and highly centralized structures of corporate governance. The former secure power, status and material rewards, while the latter get the knowledge-based expertise and technical skills they need to realize effective surveillance and control over subject populations and the complex control systems necessary to achieve sustained profitability in an intensely competitive global economy. Indeed, there is even a suggestion in some interpretations which run along these lines[33] that a new 'service class' of organization-based professions is emerging as an independent 'third force' – between 'capital' and 'labour' – in advanced societies.[34] This 'third force' of organizational professions – managers, administrators, scientists, technical experts and human services specialists – is seen to constitute a potential force for socio-political change. It advances the cause of rationalization in the name of meritocracy, equity and efficiency as against the values of privilege, preference and stability defended by traditional elites and ruling groups. Consequently, the organizational professions can be seen as a strategic source of moral regulation and cultural integration within increasingly differentiated and fragmented modern industrial societies. By advancing the cause of core values that seem to underpin the long-term developmental trajectory of modernization away from 'ascription' and towards 'achievement', they present themselves as a positive force which provides the technical expertise and organizational integration so vital to economic success and social progress.[35]

However, this overall interpretation of the dynamics of professional power in modern societies, and their positive contribution to the intensification of organizational surveillance and control combined with socio-economic progress, has been challenged on a number of counts. First, it seriously underestimates the scale and intensity of interprofessional conflict and the internally fragmenting dynamic which this generates within the 'service class'. Second, it minimizes the continued dependence, not to say subordination, of the organizational professions to ruling economic classes and/or political elites. Third, it underplays the contradictory pressures and tensions which professionalization and professional practice in modern societies necessarily entails, and their debilitating influence on the prosecution of a coherent 'service class' mobilization project which has any significant impact on the institutional power structures of modern societies.

Recent research has suggested that the new, organizational professions are as, if not more, internally divided and fragmented than their 'liberal' forebears. The former are engaged in a political and ideological struggle to prove their worth to powerful groups that dominate the decision-taking process in corporate business. This struggle fatally weakens any aspiration which the organizational professions may have to unify around a collective mobility project facilitating a cohesive power base and ideological rationale in modern societies:

the organizational professions which are said to be the major constitutional element of the new middle class are themselves part of an increasingly routinized division of labour which penetrates the profession and provides the framework for class divisions within the professional occupations themselves.[36]

This view is certainly supported by recent research on

professionalization strategies followed by managers in America and Europe and the severe difficulties which they have encountered in establishing the degree of monopolization, closure and control normally associated with 'full' professional power and status.[37] In particular, the extent to which new, organizational professions, such as management, become internally stratified between an intellectual elite and a mass of routine workers as a result of an escalating competition between different 'specialisms' to please their economic and political masters is seen as a major obstacle to achieving the degree of occupational integration, closure and control characteristic of effective professionalization.[38] The fragmenting and internally divisive effect of interprofessional competition and conflict within management is reinforced by the difficulties the latter experiences in formulating and manipulating a 'knowledge base' to facilitate an effective jurisdictional claim. As Abbot notes:

the real problem with business management is the tenuous connection between the various abstractions applied to the area and the actual work of managers. As a result of this disconnection, the management area has numerous claimants, a degree (MBA) that covers diverse forms of training and knowledge, and an equally diverse body of abstractions about how the work ought to be done. Psychology, sociology, administration, economics, law, banking, accounting and other professions all claim some jurisdiction in business management; each by extending its own abstractions emptying them of content, and claiming that they cover the whole field.[39]

Both of these points – competition within and between the organizational professions, as well as the severe problems they encounter in structuring an effective knowledge base – remind us of the continuing struggle between corporate elites and technical experts to control and manipulate the decision-taking process within large-scale, complex organizations. The proposition that the organizational professions are emerging as a 'service class' or 'third force' independent of capital and labour has been severely criticized for its lack of attention to the largely subordinate role which the former continues to play in *deciding* on corporate strategy within large organizations in both the private and public sectors.[40] While they are

seen to play a significant role in *formulating* the broad
outlines of corporate strategy through the technical expertise
they provide, choices between various strategic options are
still seen largely as the prerogative of top-level management:

The organization of the management hierarchy, with its system of
careers and compensation, the forms of control over the labour
process, and financial parameters such as rates of growth and
profitability, are all conditioned by the nature of the corporate
strategies formulated by the dominant coalitions which have control
of the large business enterprises. The composition of the dominant
coalitions, and hence the balance of power and interests which
determine corporate strategy, are a reflection of the changes which
have altered the intercorporate networks of the major capitalist
economies. . . .[41]

Scott is reminding us here of the economic and political
parameters within which organizational professions – certainly in the private sector and with increasing severity in the
public sector[42] – are forced to operate. Yet the subordination
of professional groups to private economic power and public
political dominance is far from complete; the former continue
to provide the technical expertise and ideological legitimation
on which corporate and governmental elites depend for the
formulation and justification of strategic policy. Perhaps the
critics of the service-class thesis are guilty of underestimating
the contradictory pressures which professionalization and
rationalization entail and their longer-term impact on emerging organizational forms. The codification, organization and
deployment of 'expert knowledge' is undoubtedly a strategic
component of the dynamics of power relations in modern
societies.[43] The expert divisions of labour found within the
latter contain contradictory forces pushing in the direction of
bureaucratic rationalization and professional monopolization
whose impact on institutional outcomes is still uncertain.
Under certain circumstances, bureaucratization and professionalization can be complementary, rather than contradictory, forces for organizational transitions and institutional
changes pressing in the direction of more extensive and
intensive surveillance and control.[44] Social life in modern
societies is permeated by expert systems that provide
knowledge and practices which are geared to problem-solving

from the most mundane aspects of everyday living to strategic decisions which profoundly influence the 'life chances' of millions of people. The various ways in which expert knowledge is organized in modern societies, and the organizational mechanisms through which it is mobilized and contested, provides one of the major issues directing analysis and debate in organization theory at the present time. Power struggles within and between both the 'old' and 'new professions', and their relative power position with dominant economic and political groups on the one hand and subordinate groups on the other, are likely to exert a dramatic influence on the forms of organization which develop in late twentieth-century societies. Expert knowledge is a strategic power resource which will be fought over by different groups as they attempt to establish their position within the power structures that are beginning to crystallize in advanced societies. While the old, liberal professions seem to be on the defensive, if not in retreat, in their attempt to resist the encroachment of bureaucratization and rationalization,[45] the new, organizational professions are attempting to mobilize their expert knowledge base in order to enhance the degree of closure and control which they enjoy. Both are engaged in a contest with dominant interests and subordinate labour to control the decision-taking processes which will shape the organizational structures and practices which are characteristic of global modernity. In this respect, the analysis of professional power and organizational control dovetails with the politics of organizational design as key aspects of contemporary organizational studies.

THE POLITICS OF ORGANIZATIONAL DESIGN

The significance of intra- and interprofessional power struggles for an understanding of developments in organizational structures and practices have been highlighted in the previous section. Professional disciplines and practices have played a strategic role in shaping the various forms of organizational surveillance and control developing in modern societies. This is the case in so far as they have strengthened an underlying process of bureaucratic rationalization which has been at work in the institutional bowels of modern societies since the eighteenth century. At the same time, they have opened up and expanded areas of partial or restricted 'professional' autonomy and uncertainty which have made a mockery of complete or total organizational control over collective social action. Nevertheless, the distribution, allocation and organization of 'expert knowledge' within the occupational divisions of labour and organizational regimes which are characteristic of modern societies is a central process in the development of those power structures which constitute modernity.[46]

The struggle to gain access to and control over expert power and knowledge in modern societies has to be located within a wider arena of political contestation over the organizational resources and mechanisms that shape the process, direction and outcome of institutional change. In this context, one can identify four overlapping and intersecting political arenas that structure the emergence, advance and/or decline of different forms of organizational surveillance and control in modern societies: first, what we might term 'managerial politics' and its impact on organizational strategy and structure; second, the way in which 'class politics' configures the control mechanisms deployed within work organizations and the multifarious types of worker resistance they elicit; third, the increasing emphasis given in contemporary organizational analysis to the significance of 'sexual politics' in determining the organizational discourses and practices through which gender-biased structures are institutionalized; finally, a less well-developed focus on the way in which 'racial politics' shapes discriminatory employment practices within the work organization.

Each of these overlapping and intersecting political arenas are seen to mobilize competing, and often conflicting, types of collective agency that reproduce and transform the organizational forms through which 'governance' is exercised and challenged in modern societies. The assumption that any one of them should be given explanatory or political primacy over the others has been counteracted by the pervasive intellectual and ideological pluralism which has been symptomatic of the study of organizations over the last twenty years or so. While managerial and class politics, as shapers of organizational strategy, structure and practice, still tend to predominate in current research and analysis, the growing emphasis on sexual and racial politics is simply another sign of the increasing plurality and diversity of organizational sociology – both as a field of study and as a set of interrelated intellectual practices focused on the problematic of 'organization'. The inter-relationships prevailing between these four arenas of struggle and competition, and their particular impact on emerging organizational forms, is still very much an open question. But the complexity of the political processes which structure the organizational forms through which social action is organized in modern societies cannot be denied.

Research on managerial politics has been primarily con-cerned with two major areas of interest: first, its impact on strategic change in complex organizations and second, its role in shaping the process and outcome of technological change. Work on the politics of strategic change has tended to focus on transformations in the core values which constitute 'corporate culture' and their role in directing long-term structural development.[47] Analysis of the politics of tech-nological change has been directed towards the micro-political processes within the management coalitions through which the design, implementation and circulation of new technology is mediated.[48] Research conducted in both of these areas entails a very distinctive – theoretically, metho-dologically and substantively – move away from systems-based approaches to organizational design as advocated by Donaldson.[49] This is so to the extent that they reject the latter's limited focus on internal adaptation to environmental demands or pressures and its corresponding neglect of the underlying socio-political processes and contexts along and through which organizational change is carried. In this way, organizational change is seen as an interactive, multi-level process in which strategic choices and technological transi-tions emerge out of the power struggles in which managers are routinely engaged to dominate and manipulate the central values and political alignments which shape structural transformation.

Empirical research on the politics of strategic and technological change in complex organizations has encouraged the
development of a shared concern with the 'rules of the game'
which direct the more formal decision-making processes
through which options are narrowed and final choices
selected. These are treated as legitimating norms and values
which are never openly articulated and justified, but constitute the background or 'assumptive framework' which key
actors rely upon to make sense of their involvement and
interventions within the change process. These unofficial and
undeclared 'rules of the game' are constructed and mobilized
through the unobtrusive manipulation by dominant actors of
symbols and ideologies that reinforce the organizational
*status quo*. However, they are not immune to challenge in
the sense that they often become more explicit, visible and
open to question in times of organizational crisis and
upheaval when the very foundations of normative and
political orders are under threat. As Pettigrew says of
'revolutionary change' in complex organizations:

> Once a large organization develops a coherent strategy of how it is
> going to deal with its external environment, and that strategy is
> reinforced by the structures, systems, cultures and political con-
> straints of the organization, the dominating ideas and assumptions
> which are implicit and explicit in the strategy it behaves are
> extraordinarily difficult to break down. Thus when strategic change
> does occur it tends to occur in radical packages – revolutionary
> periods interspersed with long periods of absorbing the impact of the
> radical changes. . . . Radical changes have to be preceded by and
> initiated by ideological shifts. . . . Crucial to the timing of such
> radical actions are real and constructed crises, changes in leadership
> and power, and the transformation of organizational ideologies.[50]

As we have already seen,[51] research on the role of 'class
politics' in structuring the development of organizational
forms has also taken a keen interest in power struggles to
control legitimating ideologies and allocative resources within
administrative systems geared to the protection of dominant
economic groups. However, this research has always attempted to link internal managerial politics to the wider
structures of class domination and control operative within a
capitalist political economy.[52] It has not been content to

limit its analytical focus and narrative scope to organizationally based interest group politics. Instead, it has regularly
striven – not always with a great deal of success – to link
micro-politics and macro-politics within a theoretical approach and an empirical research project that is grounded on
an understanding of intra-organizational struggles to control
allocative and administrative resources in the encompassing
social structures of class inequality and power.[53]

At one level, the general impact of this research on class-
based organizational politics and its strategic influence in
directing the overall, long-term development of organizational
structures and practices has been to lift organizational
analysis out of its limited concern with 'local' power struggles
and their impact on emerging forms. It has reminded
organizational researchers and analysts that complex organizations operate within wider structures of power and
domination that cannot be ignored. This is so to the extent
that research has shown how the mobilization of the
structural properties of capitalist political economies – in the
form of wage labour, capitalist accounting systems, legal
property rights, labour market practices, etc. – is a crucial
component of interorganizational power struggles to control
the agenda for change. Indeed, it has stressed the significance
of 'organizations' as administrative systems actively constituted by and through these wider structural properties.

But at another level, research on class politics has simply
reinforced a deep-seated trend in organizational analysis that
emphasizes the contradictory, and potentially conflicting,
principles of action and legitimation available to organizational actors in modern societies. Any remaining predilection
towards a form of class determinism which assumes a direct,
causal relationship between class politics and organizational
design has been virtually eradicated by a series of studies that
call attention to the *inherent plurality* of organizations and
the diverse structural properties through which they are
constituted.[54] While the centrality of capitalist structures for
an understanding of organizational change is reasserted in this
research, they are seen to be complemented by alternative structures – ethnicity, gender, professionalism and
managerialism – that often distort, challenge and undermine

the 'logic' of the former. In this respect, the recurring tendency of class-based research and analysis to retreat into a monolithic conception of organization has been counteracted by findings which support a much more open and pluralistic reading of the reality of organizational life in modern societies.

A prime example of this current emphasis on the relatively wide range of structural components that are mobilized in collective action directed to the process of organizing is the recent empirical research carried out on the detailed organizational practices which managers engage in to construct and sustain viable systems of corporate governance.[55] The latter has emphasized the importance of habituated forms of thinking and action in managerial practices geared to the problem of organizing. These established logics of managerial action do not need continual redefinition and relegitimation, but they continue to function as embedded ways of thinking and acting that constrain the decision-making options considered by dominant coalitions. Such habituated forms of thinking and practice will embody certain class-related prejudices and interests, but they will also generate forms of 'accepted' organizational discourse that routinely privilege certain interpretations and programmes over others.

The subtle, and not so subtle, ways in which organizational discourse is penetrated by ways of thinking and acting which routinely privilege a restricted range of sectional interests to the virtual exclusion of others is reflected in the strong emphasis currently given to the influence of 'sexual politics' on the process and products of organizational design.[56] Here, the major concern has been to reveal the gender-biased, taken-for-granted assumptions that unreflectively inform the modes of organizing that are dominant in modern societies. Thus, within this area of research on the politics of organizational design, organizations are seen as crucial sites or settings for the construction and institutionalization of gender-biased conceptions of subjectivity and identity that automatically divide men and women into distinctive, and often separate, 'organizational worlds'. As Hearn *et al.* maintains:

it is difficult to *overestimate* the depth and complexity of the ways in which dominant forms of sexuality are produced and reproduced, not just in the broad structuring of organizations but also in the minutiae of organizations.... The relationship of gender and organizational structure has in recent years become more fully recognized as an aspect of organization theory.... We see sexuality, and its social organization and social control, as fundamental to gender relations in general and patriarchy in particular, and thus to organizations.[57]

Their analysis is based on a distinction between 'sexuality' and 'gender' that stresses the ideological role of the former in legitimizing divisions of organizational labour and forms of organizational practice reinforcing male domination, and the cognitive function of the latter in routinizing systems of thought and knowledge that exclude, in often subtle and indirect ways, women from key decision-making arenas. The ideological and cognitive function of sexual discourse and gender-biased practices in organizations are brought together in a research focus on systems of institutional closure. These systems assemble very powerful and pervasive sets of organizational controls that suppress or marginalize the 'deviant' conceptions of sexuality which challenge discriminatory practices and their distorting effect on everyday organizational life.[58]

Work on 'gender politics' in complex organizations has been developed along these two analytical tracks – that is, viewing male domination over and exploitation of women as primarily a cultural phenomenon, or concentrating on the gender-biased organizational practices through which females are kept in subordinate positions. Within the former, research effort has been directed on the multifarious ways in which the 'everyday' and 'official' languages and discourses of complex organizations are biased by a pervasive set of gender-related values which favour males over females in regard of power, position, status, reward and autonomy.[59] In particular, the way in which organizational rules are pervaded by gender-biased assumptions, and the distorting effect which they exert over both allocative and administrative practices, has proved to be a rich seam of empirical research.[60] The often taken-for-granted and unquestioned nature of organizational cultures and discourses which routinely privilege males over females in terms of dominant social identities has been revealed by this research.[61]

Research on the organizational control practices through which gender inequalities are developed and maintained has focused more on the influence of 'patriarchy' as a set of socioeconomic relations operative within labour markets and employment structures through which women are systematically exploited by men.[62] Here, the emphasis is less on the ubiquitous cultural and ideological processes through which female subordination is secured and more on the situationally specific practices and relations through which male economic and political power over women is institutionalized.

Empirical inquiry on the fourth arena of political conflict and struggle through which organizational forms are constituted, maintained and transformed – that is 'ethnicity' – is far less well-developed than the other three arenas which have previously been reviewed. Most of the relatively little work which has been done on the role of 'racial politics' in shaping organizational structures and systems has been primarily concerned in the diffuse operation of discriminatory norms and practices in employment recruitment and selection based on ethnic divisions.[63] Thus, physical, religious and cultural differences between ethnic groups are transformed by racial politics into forms of social stigma which routinely exclude deviant or 'abnormal' groups from positions of power and status within paid work. The operation of ethnically-based, exclusionary practices within the labour market and internal systems of labour management control developed within particular work organizations are often difficult to detect and take on the appearance of the taken-for-granted 'naturalness' typical of habituated forms of exploitation and power. However, these practices tend to become more socially visible as a continuing source of intra-organizational conflict between different ethnic groups engaged in a struggle to gain control over workplace organization.

Work on the politics of organizational design has revealed the distinct, but overlapping, arenas of conflict and struggle through which administrative practices and allocative mechanisms are developed over time. Each of these arenas – the managerial, class, gender and ethnic – are based on different rationales or 'logics of action'; that is, different ways of engaging in and acting through organizational practices which draw on a range of rules and resources to mobilize competing definitions of organizational reality and the recipes for action which they entail. No single logic can be regarded as completely dominant in the sense of dictating the forms of organizational action engaged in by agents. The organization itself is now viewed as a setting or locale in which competing and conflicting logics of action, and the creative tensions which they generate, shape the structures and practices that emerge. While class and managerial politics are likely to remain central concerns in contemporary research, the interest in gender and ethnicity as potential bases for organizational action is growing. The structural repertoires and action-recipes provided by capitalist logic and managerial professionalism will continue to be the major research concern, but their interaction with alternative sources of identity, motivation and power can no longer be denied. The politics of organizational design currently provides a much broader research focus than was the case in the 1970s and connects with some of the most basic power struggles constitutive of institutional change and transformation in modern societies.

## ORGANIZATIONAL RATIONALITY

Research and analysis on the three themes reviewed so far in this chapter – surveillance and control, professional power and the politics of organizational design – have strongly reinforced the already existing tendency to question the status of organizations as exemplars of formal or technical rationality in modern societies. As has been repeatedly expressed throughout this book, both organizations and or-ganizational analysis are conventionally seen as expressions of the cultural and institutional dominance of a form of rationality, based on systematic calculation and control within modern societies. The development and diffusion of formal or complex organization is seen to signify the pervasive influence of rational systems of command, coordination and control that eradicate all vestiges of human emotion, prejudice and subjectivity. Within this vision, organizations are seen as the primary institutional 'carriers' of a formal rationality based on logical calculation and control within modern, and modernizing, societies.

However, the status of organizations as paradigmatic exemplars of the dominance of rational modes of thinking and acting in modern societies now looks much more problematic. With the benefit of hindsight that twenty years or more of empirical research and theoretical analysis brings, the concept of organized or organizational rationality, and its implications for explaining and practising 'organizing', are now regarded in a somewhat different light to that once prevailing. Indeed, there is every suggestion that the concept needs to be dropped altogether in so far as it refers to a state of affairs that can no longer be said to prevail – if it ever had done, even in the heyday of scientific rationalism and technocratic managerialism between the 1930s and 1960s.[64]

This has led some commentators to suggest that there is now a 'retreat from rationality' underway within organizational analysis that threatens to turn into a complete rout.[65] The proposition that organizations are based on and operate through an institutionalized system of rational calculation and control geared to the overriding imperatives of efficiency and effectiveness has been severely damaged – some might say, destroyed – by research which radically undermines any residual belief in a dominant, unified and monolithic cognitive process and cultural system directing collective action.

The most developed research area in which this 'assault on organized rationality' has become increasingly evident is in the field of organizational decision-making and its gradual infiltration by analysts drawing on ideas from cognitive psychology, cultural anthropology and business history.[66] The cumulative impact of their research has been to popularize the view that organizations do not embody any universal, instrumental or technical rationality in their decision-making structures and practices. Instead, they must be treated as consisting of different systems of thought and action which reflect the underlying and irrevocable ambiguity, uncertainty and capriciousness of organizational life in all its messy, not to say gory, detail. Thus, the full theoretical blush of organizational rationality has faded rather badly as the reality of organizational decision-making is revealed to be a process dominated by cognitive, ideological and political practices that virtually destroy any sense of pristine objectivity, neutrality, rationality and control. This supports Weick's argument that:

Rationality in newer formulations is still discussed, but in the context of a narrower set of issues. Rationality is viewed as (1) a set of prescriptions that change as issues change, (2) as a façade created to attract resources and legitimacy, and (3) as a postaction process used retrospectively to invent reasons for action.[67]

However, there is a very real danger here that we may be throwing out the baby of a more realistic and sensitive view of organizational rationality with the bath water of an unrealistic pure, universal, objective and logically calculated formal or technical rationality. If organizational decision-making is a process and an outcome that is shaped by a mix of 'rationalities' or 'rationales', then we need to be much more careful and precise about the make-up of that mixture and the way in which it is assembled and used by organizational actors. While the consistency, coherence and relevance of organizational rationality may be much more limited and fragile than the 'founding fathers' of organization theory believed, we still need to arrive at a sensible assessment of its role in building and sustaining organizations. Instrumental or technical rationality still provides a very 'powerful' – cognitively and politically – rationale for certain forms of organizational action, even if it is challenged by alternative modes of calculation and behaviour.

The most promising advances in this direction are to be found in recent attempts to develop a more discriminating conception of organizational rationality that coheres with other modes of calculation which are prominent in collective forms of life in modern societies. The study of organizations has been dominated for too long by a conception of 'strategic rationality' in which:

Action is conceptualized as the intentional, self-interested behaviour of individuals in an objectivated world; that is, one in which objects and other individuals are related to in terms of their possible manipulation. The rationality of action is correspondingly conceptualized as the efficient linking of actions – seen as means to the attainment of individual goals.[68]

This, almost exclusive, concentration on strategic rationality has led to a relative neglect of 'contextual rationality'. The latter refers to a form of cognition and behaviour which is oriented 'toward creating or maintaining institutions and traditions in which is expressed some conception of right behaviour and a good life with others'.[69] As such, contextual rationality emphasizes the moral and symbolic, rather than the utility maximizing and technical, aspects of organizational action. It emphasizes the need for social actors to create and preserve intersubjectively binding normative structures that support and re-enforce the organizational relationships in which they are implicated. The study of organizational decision-making as a technical exercise in the application of formal rationality to problems of choice and utility maximization is transformed into a study of organizational governance and the moral and political foundations on which the latter rests.

This latter development incorporates a far wider range of 'non-rational' modes of thinking and acting which intermingle with more formal and rationalized systems of control to constitute the many-sided phenomenon we label 'organization'. For instance, the concept of 'trust relations' and its significance for our understanding of the complex interdependence between cooperation and conflict within organizations surfaces as a major issue.[70] The strength of trust relations between social actors – based on mutual obligations and understandings of collective involvement – are likely to have a major impact on the patterns of cooperation and conflict that develop in work organizations and the systems of control that coalesce around them. When the number of decision-making centres increases within and between organizations, and the enhanced complexity and uncertainty which this creates, then the salience of relations based on mutual involvement, reciprocity and solidarity is likely also to be substantially increased. As Gambetta argues, 'trust becomes increasingly salient for our decisions and actions the larger the feasible set of alternatives open to others.'[71] The balance between interdependence and autonomy, which is still subject to a degree of rational calculation and control, becomes much more difficult to decide on than under the rubric of 'strategic rationality' with its overriding emphasis on narrow self-interest and the maximization of sectional benefits. Thus, trust comes to be regarded as a scarce resource that becomes more relevant in decision-making situations where the initiation and maintenance of social cooperation is highly rational in the face of problems that defy the rigid imposition of a calculus based on means/ends-related criteria which excludes all considerations of intersubjective communication and evaluation. At this point, we are a long way – theoretically and empirically – from the simplicities of formal or technical rationality, but the latter is now relocated within an appreciation of organizational cognition, culture and history which is much broader and more subtle than that prevailing in mainstream decision-making theory.

This broadening out of the underlying conception of organizational rationality to encompass both the 'contextual' and 'strategic' dimensions of such a fundamental idea may seem rather arcane and divorced from the messy realities of everyday organizational life. However, it raises some very basic and important questions about the supposedly radical and innovative organizational forms beginning to develop and take hold in what have been called 'postmodern', rather than 'modern', societies. The need to embrace a more open and flexible conception of organizational rationality may also demand a serious reconsideration of those pivotal structures and practices most closely associated with bureaucratic administration.

POSTMODERN ORGANIZATIONS

During the course of the 1980s there has been a growing perception that the organizational forms which have dominated modern societies since the second half of the nineteenth century are no longer appropriate to the economic, technological and social conditions prevailing in the closing decades of the twentieth century. In particular, rational bureaucracy, with its emphasis on rigid hierarchical discipline and control, and a highly specialized division of labour, is increasingly seen as an outmoded and obsolete organizational form for dealing with the pressures and problems that present themselves in late twentieth-century societies. Instead, the latter are deemed to require organizational forms that break with the logic of bureaucratization and its in-built drive towards centralized control and highly differentiated work processes. In place of the overriding emphasis that bureaucratic rationality gives to hierarchy and specialization, 'postmodern' or 'post-bureaucratic' organizational forms are assumed to be founded on a developmental logic that pushes in the direction of decentralized, flexible networks in which work tasks on the shop floor and in the office will be 're-professionalized'.[72] A flexible, trust-based form of work organization will require a highly and broadly skilled labour force operating within administrative structures and practices that reverse the 'modernist' trend towards greater specialization and intensified bureaucratic surveillance and control. As Clegg suggests:

Where modernist organization was rigid, postmodern organization is flexible. Where modernist consumption was premised on mass forms, postmodernist consumption is premised on niches. Where modernist organization was premised as technological determinism, postmodernist organization is premised on technological choices made possible through 'de-dedicated' microelectronic equipment. Where modernist organization and jobs were highly differentiated, demarcated and deskilled, postmodernist organization and jobs are highly de-differentiated, de-demarcated and multi-skilled. Employment relations as a fundamental relation of organizations upon which has been constructed a whole discourse of the determinism of size as a contingency variable increasingly gives way to more complex and fragmentary relational forms, such as subcontracting and networking.[73]

Clegg's description provides a useful general summary of the changes in organizational forms thought to be most 'characteristic' of postmodern societies and the set of interrelated economic, technological, social and cultural changes bringing them into existence. The former can be summarized as entailing a definite shift away from centralized bureaucracy which is based on rigidly imposed disciplinary control and detailed specialization towards network structures based on multi-skilled workforces, informal divisions of labour, high-trust work relations, participative decision-making processes and advanced information technology. Thus, the organizational structures which have directed the socio-economic, political and cultural development of modern societies since the mid-nineteenth century are seen to be fragmenting into diverse networks, loosely held together by strong cultures and information technology, within solidaristic local communities or industrial districts.

The changes bringing about this shift or metamorphosis of bureaucratic base-metal into 'network gold' can be summarized in the following way: the breakdown of mass markets entailing the regularized consumption of standardized goods and their gradual replacement with more specialized or 'customized' markets demanding high-quality products; the development of advanced, microelectronic technology and the more flexible and decentralized production and service delivery systems which it makes possible; the advance of work processes and patterns breaking down deskilled and demarcated job designs and replacing them with 'polyvalent' or multi-skilled forms of work organization; the move away from large-scale units employing large numbers of people on permanent contracts to much smaller units in which subcontracting and home-based networking become much more prominent. The cumulative impact of these changes is seen to be reflected in an underlying fragmenting or 'disorganizing' dynamic which transforms the hierarchical structures and disciplinary practices constitutive of rational bureaucracy into much more decentralized, self-regulating, diffuse and flexible arrangements.

Both the cognitive and cultural foundations of these new organizational forms are seen to be very different from those on which rational bureaucracy has been developed. The former are seen to rely on ways of thinking and modes of calculation which reject the overriding emphasis on short-term efficiency and effectiveness ingrained within the very institutional fabric of the latter. Rather than rely on a form of instrumental or technical rationality dedicated to order, stability and rigid control over a recalcitrant environment, postmodern organizations encourage the proliferation and free play of discursive rationalities through which multiple 'organizational realities' are constructed by different groups.[74] This is seen to be much more conducive to the partial and temporary institutionalization of ways of thinking and acting – cognitive and behavioural 'routines' – that facilitate a stress on longer-term considerations revolving around the problem of managing highly complex systems in an uncertain and ambiguous world.[75]

If modern organizations are constructed around a culture of repression and control, then their postmodern counterparts are thought to generate a culture of expression and involvement within which autonomy, participation and disagreement are openly encouraged. In this respect, postmodern organizations are seen to rely on much more 'emotional' cultures in the sense that they facilitate the personal development of individuals within collectivities based on trust, and the relatively high level of risk-taking which this involves. In addition, they refuse to make available the ritualized routines and formalized rules which 'bureaucrats' can hide behind and manipulate to repress emotional tension and political conflict. Indeed, the culture of postmodern organization seems to be one that celebrates, even luxuriates in, the dissolution and demise of the normative regimes and disciplinary practices associated with rational bureaucracy. Thus, Tixier welcomes the emergence of a post-rational organization which will:

recognize the subjectivity and creativity denied to the social actors by the rational organization of work. . . . The pressure of international competition upon firms, the insistence upon product quality, and the increasing segmentation of markets necessitate making organizations more flexible than under rational models. . . . This new 'post-rational' model of organization . . . constitutes an objective rationality adapted to the values of creativity, self-expression and participation . . . it introduces a new type of rationality of human action with the organization, a model pivoting around the attempt to match people, structures and human creativity.[76]

By the end of the 1980s, this view of postmodern organizational development had virtually become a new orthodoxy in the field of organizational analysis which presented itself under the banner of 'Post-Fordism' or 'flexible specialization'.[77] The latter has been most closely associated with the work of researchers such as Piore and Sabel,[78] Lash and Urry[79] and Aglietta.[80] Although each of these authors approach the development of postmodern organizational forms in very different ways, they are agreed that the trajectory of institutional development in advanced industrial or capitalist societies is inexorably pushing in the direction of a 'post-bureaucratic' organizational world. The latter, it is argued, is based on the emergence of organizational structures and practices which break with the highly centralized and rationalized systems dominating institutional growth from the early twentieth century onwards. In their place, these authors anticipate the emergence of organizational forms signifying an irreversible shift towards ways of organizing which entail an 'epochal redefinition of markets, technologies and industrial hierarchies'.[81]

This redefinition of the relationships between economic conditions, material technologies and organizational structures is seen to entail a move away from mass production economies based on the servicing of standardized mass markets towards much more specialized and 'customer-oriented' production systems in which the manufacture and distribution of high value-added goods and services becomes the key to international, national, or sectoral, economic success. In turn, the latter is seen to demand the development of organizational forms that break with bureaucratic rationality and reinforce a trend towards 'network structures' based on a much higher degree of decentralization, participation and involvement. This push towards a form of organizational specialization and coordination that is much more responsive to market change and technological advance is thought to encourage the re-emergence of patterns of work relations based on 'high-trust' ideologies.[82] The latter indicate a degree of social solidarity and community support that departs from the highly instrumental and conflict-prone industrial relations which are characteristic of mass production industries and companies. Instead, one sees the development of employment relations and industrial relations practices that presage the arrival of organizational structures and practices in which managers and unions cooperate in the collective activities necessary for locally or regionally based economic growth and stability.[83]

There were a number of interrelated economic, technological and political developments occurring in the 1970s and 1980s which are identified as bringing about this shift to postmodern forms of organization: first, the failure of Keynesian demand-management to provide the degree of economic stability and continuity characteristic of the post-Second World War period; second, the advance of microelectronic information technologies that dispense with the managerial need for highly bureaucratized control systems and push in the direction of more flexible 'network'-type organizational structures; third, a self-reinforcing lack of confidence in national governments to manage the financial and social dislocations generated by the deep-seated economic, technological and organizational transformations consequent upon the move to a global economic system in which the internal political economics of nation-states are fully exposed to the vagaries of intense and unremitting international competition. The overall cumulative impact of these changes in macro-level political economics and meso-level industrial sectors is seen to produce an environmental setting in which:

the keyword is flexibility – of plant and machinery as of products and labour. Emphasis shifts from scale to scope, and from cost to quality. Organizations are geared to respond to rather than regulate markets. They are seen as frameworks for learning as much as instruments of control. Their hierarchies are flatter and their structures are more open. The guerrilla force takes over from the standing army. All this has liberated the centre from the tyranny of the immediate. Its task shifts from planning to strategy, and to the promotion of the instruments of post-Fordist control – systems, software, corporate culture and cash.... Sector and enterprise strategies need to take on board the nature of the new competition, the centrality of skilled labour, the need for specialization and quality, and for continuous innovation.[84]

Reference to the 'new competition' has been developed by writers such as Best[85] and Urry[86] to refer to the emergence of economic systems led by business enterprises based upon production principles and organizational concepts very different to those which were dominant in the age of Fordist mass production and consumption. As Best describes the 'New Competition':

At the centre of the New Competition is the entrepreneurial firm, an enterprise that is organized from top to bottom to pursue continuous improvement in methods, products and processes. The pursuit of continuous improvement is a production-based strategy that has redefined the meaning of entrepreneurial activity from its traditional individualist approach to a collectivist concept. The entrepreneurial firm seeks a competitive edge by superior product design, which may or may not lead to lower costs, but it demands organizational flexibility which in turn requires organizational commitments to problem solving, a persistence to detail, and an integration of 'thinking and doing' in work activities.[87]

This reinforces the post-Fordist/flexible specialization 'thesis' that organizational forms in advanced capitalist economies are undergoing a fundamental restructuring away from the rigidities and constraints which are characteristic of bureaucratic command and control towards highly flexible structures and cultures which are alien to mass production/mass consumption Fordist- or Taylorist-type systems. Thus, Best maintains that the entrepreneurial firm, as opposed to the hierarchical firm, seeks strategic advantage on the basis of organizational structures and cultures institutionalizing continuous innovation in product design, process operation and management practices. Rapid strategic adjustment is made possible by a high degree of organizational flexibility in which perpetual problem-solving – that is, the pursuit of continuous improvement – is ingrained in the very social fabric of the firm and the production technologies that it relies on to 'stay ahead of the market'.

The rise of the entrepreneurial firm links with Urry's prognosis concerning the shift to post-Fordist consumption patterns in which producers are forced to become much more consumer-driven and to open their organizational structures and practices to highly specialized, temporary, individuated and dynamic markets. The latter are seen to demand a degree of organizational flexibility and adaptability inimical to the centralized command-and-control production organizations typical of the Fordist era, in which mass production and mass consumption were linked through highly bureaucratized internal management systems. The increasing dominance of specialized product markets with much shorter product life cycles, in which constantly changing consumer tastes and preferences preclude the long production runs and dedicated technology characteristic of Fordism, requires decentralized network structures held together by advanced information technology and high-trust organizational cultures solidly embedded in well-integrated localities or districts. The bureaucratized organizational forms that directed the process of industrial modernization in the West for more than a century are seen to be dissolving into fragmented and diverse structures which signify the imminent demise of Fordism and the emergence of a post-Fordist world.

The backlash against the post-Fordist/flexible specialization thesis has gathered pace and momentum over the last two to three years.[88] Criticism has focused on three major areas: first, the lack of firm empirical evidence necessary to substantiate the wide-ranging generalizations preferred by supporters of the former; second, the highly controversial theoretical constructions and interpretations which post-Fordist writers have deployed; finally, the extent to which visible organizational modifications to incorporate a strategy of continuous innovation within advanced capitalist societies can be extrapolated into a total 'institutional paradigm shift' in which one industrial order gives way to another.

Most post-Fordist writers have focused on a relatively restricted range of empirical sites to support their general thesis that new production paradigms and organizational logics which break with Fordist/Taylorist principles are increasingly prominent within advanced Western economies. The favoured examples are regional conglomerations or industrial districts in Northern Italy, Austria, West Germany and North America in which an extra-firm infrastructure of sectoral institutions – such as trade associations, financial agencies, training and educational facilities, and regulatory bodies – fosters and nurtures forms of inter-firm competition and cooperation that benefit the area as a whole. More recently, Japan is highlighted as an example of a political economy in which institutions of inter-firm cooperation provide the necessary degree of contextual stability and continuity in which the development of a competitive edge through continuous organizational innovation can be regularly achieved. In each case, these industrial districts and political economies, like Japan, are seen to facilitate the development of interorganizational networks and intra-organizational structures that are closely interlinked through a series of sectoral relationships which provide the institutional capacity to identify a common interest and to pursue it through collective agencies.

However, this interpretation of industrial districts or regions and national economies such as Japan, which are assumed to adhere to the principles of post-Fordist production and flexible specialization, has been challenged both in substantive detail and in relation to its generalization beyond the confines of these, rather distinctive, locales. Piore and Sabel[89] argue that industrial districts establish prototypes of post-Fordist organization in three major respects. First, they create products and processes for specialized markets – speciality chemicals, luxury clothes and shoes – through organizational structures and practices that reverse the logic of mass production by opening up economic organizations to their wider social context so that 'the firm' becomes an inderdependent entity with its sector. Second, they provide a highly diverse, but well-integrated, network of small- and medium-sized organizations embedded within local cultures and ideologies based on community structures which foster collective involvement and high-trust work relations. Third, they encourage a marriage between specialization and flexibility, founded on information technologies and organizational forms that violate the key assumption of classical political economy: that economy is separate from society; in other words, they forge a degree of integration between firm-level decision-making and community-level decision-making which is anathema – on both theoretical and ideological grounds – to classical economic theory.

Yet, this analysis of the underlying organizational logic of industrial districts has been attacked by researchers such as Lovering,[90] Hyman,[91] Amin and Robins,[92] and Whitaker.[93] They have argued that limited and partial moves towards more decentralized flexible business firms and industrial sectors have to be understood and explained in terms of their continued dependence on and control by highly centralized multinational corporations operating on the basis of a 'global logic' within the world economy. The latter are seen to remain the major players within the world economy who are prepared to engage in a range of strategic alliances, partnerships and networking arrangements as long as it suits their long-term economic objectives. As Whitaker summarizes this view:

the changes taking place in these regions do not represent some kind of structural transition from one regime of accumulation to another. . . . Rather the related changes in production and consumption are most appropriately interpreted as being part of strategies by capital to preserve old modes of accumulation in a political climate very different from the welfare state Keynesianism of the 1960s. . . . what is occurring is best understood as a 'selective reworking' which reproduces, in a modified form, pre-Fordist and Fordist methods of production, rather than a fundamental transformation.[94]

Growing doubts over the empirical depth, scale and significance of the organizational changes associated with the post-Fordist/flexible specialization thesis, and its too-easy presumption in favour of a sustained move towards 'postmodern' organizational structures, have helped to focus critical attention upon the theoretical framework and logic which the former generates. In particular, the marked propensity of post-Fordist writers to fall back on rather abstract ideal-type constructs, presuming generalized patterns of structural change inexorably pushing in the direction of irreversible organizational tendencies, has been severely criticized. As Rustin has maintained, the post-Fordist/flexible specialization thesis is most appropriately interpreted as 'one ideal-typical model or strategy of production and regulation, co-present with others in a complex historical ensemble, rather than as a valid totalizing description of an emerging social formation here and now.'[95] Viewed in this theoretical light, the post-Fordist/flexible specialization thesis is clearly guilty of over-generalizing emergent and contradictory tendencies into finalized institutional outcomes. The pattern of organizational change and institutional transformation which it envisages is based upon a theoretical strategy that sacrifices detail and complexity on the altar of generalization, while at the same time presuming the arrival of 'outcomes' more appropriately treated in terms of, as yet, unrealized possibilities.

This also raises the whole question of the credence which can be attached to the anticipation of an unstoppable movement towards an organizational exemplar and institutional structure that entails a fundamental and irreversible break with rational bureaucracy. Is the post-Fordist/flexible specialization thesis more appropriately assessed as providing a partial insight into a number of significant, but limited, organizational developments in advanced capitalist economies, rather than specifying a decisive structural shift or historical movement in the direction of a radically new industrial and social order? Recent critical response would suggest that the former carries more weight than the latter. This is so to the extent that post-Fordism has some credence as referring to an interrelated set of organizational changes which modify the logic of capitalist-led bureaucratization, but fails to stand up as a fully fledged and well-grounded alternative theory of long-term institutional development. In short, the post-Fordist thesis is evidently 'not-proven' as Whitaker puts it, and is in need of serious revision as a *general* interpretation of organizational transformation in Western capitalist economies.

Nevertheless, the thesis has presented a very serious challenge to evolutionary theories of institutional and organizational change in advanced capitalist societies which draw on the Weberian prognosis of unstoppable bureaucratic rationalization. It suggests that Western societies are now locked into a very different trajectory of long-term institutional and organizational development to those specified by 'mainstream' social science. At the very least, it has raised a series of very important questions concerning the dynamics, potentialities and trajectories of organizational development in contemporary capitalism. These questions have prompted a serious reconsideration of the key assumptions which have underpinned our view of modern organizations, and 'the story' that organizational analysis has to tell from its intellectual origins in the seminal work of Max Weber. In short, both the nature of the phenomena which organizational analysis focuses upon and the manner in which that analysis proceeds are now subject to a degree of self-reflection and questioning that is unprecedented in the history of the sociology of organizations as a field of inquiry. As Harvey has concluded:

> The current conjuncture is characterized by a mix of highly efficient Fordist production (often nuanced by flexible technology and output) in some sectors and regions (like cars in the U.S.A., Japan or South Korea) and more traditional systems (such as those of Singapore, Taiwan or Hong Kong) resting on artisanal, paternalistic or patriarchical (familial) labour relations, embodying quite different mechanisms of labour control ... it does seem important to emphasize to what degree flexible accumulation has been seen as a particular and perhaps *new combination of mainly old elements within the overall logic of capital accumulation.*[96] (My emphasis)

This is the highly diverse and complex organizational and institutional reality that contemporary organizational analysis has to confront. The latter has to provide some coherent account of this historical and institutional conjuncture if it is to continue to speak to problems and themes that shape the agenda for present-day social science. Any attempt to provide such an account will necessarily demand that students of organization reconsider the location and significance of their efforts in relation to the wider social scientific enterprise in the closing years of the twentieth century.

## CONCLUSION

This chapter has surveyed the substantive agenda currently being developed within the sociology of organizations. Taken as a whole, the working through of this agenda raises some very basic questions about the theoretical capital on which organizational analysis has traded for most of this century. More specifically, it challenges the conventional view that modern organizations represent a mode of institutional thought and action based upon 'objective' rational calculation and bureaucratic control which are presumed to direct the trajectory of structural transformation in all advanced Western industrialized societies.[97] It also requires us to reconsider the theoretical options available for future intellectual development within a field of study that has certainly lost its 'age of innocence' and is forced to confront the complex organizational realities of collective life in modern societies at the end of the twentieth century.

This issue – that is, the range of theoretical options available for organizational analysis and research at the end of the twentieth century, as well as a consideration of those options which look most promising for advancing an intellectual project that has been in the making for over a century or more – is discussed in the following chapter.

### REFERENCES

1. Reed, M., 'Scripting Scenarios for a New Organization Theory and Practice', *Work, Employment and Society*, vol. 5 (1), 1991a, pp. 119–32.
2. Giddens, A., *The Nation State and Violence* (Polity Press, Cambridge, 1985).
3. Butler, R., *Designing Organizations: A Decision-Making Perspective* (Routledge, London, 1991).
4. Turner, B., 'The Rise of Organizational Symbolism' in Hassard, J. and Pym, D. (eds), *The Theory and Philosophy of Organizations: Critical Issues and New Perspectives* (Routledge, London, 1990), pp. 83–96.
5. Clegg, S.R., *Modern Organisations: Organisation Studies in the Postmodern World* (Sage, London, 1990).
6. Reed, M., 'The End of Organised Society: A Theme in Search of a Theory?' in Blyton, P. and Morris, J. (eds), *A Flexible Future?: Prospects for Employment and Organization* (De Gruyter, Berlin, 1991b), pp. 23–41.

7. Dandeker, C., *Surveillance, Power and Modernity* (Polity Press, Cambridge, 1990).
8. *ibid.*, p. 38.
9. *ibid.*, p. 37.
10. Giddens, A., 'Time and Social Organizations' in Giddens, A., *Social Theory and Modern Sociology* (Polity Press, Cambridge, 1987), pp. 140–65 (p. 162).
11. The concept of 'areas of uncertainty' was originally developed by Michel Crosier in his book *The Bureaucratic Phenomenon* (University of Chicago Press, Chicago, 1964). For a further development of the concept and its implications for analyzing intra- and interorganizational power relations see Reed, M., *Redirections in Organizational Analysis* (Tavistock, London, 1985).
12. Dandeker, C., *op. cit.* (1990), p. 196.
13. For an extended discussion of this point see Larson, M.S., 'In the Matter of Experts and Professionals' in Torstendahl, R. and Burrage, M. (eds), *The Formation of Professions* (Sage, London, 1990), pp. 24–50.
14. Dandeker, C., *op. cit.* (1990), p. 197.
15. Giddens, A., *op. cit.* (1987), p. 155.
16. Hopwood, A.G., 'The Archaeology of Accounting Systems', *Accounting, Organizations and Society*, vol. 12 (3), 1987; Miller, P. and O'Leary, T., 'Accounting and the Construction of the Governable Person', *Accounting, Organizations and Society*, vol. 12 (3), 1987, 235–66; Morgan, G., *Organizations in Society* (Macmillan, London, 1990), pp. 106–20.
17. Anthony, P.D., *The Foundation of Management* (Tavistock, London, 1986).
18. Storey, J. (ed.), *New Perspectives on Human Resource Management* (Routledge, London, 1989).
19. Armstrong, P., 'Management Control Strategies and Inter-Professional Competition: The Cases of Accountancy and Personnel Management' in Knights, D. and Willmott, H. (eds), *Managing the Labour Process* (Gower, Aldershot, 1986); Townley, B., 'Foucault Power/Knowledge and its Relevance for HRM', unpublished conference paper, Cardiff Business School, 1990; Wilkinson, A., Allen, P. and Snape, E., 'Total Quality Management and The Management of Labour', *Employee Relations*, vol. 13 (1), 1991, p. 24–31.
20. Legge, K., 'Human Resource Management: A Critical Analysis' in Storey, J. (ed.), *op. cit.* (1989), pp. 19–40 (p. 36).
21. Watson, T., 'Towards a General Theory of Personnel and

Industrial Relations Management', *Trent Business School, Occasional Paper Series*, no. 2 (1983), p. 24.

22. Scott, W.R., 'The Adolescence of Institutional Theory', *Administrative Science Quarterly*, vol. 32 (4), 1987, pp. 493–511.

23. Johnson, T.J., 'The State and the Professions: Peculiarities of the British' in Giddens, A. and MacKenzie, G. (eds), *Social Class and the Division of Labour* (Cambridge University Press, Cambridge, 1982), pp. 186–208.

24. Hall, R.H., 'Professionalization and Bureaucratization', *American Sociological Review*, vol. 69 (July), 1963, pp. 32–40.

25. Dandeker, C., *op. cit.* (1990), pp. 206–10.

26. This point has already been dealt with at some length in Chapter 1.

27. Murphy, R., 'Proletarianization or Bureaucratization: The Fall of the Professional' in Torstendahl, R. and Burrage, M., *op. cit.* (1990), pp. 71–96.

28. Abbott, A., *The System of Professions* (University of Chicago Press, Chicago, 1988), p. 60.

29. Murphy, R., *op. cit.* (1990), pp. 91–2.

30. Larson, M.S., *The Rise of Professionalism* (University of California Press, Berkeley, 1977); Child, J., 'Professionals in the Corporate World: Values, Interests and Control' in Dunkerley, D., and Salaman, G. (eds), *The International Yearbook of Organizational Studies* (Routledge, London, 1982), pp. 212–41.

31. Johnson, T.J., *Professions and Power* (Macmillan, London, 1982).

32. Morgan, G., *op. cit.* (1990), pp. 101–2.

33. For a review of the 'service class' thesis see Reed, M., *The Sociology of Management* (Harvester Wheatsheaf, Hemel Hempstead, 1989), pp. 124–49.

34. Roomkin, M. (ed.), *Managers as Employees: An International Comparison of the Changing Character of Managerial Employment* (Oxford University Press, Oxford, 1989); Lane, C., *Management and Labour in Europe* (Edward Elgar, Aldershot, 1989).

35. Crompton, R., 'Professions in the Current Context', *Work, Employment and Society*, additional special issue: A Decade of Change?, May 1990, pp. 147–66.

36. Clegg, S.R., Boreham, P. and Dow, G., *Class, Politics and the Economy* (Routledge, London, 1986), p. 192.

37. Reed, M., *op. cit.* (1989); Reed, M. and Anthony, P.D., 'Professionalizing Management and Managing Professionalization: British Management in the 1980s', *Journal of Management Studies*, special issue, June 1992; Abbott, A., *op. cit.* (1988).

38. Armstrong, P., 'Competition between the Organizational Professions and the Evolution of Managerial Control Strategies' in Thompson, K. (ed.), *Work, Employment and Unemployment* (Open University Press, Milton Keynes, 1984), pp. 97–120.

39. Abbott, A., *op. cit.* (1988), p. 103.

40. Scott, J., *Corporations, Classes and Capitalism* (Hutchinson, London, second edition, 1985).

41. *ibid.*, p. 193.

42. Cousins, C., *Controlling Social Welfare: A Sociology of State Welfare Work and Organization* (Harvester Wheatsheaf, Hemel Hempstead, 1987); Pollitt, C., *Managerialism and the Public Services: The Anglo-American Experience* (Basil Blackwell, Oxford, 1990).

43. Giddens, A., 'Structuration Theory: Past, Present and Future' in Bryant, C.G. and Jary, D., *Giddens' Theory of Structuration* (Routledge, London, 1988), pp. 201–21.

44. For a more detailed elaboration of this point see Dandeker, C., *op. cit.* (1990) and Scott, W.R., *Organizations: Rational, Natural and Open Systems* (Prentice-Hall, Englewood Cliffs, NJ, second edition, 1981).

45. On this point see Larson, M.S., *op. cit.* (1990) and Murphy, R., *op. cit.* (1990).

46. Rueschemeyer, D., *Power and the Division of Labour* (Polity Press, Cambridge, 1986).

47. Pettigrew, A., *The Awakening Giant: Continuity and Change in ICI* (Basil Blackwell, Oxford, 1985); Pettigrew, A. (ed.), *The Management of Strategic Change* (Basil Blackwell, Oxford, 1988); Jackall, R., *Moral Mazes: The World of Corporate Managers* (Oxford University Press, Oxford, 1988); Wood, S., 'New Wave Management?' *Work, Employment and Society*, vol. 3 (3), 1989, pp. 379–402.

48. Wilkinson, B., *The Shop Floor Politics of New Technology* (Heinemann, London, 1983); Francis, A., *New Technology at Work* (Oxford University Press, Oxford, 1986); McLoughlin, I. and Clark, J., *Technological Change at Work* (Open University Press, Milton Keynes, 1988).

49. Donaldson, L., *In Defence of Organization Theory* (Cambridge University Press, Cambridge, 1985).

50. Pettigrew, A., *op. cit.* (1985), pp. xix–447; on this point also see Hickson, D.J., Butler, R.J., Cray, D., Mallory, G.R. and Wilson, D.C., *Top Decisions: Strategic Decision-Making in Organisations* (Blackwell, Oxford, 1986); and Smith, C., Child, J. and Rowlinson, M., *Reshaping Work: The Cadbury Experience* (Cambridge University Press, Cambridge, 1990).

51. See Chapter 4.
52. Burawoy, M., *The Politics of Production* (Verso, London, 1985); Thompson, P., *The Nature of Work: An Introduction to Debates on the Labour Process* (Macmillan, London, second edition, 1989); Knights, D. and Willmott, H., *Labour Process Theory* (Macmillan, London, 1990).
53. Littler, C. and Salaman, G., *Class at Work: The Design, Allocation and Control of Jobs* (Batsford, London, 1984).
54. Whittington, R., *Corporate Strategies in Recession and Recovery: Social Structure and Strategic Choice* (Unwin Hyman, London, 1989).
55. Clark, P. and Starkey, K., *Organization Transitions and Innovation Design* (Pinter Press, London, 1988).
56. Hearn, J., Sheppard, D.L., Tancred-Sheriff, P. and Burrell, G. (eds), *The Sexuality of Organization* (Sage, London, 1987); Mills, M.J. and Murgatroyd, S.J., *Organizational Rules: A Framework for Understanding Organizational Action* (Open University Press, Milton Keynes, 1991); Burrell, G., 'Sex and Organizational Analysis', *Organization Studies*, vol. 5 (2), 1984, pp. 97–118; Davies, S., 'Inserting Gender into Burawoy's Theory of the Labour Process', *Work, Employment and Society*, vol. 4 (3), 1990, pp. 391–406; Mills, A.J., 'Organizational Discourse and the Gendering of Identity', in Parker, M. and Hassard, J. (eds) *Postmodernism and Organizational Theory* (Sage, London, 1992).
57. Hearn, J. *et al.*, *op. cit.* (1989), pp. 179–80.
58. Walby, S., *Patriarchy at Work* (Polity Press, Cambridge, 1986); Thompson, P., *op. cit.* (1989), pp. 180–209.
59. Morgan, G., *Images of Organization* (Sage, London, 1986).
60. Mills, A.J. and Murgatroyd, S.J., *op. cit.* (1991), pp. 68–96.
61. Mills, A.J., *op. cit.* (1991).
62. Walby, S., *op. cit.* (1986); Davies, S., *op. cit.* (1990).
63. Jenkins, R. and Parker, G., 'Organizational Politics and the Recruitment of Black Workers' in Lee, G. and Loveridge, R. (eds), *The Manufacture of Disadvantage* (Open University Press, Milton Keynes, 1987), pp. 58–70; Dhooge, E., 'Ethnic Difference and Industrial Conflicts', *Social Science Research Unit on Ethnic Relations*, Working Paper on Ethnic Relations, no. 13, 1981. For a more detailed review of the impact of race and ethnicity on labour markets and work organizations see Grint, K., *The Sociology of Work: An Introduction*, (Polity Press, Cambridge, 1991).
64. On this point see Reed, M., *op. cit.* (1985).
65. Bryman, A., 'Organization Studies and the Concept of

Rationality', *Journal of Management Studies*, vol. 21 (4), 1984, pp. 391–404; Brunsson, N., 'The Irrationality of Action and Action Rationality: Decisions, Ideologies and Organisational Actions', *Journal of Management Studies*, vol. 18 (1), 1982, pp. 29–44; Brunsson, N., *The Irrational Organization: Irrationality as a Basis for Organizational Action and Change* (Wiley, New York, 1985); March, J.G., *Decisions and Organizations* (Blackwell, Oxford, 1988); Brunsson, N., *The Organization of Hypocrisy: Talk, Decisions and Actions in Organizations* (Wiley, New York, 1989); Reed, M., 'Organizations and Rationality: The Odd Couple?', *Journal of Management Studies*, vol. 28 (5), 1991, pp. 559–67.

66. Weick, K., *The Social Psychology of Organizing* (Addison-Wesley, Reading, Mass., 1969); Lincoln, Y.S. (ed.), *Organizational Theory and Inquiry: The Paradigm Revolution* (Sage, Beverly Hills, 1985); March, J.E., *Decisions and Organizations* (Basil Blackwell, Oxford, 1989). Two other areas in which this retreat from 'hard' versions of organizational rationality has been well underway for some time and is currently gathering momentum are the psychodynamics of work organization and economic theory. On the former, see Hirschorn, L., *The Workplace Within: Psychodynamics of Organizational Life* (MIT Press, Cambridge, Mass., 1988) and Doray, B., *From Taylorism to Fordism: A Rational Madness* (Free Association Books, London, 1988). On the latter see Etzioni, A., *The Moral Dimension: Toward a New Economics* (Free Press, New York, 1988).

67. Weick, K., 'Sources of Order in Underorganized Systems: Themes in Recent Organizational Theory' in Lincoln, Y.S. (ed.), *op. cit.* (1985), pp. 106–36 (p. 110).

68. White, S.K., *The Recent Work of Jürgen Habermas: Reason, Justice and Modernity* (Cambridge, Cambridge University Press, 1988), pp. 10–1.

69. *ibid.*, p. 16.

70. Gambetta, D. (ed.). *Trust: Making and Breaking Co-operative Relations* (Basil Blackwell, Oxford, 1988); Giddens, A., *The Consequences of Modernity* (Polity Press, Cambridge, 1990).

71. Gambetta, D., *op. cit.* (1988), p. 219.

72. Streeck, W., 'The Uncertainties of Management in the Management of Uncertainty: Employers, Labour Relations and Industrial Adjustment in the 1980s', *Work, Employment and Society*, vol. 1 (3), 1987, pp. 281–308.

73. Clegg, S.R., *op. cit.* (1990), p. 181.

74. Power, M., 'Modernism, Postmodernism and Organization' in Hassard, J. and Pym, D., *op. cit.* (1990), pp. 109–24.
75. Heydebrand, W., 'New Organizational Forms', *Work and Occupations*, vol. 16 (3), 1989, pp. 323–57.
76. Tixier, P.E., 'The Labour Movement and Post-Rational Models of Organization: A French Case or a Trend in Western Societies? in Lammers, C.J. and Szell, G. (eds), *International Handbook of Participation in Organizations*, vol. 1, (Oxford University Press, Oxford, 1989), pp. 26–37 (pp. 2–28).
77. Bagguley, P., 'Post-Fordism and the Enterprise Culture: Flexibility, Autonomy and Changes in Economic Organization', in Keat, R. and Abercrombie, N. (eds), *Enterprise Culture* (Routledge, London, 1991), pp. 151–70.
78. Piore, M. and Sabel, C., *The Second Industrial Divide: Possibilities for Prosperity* (Basic Books, New York, 1984).
79. Lash, S. and Urry, J., *The End of Organized Capitalism* (Polity Press, Cambridge, 1987).
80. Aglietta, M., *A Theory of Capitalist Regulation* (Verso, London, 1979).
81. Sabel, C., *Work and Politics* (Cambridge University Press, Cambridge, 1982), p. 231.
82. Fox, A., *Beyond Contract: Work, Power and Trust Relations* (Faber, London, 1974).
83. Lane, C., *op. cit.* (1989).
84. Murray, R., 'Fordism and Post-Fordism' in Hall, S. and Jacques, M. (eds), *New Times: The Changing Face of Politics in the 1990s* (Lawrence and Wishart, London, 1989), pp. 38–54 (pp. 47–51).
85. Best, M.H., *The New Competition: Institutions of Industrial Restructuring* (Polity Press, Cambridge, 1990).
86. Urry, J., 'Work, Production and Social Relations', *Work, Employment and Society*, vol. 4 (2), 1990, pp. 271–80.
87. Best, M.H., *op. cit.* (1990), pp. 2–3.
88. Wood, S., *op. cit.* (1989); Reed, M., *op. cit.* (1991b); Amin, A. and Robins, K., 'The Re-Emergence of Regional Economies?: The Mythical Geography of Flexible Accumulation', *Environment and Planning: Society and Space*, vol. 8, 1990, pp. 7–34; Hyman, R., 'Plus Ça Change?: The Theory of Production and The Production of Theory' in Pollert, A. (eds), *Farewell to Flexibility?* (Blackwell, Oxford, 1991), pp. 259–83; Thompson, P., 'Fatal Distraction: Postmodernism and Organizational Analysis', in Parker, M. and Hassard, J. (eds) *Postmodernism and Organizational Theory* (Sage, London, 1992); Cooke, P., *Back to the Future: Modernity, Post-*

*modernity and Locality* (Unwin Hyman, London, 1990).

89. Piore, M. and Sabel, C., *op. cit.* (1984).
90. Lovering, J., 'A Perfunctory Sort of Post-Fordism: Economic Restructuring and Labour Market Segmentation in Britain in the 1980s', *Work, Employment and Society: The 1980s a Decade of Change?*, additional special issue, May 1990, pp. 9–28.
91. Hyman, R., *op. cit.* (1991).
92. Amin, A. and Robins, K., *op. cit.* (1990).
93. Whitaker, A., 'The Transformation in Work?' in Reed, M. and Hughes, M.D. (eds), *Rethinking Organization: New Directions in Organization Theory and Analysis* (Sage, London, 1992).
94. *ibid.*, pp. 184–206. For empirical confirmation of Whitaker's conclusions see Lawson, A., Morgan, K., Weber, D., Holmes, P. and Stevens, A., *Hostile Brothers: Competition and Closure in the European Electronics Industry* (Clarendon Press, Oxford, 1990), pp. 315–18.
95. Rustin, M., 'The Politics of Post-Fordism or the Trouble with New Times', *New Left Review*, 1989, pp. 54–77 (p. 61).
96. Harvey, D., *The Condition of Postmodernity* (Basil Blackwell, Oxford, 1989), pp. 191–6.
97. Leggatt, T., *The Evolution of Industrial Systems* (Croom Helm, London, 1985).

# / 6 /

## FUTURE PROSPECTS

### INTRODUCTION

Discontinuity has been the dominating issue or problematic within the sociology of organizations over the last two decades or so. The period has been characterized and represented by a discourse which lays overwhelming emphasis on institutional and intellectual ruptures with the past. Both in relation to the organizational forms which constitute the discipline's subject matter and the theoretical frameworks through which they are analyzed, the recurring theme is one of a deep-seated, fundamental transformation that breaks with previously established trajectories of institutional and intellectual development. Any sense of historical continuity and narrative coherence is lost in the clamour of voices announcing the 'end of history' and extolling the virtues of root and branch transformation from the 'old' to the 'new' organization theory.

The most obvious example of this 'celebration of discontinuity' is the recent impact of 'postmodernist' thinking in relation to explanations of changing organizational forms and the theoretical frameworks through which they are most appropriately explored.[1] But this is merely one illustration of a continuing series of interventions within the field over the last two decades which have either implicitly entailed or explicitly demanded a fundamental 'break with the past' in terms of projected organizational forms and preferred theoretical frameworks. Ethnomethodology, labour process theory, population ecology, organizational symbolism and poststructuralism, amongst others, have vied for our attention as perspectives and/or research programmes that seem to signify the intellectual exhaustion of functionalist orthodoxy and the proliferation of alternative languages and problematics which 'blow the field wide open'.

In this respect, the 'disorganizing dynamic' which is thought to be at work within the longer-term institutional development of advanced industrial societies is assumed to be mirrored in the trajectory of intellectual development into which the study of organizations has fallen. In the former context, the previously assumed evolutionary trend towards bureaucratic rationalization and centralization has been displaced by analyses suggesting a developmental logic pushing in the direction of much more fragmented social structures and flexible organizational forms. In the latter context, the shift from bureaucracy to networks is seen to be paralleled by an intellectual retreat from formal rationality and functionalist evolution which eventually embraces, indeed luxuriates in, the delights of theoretical plurality and methodological eclecticism.[2]

Previous analysis in this book has already questioned this overpowering emphasis on discontinuity and its tendency to legitimate interpretation of the discipline's development which either downplay or ignore the deeper, underlying continuities that shape current debates and their projected outcomes. The need to achieve a more sensible and accurate assessment of the shifting balance between continuity and discontinuity, as well as its implications for future intellectual development within the field, is the major objective pursued within this final chapter.

The latter is carried through in four phases. First, an overview is provided of some of the most recent debates concerning theoretical developments, organizational change and emerging problematics within the field as a whole. Second, an assessment is made of the various recipes for future intellectual development which are currently on offer – within the broader setting provided by the previous overview. Third, a case is made which suggests that the concept of organization needs to be 'reclaimed', *in a particular way*, as the strategic analytical focus and research site for the sociology of organizations. Finally, some selected examples of recently published organizational research and analysis are discussed as providing exemplars of the type of work which needs to be done if the concept of organizations is to be reclaimed as *the* strategic focus and site for future advance.


FROM ORTHODOX CONSENSUS TO PLURALISTIC DIVERSITY


As previous discussions has indicated, the last two decades have witnessed very significant changes in the way in which the concept of organization is defined and the practice of organizational analysis conceived. Generally speaking, one can separate the period into three phases of theoretical change and development during which very different conceptions of organization and organizational analysis have been influential. These three phases convey very different impressions of what the sociology of organizations is about and the manner in which it can be most fruitfully prosecuted. During this period, there have been significant changes in the way in which both subject matter and theoretical approach have been regarded, but these changes have to be set and interpreted within a longer-term context. Overall, the underlying trajectory revealed through an examination of the three phases of theoretical development seems to press in the direction of enhanced plurality, diversity and controversy, as well as the underlying fragmenting dynamic which they have set in motion.

By the late 1960s, various strands of theoretical development in organizational analysis seemed to be converging around a systems-based contingency approach that focused on the adaptability of organizational designs to environmental imperatives of one sort or another.[3] However, the subsequent decade witnessed a sharp move away from this presumptive orthodoxy in the shape of critiques and alternative formulations that substantially devalued the theoretical capital on which systems-based approaches had traded. In particular, the latter were seen to rely on static conceptions of 'organization' as distinctive, indeed partially sealed, social units that were constrained, if not determined, by the larger environmental settings in which they operated. Alternative formulations suggested that organizations were reproduced and transformed through cultural and political processes which could not be caught in the analytical net provided by systems theory, with its theoretical trawl for isolatable 'dimensions' of formal organizational structure and environmental context which could be aligned through one assumed 'logic of effectiveness'.[4] Instead of a presumed logic of organizational adaptation that reinforced an ingrained theoretical predilection favourably disposed towards environmental determinism, alternative perspectives – the action frame of reference, negotiated order, ethnomethodology and political theories of organization decision-making – promulgated conceptions of 'organization' that highlighted the *construction* of organizational reality by means of power processes and symbolic interventions which manipulated and interpreted 'external' pressures in such a way that simultaneously buttressed and undermined established arrangements. Consequently, organizational design was perceived to be less a matter of an impersonal, objective force exerting its dominance and more a question of a constructed and manipulated social artefact. In turn, this development seriously undermined the conceptual separation between 'organization' on the one hand and 'environment' on the other. The boundaries between the two were perceived to be much more porous than contingency theory had admitted.

Ten years later, by the late 1970s, the disenchantment with systems-based conceptualizations of organization and the scientific legitimations of organizational analysis which they reinforced – that is, the commitment to organizational studies as a social *science* geared to the identification of causal relationships between 'organization' and 'environment' – had turned into a veritable backlash against conventional thinking. By this time, orthodox organization theory was increasingly perceived as being in a state of intellectual crisis, or disarray, in which the once solid conceptual foundations of systems orthodoxy had all but been eaten away in the 'locust years' of deepening dissension and counter-movement.[5] Thus, systems orthodoxy, by the late 1970s, was perceived to have no answer to the mounting demand for theoretical frameworks which could effectively deal with:

the social production of organizational reality, including the reality-constructing activity of the organization scientist; the political bases of organizational realities, including the ties of theorists to power structures; the connection of organizations to the larger set of structural arrangements in the society; and the continuously emergent character of organizational patterns.[6]

Around these strategic conceptual and methodological issues, a series of theoretical flows began to coagulate that considerably widened the agenda for organizational studies. They also presented an, often bewildering, array of alternative approaches that defied accommodation within the once impregnable aegis of intellectual orthodoxy. As the latter began to dissipate, the ability to establish a, or *the*, defining problematic and framework for organizational analysis became increasingly difficult, if not impossible, to achieve. Organization theory seemed to be moving into a state of 'intellectual anomie'. The *fin de siècle* of intellectual orthodoxy coincided with a proliferation of theoretical options which created a deepening sense of academic normlessness.

Between the late 1970s and the late 1980s an ever-widening range of theoretical perspectives were offered as alternatives to the unacceptable constrictions of orthodoxy and as potential correctives to the miasma of conceptual proliferation into which organizational theory was being seduced. First, there was an increasingly potent emphasis on the cultural and symbolic processes through which organizations were socially constructed and organizational analysis academically structured. Second, the macro-level power relations and ideological systems through which organizational forms were shaped became a central focus for analysis. Third, the retreat from natural science conceptions of organizational analysis seemed to make intellectual and institutional space available for approaches that focused on the complex interaction between theoretical innovation and social context.[7] At one level, these developments seemed to signify the dissolution of organizational analysis as an identifiable field of study and a coherent body of knowledge.

At another level, they seemed to open up attractive possibilities for research and explanation that forged connections between philosophical debate, theoretical development and institutional change – connections that had either been ignored or inadequately treated in previous work. Organization theory seemed to have finally left its period of 'intellectual innocence' far behind; by now, it was participating in fundamental debates about the nature of social scientific research and explanation that moved beyond the narrow confines of established disciplinary orthodoxy.

Intensified debate and controversy over the theoretical foundations of organizational studies has been paralleled by growing awareness of and sensitivity to substantive changes in those organizational forms which provide the empirical focus for research and analysis. Whether these structural changes should be regarded as signifying a fundamental transformation in the institutional fabric of advanced industrial societies, or more appropriately as the working through of older, well-established forms to their more developed state, is a moot point.[8] Nevertheless, however these changes in organizational forms are characterized and explained, there is general agreement that they signify the theoretical importance and practical relevance of a far wider range of structural options than were considered under the rational model or systems perspective.

The belief that rational bureaucracy, as exemplified in formal organization structures characterized by extreme internal differentiation and rigid hierarchical control, constituted a universalizable solution to the problem of achieving operational efficiency and effectiveness in conditions of environmental uncertainty had petrified into a rigid orthodoxy that the dominant systems approach maintained. While such structures were seen to require some 'fine tuning' to align them more closely with specific configurations of environmental contingencies, they were presumed to provide a core repertoire of universalizable principles and mechanisms that equipped organizations to face competitive pressures and the implacable demands which the latter generated for effective coordination of large-scale, complex operations. External pressures for economic efficiency and administrative effectiveness were assumed to exert a predominant influence over organizational design.

Over the last decade or so, historical and comparative research on organizational forms has revealed the inherent limitations and inadequacies of this 'universalistic' thesis. It has shown that different historical periods and institutional locations within and between different societies produce and reproduce a wide range of organizational forms which cannot be accommodated with the universalizing logic of the rational/systems model. Indeed, this research has shown that the conventionally accepted functional relationship between highly differentiated and formalized organizational structures and socio-economic contexts defined by competitive pressures pressing in the direction of market efficiency may be much more tenuous than supporters of the dominant orthodoxy have suggested. In addition, such research has also called into question the conventional conceptual and methodological apparatus through which comparative organizational forms have been studied within the analytical confines presented by the rational/systems approach. Thus, a growing interest in the social rationalities and practices which shape economic organization,[9] the power struggles through which they are formulated, implemented and contested and the varying conceptions of historical and institutional time in which such rationalities and struggles are contextualized, all signal a dramatic shift of emphasis in the study of organizational forms towards the dynamics of change and the logics through which it proceeds. As Clegg has concluded:

When we study the question of why it is that organization structures are as they are, the answer is likely to be far more complex than the simple surmise that they are subject to efficiency and effectiveness pressures. . . . The efficiency imperative can rarely be untangled from the institutional framework within which calculations both of what efficiency is and how it is to be achieved are made. . . . Increasingly, current organization theory is aware of the independence of power, institutions and efficiency. . . . Organizational modernities contain a number of diversities, rather than a more limited horizon of possibilities.[10]

If this view is accepted, than the interaction between

organizational forms and contexts over time needs to be rethought within a much more sensitive appreciation of the interrelationships between power, institutions and efficiency. As Clegg has indicated, this is likely to take the theoretical form of a much stronger emphasis on the historical, comparative and political dimensions of the *process* of organizational design.

As well as internal theoretical innovation and external institutional/organizational change, contemporary organizational analysis has also witnessed significant movement in the central 'problematics' which give the field some kind of coherent identity and shape as a going intellectual concern. If we regard a problematic as a general conceptual scheme organized around a core idea or problem which then provides a range of specific issues or puzzles for people working within the framework to get their intellectual teeth into, then it is possible to trace the emergence of alternative problematics over the last two decades which have challenged the intellectual *status quo* in varying ways and to differing degrees.

By the late 1960s the problematic of order had structured the field to the virtual exclusion of alternative formulations. This problematic centred on the question of how organizational survival was possible in the face of environmental forces and pressures which threatened the organization's very existence as a viable social unit.[11] The conceptual framework woven around this core problem rested on an ontological commitment to 'organization' as a distinctive and separate entity, dependent on certain stability maintaining and integrating mechanisms facilitating long-term survival in a potentially hostile environment.[12] These mechanisms were presumed to facilitate the 'fine tuning' in organizational design that equipped them to cope with uncertain and complex environments. Organizations seemed to possess the equilibrating mechanisms required to ensure long-term survival in hostile environmental conditions.

Ten years later, the problematic of order had been largely displaced by the problematic of domination – that is, a significant shift away from a primary concern with survival and stability towards an emphasis on the social and political processes through which organizational power is mobilized and legitimated.[13] This movement entailed a drastic reappraisal of the explanatory priorities which had traditionally shaped the substantive agenda for organizational analysis, as well as the theoretical and methodological tools thought most appropriate to the working through of that agenda. Instead of concentrating theoretical resources and methodological strategies around the establishment of causal relationships between environmental contingencies and formal organizational designs, the focus of attention shifted to an unearthing of the political and ideological manipulations which operated behind the public façade of stability and order.[14] The power of non-decision-making and institutional bias became the orienting themes in organizational analysis. The manipulation of ideologies to secure the continued power of dominant groups and their preferred institutional designs emerged as a central research theme.[15]

The last ten years have seen another transition in problematic in which the construction of organizational reality, through the skilled utilization of largely arbitrary linguistic and cultural representations or 'language games',[16] has become the central concern. This has given added intellectual momentum to approaches which reject the rationalistic predilections of earlier formulations and call attention to the complex negotiating processes through which a precarious, and unavoidably unstable, collective sense of organizational reality is sustained.

This third movement in problematic – the linguistic or cultural 'turn' in contemporary organizational analysis – also owes much to the widening impact of postmodernist thinking within the field. This latter development – and its potentially far-reaching implications for the way in which we conceptualize 'organization' – provides another intervention into a crowded field of study that has been inundated by contributions which are highly critical of the established intellectual capital on which mainstream organizational analysis has continued to trade. Indeed, postmodernist thinking seems to hammer the last nail into the coffin of intellectual orthodoxy in that it anticipates an irreversible move towards a state of affairs in which the certainties and stabilities once provided by the latter are no longer available. Instead, it presumes that we presently inhabit an intellectual world of competing perspectives and paradigms in which any sense of sustained conceptual continuity or basic epistemological foundations is very difficult, if not impossible, to maintain:

The view of knowledge-making as a transcendent pursuit, removed from the trivial enthralments of daily life, pristinely rational and transparently virtuous, becomes so much puffery. We should view these bodies of language we call knowledge in a lighter view – as ways of putting things, some pretty and others petty – but in no sense calling for ultimate commitments, condemnations, or profound consequences. We should be rather more playful with our sayings.[17]

It is these wider, and potentially seismic shifts, in theoretical orientations and institutional forms which provide the larger backdrop against which current prescriptions for longer-term intellectual advance need to be situated.

### THEORETICAL FUTURES

It is against the backdrop provided by the general developments that have been adumbrated in the previous section that current prescriptions for future advance within the field need to be set. They establish the immediate context in which recipes for longer-term intellectual progress within the sociology of organizations needs to be located. As has been indicated on several previous occasions, it is a context characterized by considerable uncertainty and controversy over the way in which organizational analysis should be prosecuted. This is particularly true at a time when both the definition of subject matter and the rules for theory building and research practice are so open to debate and conflicting interpretations.

However, a number of potential strategies for longer-term intellectual development can be discerned. Summarized somewhat crudely, these can be separated out into four basic options: first, 'back to basics'; second, 'separate development'; third, 'anything goes'; and fourth, a 'partial synthesis' movement which will be supported by the present author. Each of these options, and their programmes for intellectual advance, will be received in turn. This will be followed by a more detailed conceptual elaboration and empirical illustration of the fourth option as building on the practice perspective that has been recommended in Chapter 4.

On the whole, the first of these options – 'back to basics' – takes a very dim view of the disruptive forces that have been let loose within the field over the last two decades and attempts to mobilize support behind a conservative strategy that reaffirms the benefits to be derived from theoretical and methodological orthodoxy. Its clearest expression is to be found in the work of Donaldson,[18] but it also finds support in the work of those who take a less fundamentalist, but none the less 'sound', view of what the present position calls for by way of managed theoretical development and appropriate research initiatives.[19]

For Donaldson, the events of the last twenty years or so have culminated in a once well-regarded, if somewhat loosely structured sub-discipline being in a state of potential terminal disarray and disintegration. In his view, any overarching sense of intellectual coherence and practical relevance has been submerged beneath the welter of disputation and controversy released by the anticipated decay and eventual decomposition of theoretical and methodological orthodoxy. He conveys this perception of impending intellectual dissolution as follows:

The consequences of this growing tide of criticism has been extraordinary. Organization Theory has come into disrepute in many quarters. Though widely offered in courses, organizational sociology is often treated in a superficial and scathing manner, which is light in understanding and heavy in critique . . . the criticism of funda mentals has gone unanswered – and for too long. . . . Hopefully, this may serve as a rallying point for other students of organization and lead to a re-assertion of our sub-discipline as purposeful, coherent and with its own criteria. . . . It would seem that the challenge to orthodoxy has breached the castle walls of positivism, and penetrated its keep. . . . What was once a fringe counter-movement has become an incipient hegemony. . . . The lack of an effective counter-discussion and the growing influence of this movement are undesirable, for the sub-discipline, for sociology and for society.[20]

Donaldson's defence of organization theory can be read as a polemic advocating a return to the hard-won verities of functionalist theory and positivist methodology that once 'held court' within the field. He advocates a return to these previously dominant positions as providing a redoubt from which the rolling back of the critical tide can be mounted. Thus, a combination of functionalist theory and positivist methodology geared to the generation of a problem-solving, policy science is seen to provide a privileged intellectual standpoint from which criticism can be resisted and sub-disciplinary rectitude re-established. Consequently, Organization Theory (always in capitals for Donaldson) is repositioned as a specialist sub-discipline with its own subject matter, theoretical framework and research methodology. The subject matter is defined in terms of organizations as purposeful systems, directed to the achievement of collective goals requiring structured coordination and control amongst individuals. The theory is articulated in relation to supra-individual structures and processes that meet this functional need for regular coordination and control. The research methodology is projected in terms of data-gathering and interpreting techniques that account for varying relationships between internal structural design and external environmental contingencies through the manipulation of statistical correlations between operationalized dimensions of formal organization. This recombination of functionalism, positivism and operationalism is deemed to provide the revitalized intellectual regime from which the regeneration of orthodoxy can be effectively pursued. This revitalized regime, Donaldson assures us, will return organizational sociology to a focus on the core relationship between structure, environment and performance that had once been the intellectual and technical staple diet of conventional research and analysis.

More recently, Donaldson has advocated a 'liberal theory of organization' which anticipates a much closer relationship between organizational analysis and economic theory.[21] In this context, he envisages a much closer working relationship between selected aspects of institutional or organizational economics – such as agency theory and transaction cost theory[22] – and organizational analysis. While he is highly critical of some of the cruder axioms that underpin economic theory – such as the model of the actor as a utility-maximizing, rationally motivated individual shorn of all cultural accoutrements and ideological commitments – he envisages a new synthesis of organization theory and economic theory in which conceptual order and methodological rigour will be reimposed. By defining and constructing a new theory of organizations in this fashion, Donaldson argues, organizational sociology can play a much more 'positive' role than it has done in recent years by formulating empirically confirmed propositions on the relationships between key aspects of structural design and institutional context. In turn, this will help to re-establish the credentials of organizational analysis as a policy science that speaks to the concerns of policy-makers and implementors, rather than being seen as an exercise in intellectual self-indulgence which has nothing or little to say to powerful interest groups.[23]

Donaldson defines the subject matter of organizational analysis in terms of 'the phenomena of goal-oriented behaviour, coordination amongst individuals and other properties such as degree of differentiation, integration mechanisms, extent of concentration of power, authority, communication, legitimation, conflict and so on.'[24] These common underlying abstract variables or properties of organization structure are applicable to several different levels of analysis – individual roles, departmental sections, operating divisions and corporate structures – and can be used to analyze more than one level simultaneously. They are to be studied through the deployment of a systems approach that conceptualizes events involving organizations 'in terms of supra-individual concepts of structure, such a specialization of functions, centralization of decision-making, or adaptation to the environment'.[25] The focus for this approach is the complex relationship between different properties of formal organization structure and the environmental contingencies – size, diversification, public accountability and task uncertainty –

to which they are related. The underlying policy objective is to match organization structure and contextual contingencies in such a way that managers are in a position to implement structural designs maximizing operational efficiency and longer-term strategic effectiveness in their respective environmental 'domains'. In this way, Donaldson sees himself reasserting the overriding theoretical and practical value of a research tradition that had been badly mauled by – for the most part – ill-informed and tendentious critiques that had led organization studies up a theoretical blind alley and left it practically impotent in relation to policy advice.

His attempt to revive the systems approach and to reassert its claim to intellectual pre-eminence within the field has received substantial support from influential figures who believe that the theoretical coherence and practical utility of organization theory have been severely damaged by the successive waves of critical assessment that have washed over it during the last two decades. Thus, Hinings[26] and Aldrich[27] suggest that the intellectual fragmentation and policy paralysis induced by excessive philosophical debate and sociological theorizing can only be resisted by a return to the general 'positivist-functionalist' frame of reference that informed the analysis of organizations for most of its historical development as a recognized field of study. This may also generate cumulative empirical research programmes that will provide the knowledge base for transmitting informed policy advice to organizational elites, while at the same time facilitating a greater degree of 'institutionalization' for organization theory as an accepted discipline with its own specialized journals and research institutes.

In many respects, this programme of intellectual reorientation would entail a return to the 'technical' design questions and problems that dominated the study of organizations from the early decades of the twentieth century onwards.[28] These issues would be framed in a rather different theoretical idiom – in the sense that the language and logic of modern systems theory rejects the universalistic assumptions underpinning 'classical' management theory and its unremitting search for the 'one best way' to organize – but it would entail the acceptance of a technical view of organization as a rational instrument of coordination and control shaped by various environmental demands and the functional imperatives that they impose. In this sense, formal organization structure and its environmental determinants would once again become the analytical focus for organizational analysis, with the objective of providing theoretical knowledge that could be utilized by management in their attempt to effect a good functional match between structural design and situational contingencies.

The belief that 'separate development' provides the best way forward for organizational analysis is based on a very different rationale than Donaldson's prescriptions for future intellectual growth. However, it does possess some interesting, and perhaps surprising, parallels with his approach. Both prescribe a degree of theoretical closure and isolationism which is fundamentally incompatible with the advocacy of intellectual openness and debate by the other two developmental options which we will be considering. They also resonate with an ethos of intellectual rectitude and ideological exclusivity foreign to the latter.

The argument that the longer-term expansion of the knowledge base in organizational analysis will be most appropriately furthered through the separate development of perspectives and approaches located within distinctive 'paradigms' has been particularly influential during the 1980s. It was originally developed with some panache and force by Burrell and Morgan[29] in the late 1970s and has continued to exact a powerful influence on thinking about strategic intellectual development within the field since that time.[30]

Building on their conception of paradigms as constituting overarching frameworks of basic or foundational assumptions defining the nature of organizations and the manner in which they are to be 'properly' analyzed, Burrell and Morgan contend that:

Each paradigm needs to be developed in its own terms. In essence, what we are advocating in relation to developments within these paradigms amounts to a form of isolationism. We firmly believe that each of the paradigms can only establish itself at the level of organizational analysis if it is true to itself. Contrary to the widely held belief that synthesis and mediation between paradigms is what is required, we argue that the real need is for paradigmatic closure. In order to avoid emasculation and incorporation within the functionalist problematic, the paradigms need to provide a basis for their self-preservation by developing on their own account. Insofar as they take functionalism as their reference point, it is unlikely that they will develop far beyond their present embryonic state – they will not develop coherent alternatives to the functionalist point of view.[31]

It is clear from this manifesto that Burrell and Morgan advocate separate intellectual development within each paradigm (functionalist, interpretive, radical humanist and radical structuralist). They justify this strategy on the grounds that it offers the only viable way for organizational analysis to break free from the stultifying embrace of functionalist orthodoxy and nurture 'deviant' approaches that can be eventually established in their own right as constituting fully fledged visions of alternative 'organizational realities'. This is entirely in keeping with their underlying treatment of paradigms as constituting 'mutually exclusive ways of seeing the world';[32] that is, of providing different *languages* of organization and *rationales* for organizational analysis which cannot be accommodated to each other, or incorporated within a wider synthesis, because they inhabit mutually opposed cognitive and cultural universes. They are fundamentally and irrevocably *incommensurate* with each other in the sense that they are unable to communicate across inter-paradigmatic boundaries – much less be successfully incorporated or synthesized into a more all-inclusive framework. This is due to the fact that they 'speak' with divergent conceptual tongues which cannot be translated into a universal 'organizational esperanto!' In addition, they make mutually exclusive knowledge claims about organizational reality, and the behavioural and moral implications that the former convey, which cannot be reconciled through reliance on an objective adjudicatory mechanism untainted by intra-paradigmatic prejudices. Separate development remains the only viable intellectual strategy likely to produce and protect genuine theoretical diversity and plurality within a field of study dominated by such a well-entrenched orthodoxy.

This strong version of the 'incommensurability' thesis has been criticized on several grounds. This is particularly so in relation to whether it provides a sustainable description of *how* organizational analysis has developed historically, or a supportable prescription of the way in which it *ought* to be advanced as a body of knowledge in the future. However, it still continues to attract substantial support – perhaps in a somewhat diluted form – from within the heterogeneous community of researchers and scholars concerned with the study of organizations. A recent example of this is Jackson and Carter's defence of paradigm incommensurability as providing the only adequate foundation and protection for theoretical pluralism and political emancipation in the face of 'the imperialistic aspirations of an orthodoxy whose interests are rooted in performance and control'.[33] They suggest that while communication across paradigmatic boundaries is possible and healthy, each paradigm must be considered as distinctive in its own terms and possessing a separate language which sets it apart from the others. This opposition and sense of 'otherness' between paradigms provides the intellectual conflict and energy from which longer-term advance can occur. Any attempt to abandon paradigm incommensurability and the strategy of separate intellectual development which it legitimates will inexorably lead, in their view, towards a regime of epistemological and theoretical authoritarianism.

Yet Gioia and Pitre[34] have shown that paradigmatic boundaries are much *more* permeable than Jackson and Carter or Burrell and Morgan allow in that they are most appropriately conceived as 'transition zones' rather than as hard and fast domains. The former do not suggest that different paradigms or perspectives can be collapsed or synthesized into an integrated framework. Instead, they suggest that a pluralistic, multiple-perspective view can be developed by building conceptual bridges across transition zones in such a way that complementary interpretations of organizational reality are made available.[35] Thus, they reject the strong version of paradigm incommensurability and closure associated with the 'separate development' approach and argue for a strategy which establishes links between different perspectives and ways of juxtaposing or meshing these alternatives into a multi-faceted analysis. This calls for a more sensible balance between diversity and complementarity or accommodation than that made possible by a commitment to fundamentalist conceptions of incommensurability and closure. Diversity, plurality and conflict are recognized as facts of intellectual life, but they are not regarded in such a way that epistemological incommensurability and strict closure become the only basis on which long-term intellectual development can be realized. The intellectual 'puritanism' of separate development may be as unattractive as a strategy for long-term development as the 'authoritarianism' of positivist/ functionalist orthodoxy.

There are certain respects in which the 'separate development' recipe for intellectual advance shades into the 'anything goes' option. Both strategies reject the presupposition that there is a neutral or privileged epistemological and theoretical vantage-point from which competing explanations can be compared and assessed. In this sense, they both deny the superiority of the methodological orthodoxy or 'scientism' that Donaldson wishes to defend as providing a basis for counteracting deviant approaches and re-establishing the credentials of organizational analysis as a coherent sub-discipline.

But the 'anything goes' viewpoint departs from a strategy of separate development in so far as it takes a much more eclectic and pragmatic – not to say, promiscuous – view of what constitutes 'intellectual progress' and the manner in which 'it' is to be advanced. In this respect, it rejects the proposition that there is any universal objective or rational basis on which competing perspectives and conflicting theories can be judged or evaluated. Instead, it proposes that these activities can only be meaningfully pursued on the basis of what 'works', pragmatically, within a particular problem domain or area of analysis. This approach also legitimates a focus on the power relationships which shape knowledge production and development, as well as the political and administrative practices – including specialized 'technical' languages and epistemological/methodological procedures – through which micro-level control is sustained. Consequently, the emphasis shifts towards the control regimes in which the production, dissemination and evaluation of organizational knowledge are directly implicated.[36] A rather idealistic and pristine belief in the distinctiveness of, if not separation between, intellectual discourse and political practice is superseded by a viewpoint that tends to collapse the former into the latter.[37] The organizational needs of identifiable power groups within society now becomes the ineluctable driving force behind intellectual development and change. All pretence of 'neutrality', 'objective' or 'rationality' is swept away in the subordination of organizational analysis to organizational power relations and the struggles through which they are reproduced.[38] Those organization theories which will survive and prosper are those which will be most closely and effectively aligned to the interests and needs of powerful groups within the wider society.[39] Thus, organizational knowledge becomes one vital ingredient amongst a number of socio-technical resources that power groups mobilize to construct and maintain viable coalitions or 'actor networks'.

In some respects this view resonates with the 'demythologizing' and 'debunking' motives that underpinned the Marxist or 'Radical' critique of mainstream organizational analysis in the 1970s. This aspired to reveal and uncover the covert ideological prejudices and political interests on which orthodox approaches traded to legitimate their claims as a scientific enterprise geared to the 'general' good of society as a whole. It contended that a deeper, more penetrating, analysis would show how the development of organization theory, as a body of knowledge and a related set of socio-political practices, was intimately related to the changing control needs of dominant class interests and their primary concern with sustained capital accumulation. Organization theory came to be regarded as a refined form of ideological legitimation which obscured the material interests on which it rested and which it served.

More recently, the reductionist tendencies and ideological certainties of Marxist critique have been overtaken by a version of this thesis which emphasizes the socio-political power struggles to which organizational knowledge is subordinated, but without the moralizing or universalizing overtones associated with the former. The work of Foucault often provides an inspiration for this 'realistic' interpretation of knowledge growth and development within organizational analysis. This is so to the extent that:

practice now becomes much more important than theory ...
moreover, practices become viewed from the inside rather than the
viewpoint of the detached observer.... Organizations come to be
seen, therefore, as episodic and unpredictable manifestations of a
play of dominations ... it is important to know that the reality of
organizations is that they reflect and reproduce a disciplinary
society. But to talk about them, to develop discourses and
classification schemes for their analysis, actively contributes to the
reproduction of this discipline. Reality, and our discourse about
reality, are both ever more closely confining. Thus, we are imprisoned by our knowledge and made freer by our ignorance. Only to
the extent that we stop talking about types of organizations do we
succeed in *not* reproducing the disciplinary society.[40]

The problem with this kind of prognosis for the way in
which organizational knowledge should be regarded and
advanced is that it grossly overstates the internal coherence of
those practices and networks which generate knowledge
claims. It also overestimates the 'totalizing' achievements of
specific disciplinary regimes or technologies. In addition, it
tends to treat organizational analysis as a discursive formation which: 'unites thought and practice in a seamless and
circular web. Practices set the conditions for discourse and
discourse feeds back statements that will facilitate practice.
Discourse appears completely incorporated into practice. It
has no autonomous identity or distance.'[41] Consequently, intellectual growth and development tends to be rendered down
to the practical political and administrative interests which it
serves. At the same time, these disciplinary regimes are
presumed to display a degree of intellectual and organizational coherence that is belied by the findings of historical
research. The latter suggests a much less deterministic
relationship between 'thought' and 'action' than the supporters of the Foucauldian perspective imply.[42] Thus, both on
the grounds of historical/empirical accuracy and in relation to
the rather crude reductionist relationship between intellectual development, social interests and power struggles which
the Foucauldian metaphysic envisages, a rather different
conception of the interaction between 'ideas', 'interests' and
'actions' has emerged and begun to attract support.

This final developmental strategy of 'partial synthesis' is

based on the argument that some degree of limited reconciliation is possible within organizational analysis by 'juxtaposing
or meshing alternative theoretical perspectives into multi-
faceted theoretical views of organizational phenomena'.[43]
Rather than assuming that advocates of competing perspectives or paradigms are entirely the prisoners of their preferred
frameworks and the cognitive categories which these legitimate, supporters of limited synthesis have consistently maintained that mutual exclusivity and separate development are
not 'the only games in town'. Instead, the latter have argued
that selected theoretical elements of different general approaches can be recombined and reworked in such a way that
a richer and deeper understanding of organizations is made
possible. The recognition of diversity and divergence does not
necessitate an almost metaphysical commitment to the
existence of epistemological and theoretical oppositions, or
linguistic oppositions, which cannot be bridged or mediated
in any way. As Willmott maintains:

> by denying the presence (and the possibility!) of approaches that are
> either exclusively 'subjective' or 'objective', and which are not
> governed solely by the principles of 'regulation', nor by those of
> 'radical change', *Sociological Paradigms* exerts an inadvertently
> repressive force as it denies the very possibility of analysis that is
> much more sensitive to the ambiguous and contradictory nature of
> social reality than is allowed by its own one-dimensional vision of
> the mutual exclusivity of paradigms.[44]

Again, this argument for interparadigmatic mediation and
selective reworking does not entail a marginalization of
fundamental ontological and epistemological differences which
exist, and will continue to exist, between different frameworks. But it does presume that the sociological analysis of
organizations requires concepts, theories and methodologies
which are much more sensitive to the complexity of
organizational phenomena and the multi-faceted nature of the
analytical frameworks through which they are to be understood amnd explained. In short, that the longer-term theoretical development of organizational analysis must be based
upon a shared conception of 'organization' which will
facilitate a deeper understanding of the social practices that
are constitutive of such a strategic institution.

## RECLAIMING ORGANIZATION

Reference has already been made to a model of 'organization' as entailing a set of social practices geared to the assembly of highly complex and diverse social interactions into structured institutional forms.[45] Subsequent analysis builds on this practice framework by developing a generic conception of organization and its strategic role in reproducing the social structures through which modern life is carried on. Subsequent discussion will provide a brief résumé of a number of empirically based research studies which are seen to reflect the underlying approach embodied within this generic conception of organization.

A recurring theme throughout this book has been the strategic role which complex organizations have played in providing an interrelated set of social practices and mechanisms through which the transition from 'traditional' to 'modern' society has been made possible. As such, the former have been viewed as embodying certain general principles and properties which, when combined in the appropriate manner, provided the social and administrative technology required to make the transition from pre-industrial to advanced industrialized societies.[46] As Giddens has recognized, modern organizations provide the administrative power or capacity necessary to 'bracket' time and space in such a way that they are able to span greater or lesser time zones and geographical distances.[47] Thus, interrelated sets of social practices are integral to the bracketing or stretching function which modern organizations perform and the greatly extended managerial control over social interaction which this makes possible. First, those practices that allow a continual monitoring and correcting of the conditions under which social systems are reproduced ('reflexive monitoring'). Second, those practices that permit the documentation, articulation and storage of discursive history in such a way that the routine, and relatively unobtrusive, supervision of collective action is made possible (articulation of discursive history). Taken together, these two sets of social practices – and the mobilization of those administrative and allocative resources which their performance requires[48] – provide a degree of effective coordination and control over social life which is unavailable in pre-modern societies. Thus, modern organizations can be seen, Giddens argues, as time/space ordering devices through which social system reproduction and transformation in modern societies is achieved. These devices provide the essential institutional mechanisms through which the transition to modern societies was realized, by facilitating the stretching and overcoming of time/space constraints which the latter needed. In addition, they establish the conditions under which 'modernity' is made possible, in that they exercise a ubiquitous and pervasive influence over 'localized' everyday life and its articulation with 'globalized' structures. Thus, modern organizations make possible the interpenetration of the local and the global in such a manner that the reflexive reproduction of social systems can be routinely achieved.

Giddens has developed this latter point more fully in his most recent book.[49] Here he argues that modern organizations provide 'containers' in which administrative power is concentrated to a much higher degree and used with much greater effect than was the case under pre-modern forms of coordination and control. This is the case not only in relation to the centralized governmental or corporate structures which are characteristic of modernity, but it is also found in more dispersed, yet pervasive, forms of coordination and control such as 'expert systems'. The latter provide coordination of collective action across time and the control of space which lift social relations out of their 'local' context and restructure or stretch interaction across indefinite spans of historical and geographical terrain:

By expert systems I mean systems of technical accomplishment or professional expertise that organize large areas of the material and social environments in which we live today ... the systems in which the knowledge of experts is integrating, influences many aspects of what we do in a *continuous* way. Simply by sitting in my house, I am involved in an expert system, or a series of such systems, in which I place my reliance.... Expert systems are disembedding mechanisms because, in common with symbolic tokens, they remove social relations from the immediacies of context.... This 'stretching' of social systems is achieved via the impersonal nature of tests applied to evaluate technical knowledge and by public critique (upon which the production of technical knowledge is based), used to control its form.[50]

Giddens also uses this analysis to explore the dynamics and dilemmas of 'trust relations' within contemporary social settings which are organized through social practices of the kind previously outlined. He shows that we have no choice but to put our confidence – 'faith' even – in administrative and expert systems to produce a certain set of outcomes or events. Yet, at the same time, this will unavoidably entail a calculation of the degree of risk involved in putting our faith in such abstract systems to reduce or minimize the dangers to which everyday modern social life is routinely subjected – when travelling in a train, car or aeroplane, for instance. This balance between trust and the calculation of risk involved is made even more difficult by the *inherently dynamic* nature of modern organizations. The latter are pervaded by a constant monitoring, examining and re-evaluation of established social routines and methodologies in the light of incoming information about their performance. Consequently, the design and operation of modern administrative and expert systems is continuously up-dated and revised on the basis of technical knowledge and judgements which the ordinary citizen – and we are all 'ordinary citizens' for most of the time within the conditions prevailing under 'high' (rather than 'post') modernity – will be unable or unwilling to appreciate. Once again this reveals the nature of:

that distinctive feature of modern social life, the rationalized organization. Organizations (including modern states) may sometimes have the rather static, inertial quality which Weber associated with bureaucracy, but more commonly they have a dynamism that contrasts sharply with pre-modern orders. Modern organizations are able to connect the local and the global in ways which would have been unthinkable in more traditional societies and in so doing routinely affect the lives of many millions of people.[51]

It is this inherent dynamism and restlessness of modern organizations, as strategic mechanisms which lift social inter-action out of restricted, localized contexts and restructure it across vast time/space distances, which must provide the strategic problematic for contemporary organizational analysis. As strategic mechanisms for reflexively monitored system reproduction and change, modern organizations provide one of the most important sites or arenas in which the conflicts and power struggles to control the future are fought out.[52] A deeper understanding of how these, inherently dynamic, mechanisms operate – and provide sites or arenas in which the continuing struggle to gain access to and control over vital administrative and allocative resources is engaged in – can be seen as establishing the major research task for the sociology of organizations in the coming decades.

## RESEARCHING ORGANIZATIONS

Three, recently published, research studies will be reviewed as providing examples of the kind of 'sociology of organizations' which has been advocated in the previous section. In very different ways, each of these studies exemplifies the types of research which need to be pursued now and in the future, if the task of furthering our understanding of and explanations for the strategic role which modern organizations play in 'reflexively monitoring system reproduction and change' is to be advanced. The three studies reviewed in this light are Sabel's *Work and Politics*,[53] Zuboff's *In the Age of the Smart Machine*[54] and Jackall's *Moral Mazes*.[55] It will be argued that each of these studies provides us with a deeper understanding of the multifarious, and often contradictory, ways in which modern organizations simultaneously constitute disembedding mechanisms which rip social action from their localized contexts and link them into a globalized process of structural change and transformation. They also convey an appreciation of the specific power struggles that shape the changing relationship between the 'micro-politics of control' and the 'macro-politics of order'.

Each of these three research studies will be discussed in terms of a common format. First, a brief overview will be provided of the central themes tackled within each study and the manner in which they are approached. Second, this introductory review will be developed into a more substantial illustration of how each piece of research and analysis furthers the general problematic articulated in the previous section. Third, an overall assessment will be provided of the substantive conclusions drawn from the research carried out in each study and the way in which these help us to reflect back on the wider themes/problematic previously outlined.

Sabel's book provides an historical/comparative study of the way in which political and industrial conflicts within societies and workplaces have shaped economic and technological change. He focuses on the complex processes through which 'unpretentious claims for decency, defined in various and sometimes conflicting ways, can contribute to profound transformations in the structure of society'.[56] Thus, the interweaving of 'politics in the broadest sense' – that is, a complex clash of moral and social visions supported by economic and administrative power – and 'politics in the narrower sense' – that is, the conflicts between workers' demands for autonomy and managers' attempts to regain and establish control – produce the particular trajectories of socio-economic transformation which stand at the core of Sabel's analysis.

In particular, he is concerned to explain the rise of 'Fordism' as a specific form of production regime, as well as the socio-economic and political forces currently at work within advanced capitalist societies which may eventuate in a radically different type of production regime. Using 'Fordism' as a conceptual shorthand for the organizational and technological principles associated with large-scale factory production, he argues that the triumph of this system, incomplete as it was, has to be accounted for as the consequence of a series of complex, often unintended, political conflicts and choices in different places and at different times. He rejects any form of explanation couched in terms of technological determinism or 'logics of organizational efficiency and effectiveness'. In their place, he strenuously advocates analyses which show how the organization of markets and production systems is shaped by the outcome of power struggles between contending groups and the 'visions' of moral and social order which their strategies embody.

At the core of these conflicts, Sabel indicates, lies a 'struggle for place'; that is, the struggle to mesh workplace conditions, labour markets and the collective cultures of certain groups in such a way that patterns of strategic choices become related to transformations in socio-economic structures. In this context, 'organization' becomes a vital resource linking local contests and struggles to the wider, global arenas in which they are situated. It is regarded as a mechanism that, temporarily and unpredictably, harnesses the values and interests of workers and managers to collective forms of action which can transform or preserve the 'local' structures and practices through which their interaction is configured.

He maintains that industrial capitalist societies have reached a point in their socio-economic development when new forms of collective action and organizational resources are beginning to emerge that call into question and challenge established forms of the division of labour.[57] The eventual institutional outcomes which these challenges will generate cannot be predicted with any certainty, but they hold out the possibility of alternative visions of socio-economic order carried forward by organizational strategies and practices that break with the dominant Fordist regime. Movers in this direction destabilize existing 'low-trust' ideologies and relationships within workplace and societies. Indeed, they generate new forms of social and industrial conflict in which the established authority structures and power relations of advanced capitalist societies are made much more socially visible and explicit. Consequently, the social and economic benefits to be derived from low-trust work relations are called into question to the extent that they are seen to stifle innovation and restrict the range of human capacities displayed at work:

Mistrust freezes the technological progress of a whole sector; trust fosters it. The same logic applies to every phase of the business: when invention creates demand and invention is collective, this is a natural result . . . economic structure is fixed by political choices. By the end of the 1980s it is likely that comparable stories, different in substance but with equally uncertain ends, will be told for each of the advanced industrial countries.[58]

Zuboff's book attempts to unearth the 'deep structure' of

those strategic choices which shape the long-term process of socio-technical transformation and its wider impact on struggles to control the organizational knowledge bases which are constitutive of advanced industrial capitalism. Her generic theme is one of organizational transformation and the succession of political dilemmas that it presents to key actors located within the changing power structures of contemporary societies which are radically destabilized by the shock of rapid technological advance. Her basic premise is that:

a powerful new technology, such as that represented by the computer, fundamentally reorganizes the infrastructure of our material world. It eliminates former alternatives. It creates new possibilities. It necessitates fresh choices. The choices that we face concern the conception and distribution of knowledge in the workplace.... The choices that we make will shape relations of authority in the workplace.... The new technological infrastructure becomes a battle field of techniques, with management inventing novel ways to enhance certainty and control, while employees discover new methods of self-protection and even sabotage.... Computer-based technologies are not neutral: they embody essential characteristics that are bound to alter the nature of work within our factories and offices, and among workers, professionals, and managers. New choices are laid open by these technologies and these choices are being confronted in the daily lives of men and women across the landscape of modern organizations.[59]

As was the case with Sabel, Zuboff develops an historical/comparative approach to her analysis of these issues and processes which integrates ethnographic studies of changing workplace relations with institutional research on developing socio-technical structures. In this context, she gives particular attention to the role of advances in information technology in reinforcing the rationalization and centralization of knowledge associated with the growth and diffusion of industrial bureaucracy. She chronicles, in the form of a series of analytically structured narratives, the advance of information technology and administrative bureaucracy in terms of a succession of attempts on the part of employees and managers to grapple with the problem of 'the body's role in production'.[60] This chronicle highlights the strategic role of information technology and bureaucratic organization in providing devices and mechanisms which 'lift' social relations out of their local settings and bracket them in such a way that 'control at a distance' can be routinely achieved by employers and managers.[61] Thus, Zuboff documents the development of what she refers to as an 'information panopticon' which generates much more powerful forms of surveillance and control within advanced industrial societies. The latter equip dominant groups with a material and social technology which facilitates the intermeshing of the local and the global in ways that advance their 'control interests', but also release new areas of operational uncertainty and limited autonomy which can be exploited to their advantage by subordinate groups:

Information systems that translate, record, and display human behaviour can provide the computer age version of universal transparency with a degree of illumination that would have exceeded Bentham's most outlandish fantasies. Such systems can become information panopticons that, *freed from the constraints of space and time*, do not depend upon the physical arrangements of buildings or the laborious record keeping of industrial administration. They do not require the mutual presence of objects of observation. They do not even require the presence of an observer. Information systems can automatically and continuously record almost anything their designers want to capture, regardless of the specific intentions brought to the design process or the motives that guide data interpretation and utilization. The counterpart of the central tower is a video screen.[62]

While the allure of panopticon power of this sort is highly seductive from a managerial perspective, Zuboff rejects the technological determinism and political pessimism often associated with analyses of these developments and their longer-term implications. She consistently maintains that the vastly enhanced potential for control and disembedding that panopticon power makes available to employers and managers does not necessarily guarantee their success – their actual implementation and organizational consequences are unavoidably the subject of unpredictable socio-political conflict and struggle. The information systems constitutive of 'panopticon power' can 'alter many of the classic contingencies of the superior–subordinate relationship, providing certain information about subordinates' behaviour while eliminating the necessity of face-to-face engagement; they can transmit the presence of the omniscient observer and so induce compliance without the messy conflict-prone exertions of reciprocal relations'.[63] But, at the same time, they open up new areas of uncertainty – which can be manipulated by politically skilful groups of managers and workers to undermine the universalizing and totalizing 'transparency' and control which the information panopticon promises:

Unilateral techniques of control tend to evoke techniques of defence from subordinates who resent their own involuntary display. While these defensive measures can be thwarted, they can also contaminate the validity of data. Even more important, this battle of techniques of control versus techniques of defence signals the erosion of reciprocal relations as information becomes the field on which latent antagonisms are let loose. . . . The electronic text can so insulate managers from the felt realities of their workplace that they will no longer have available the means with which to rekindle reciprocities if they should want to. Paradoxically, that very insularity increases the vulnerability of the text to contamination while it simultaneously heightens the requirements for valid objective data. Thus insulated, managers often collude in ignoring the ever more *slender relationship between their data and the organizational realities they are meant to reflect*.[64] (My emphasis)

In this respect, 'panopticon power' has a crippling effect on the managerial potential to control which operates simultaneously with the vastly extended disembedded control capacity that it makes available. How the balance between these contradictory consequences will be worked through, and what its longer-term impact on organizational design will be, are matters which will be primarily determined by the strategic choices emerging from the power struggles engaged in by conflicting social, political and economic interests to impose their priorities on organizational change and development. The new control possibilities released by greatly enhanced technological and organizational power *can* restructure the 'rules of the political game' in which the major players are involved. But the subtle interplay between technological potential and political choice will be the social crucible in which new alliances are forged and new strategies pursued.

*None* of the organizations that Zuboff researched had succeeded in implementing the 'information panopticon' to its full theoretical or technical potential. Alternative logics of technological and organizational change were beginning to evolve that broke with the rationale of the latter. In particular, managers often found themselves in situations where the control promise of panopticon was in the process of being critically assessed against alternative strategies and structures grounded in a philosophy of participative decision-making, worker involvement and decentralization. The viability and success of these alternative strategies, she concludes, will largely depend on the development of new ideological contexts and political skills in which the 'God' of bureaucratic rationalization and control can be rejected for visions and practices of socio-technical transformation that resonate with the values and interests of 'high-trust' relations in work and society.

Finally, we come to Jackall. His study examines the organizational worlds of American corporate managers and the occupational strategies and tactics that they follow to survive and flourish in the highly pressurized contexts in which they operate. More specifically, he is interested in the occupational ethics or 'moral rules-in-use' that American managers rely on to guide their behaviour in the performance of their individual work roles and the wider corporate settings in which they strive to progress within the bureaucratic universes which they inhabit. He is particularly interested in the way in which bureaucratic ideologies and systems provide managers with a practical morality that allows them to *bracket or suspend* 'the moralities that they might hold *outside* the workplace or that they might adhere to privately and to follow instead of the prevailing morality of their particular organizational situation'.[65] In this way, he presents a vision of corporation morality and organizational survival in which what is right for the organization becomes the 'categorical imperative' which most, if not all, managers have to follow. The moral vacuum or 'anomie' at the heart of the business corporation reproduces an amoral strategy of personal survival and collective advancement within corporate management.

Jackall's analysis of the interconnections between managerial work, corporate bureaucracy and occupational ethics locks into the wider historical and structural transformations that have produced 'management' as an identifiable category and group within the division of labour. More specifically, he focuses on the way in which the organizational landscape of corporate managers has been transformed by the bureau-cratization of industrial life and the work regimes to which they are subjected. This transformation, he argues, has produced an organizational milieu in which the 'moral dilemmas posed by bureaucratic work are, in fact, pervasive, taken for granted, and at the same time, regularly denied'.[66] Thus, the hierarchical structure of American business life is seen as the organizational linchpin of a system that subjects the personal and professional ethics of mangers to a form of ideological indoctrination and occupational socialization which marginalizes public concerns and prioritizes private motivations that congeal with institutional morality:

> Bureaucracy breaks apart the ownership of property from its control, social independence from occupation, substance from appearances, actions from responsibility, obligation from guilt, language from meaning, and notions of truth from reality. Most important, and at the bottom of *all these fractures* it breaks apart the older connection between the meaning of work and salvation. In the bureaucratic world, one's success, one's sign of election, no longer depends on an inscrutable God, but on the capriciousness of one's superiors and the market; and one achieves economic salvation to the extent that one pleases and submits to new Gods, that is one's bosses and the exigencies of an impersonal market. In this way, because moral choices are inextricably tied to personal fates, bureaucracy erodes internal and even external standards of morality not only in matters of individual success and failure but in all the issues that mangers face in their daily work. Bureaucracy makes its own internal rules and social context the principal moral gauges for action.[67]

Once again, it is the restless dynamism of bureaucratic organization and its inherent ability to rip substantive moral values and practices from their local contexts and relocate them within abstract globalized structures which inexorably push in the direction of an instrumental rationality that lies at the analytical core of Jackall's study. However, this rationality or morality-in-use does not provide a stabilized organizational environment in which managers can rely on a degree of certainty and security that will make their occupational lives easier. Instead, the bureaucratized and rationalized organizational worlds which they inhabit present them with a highly complex and intricate set of 'moral mazes' within which ambiguity, anxiety, patronage and politicking are the prevailing social mores and dominant occupational realities. Consequently, a great deal of managerial work and behaviour consists of ongoing struggles for power and status within an organizational setting which is characterized by constant upheaval, unprincipled capriciousness and personal angst.

What one might term 'traditional' morality – notions of fairness, justice, equity and trust – is seriously compromised or socially marginalized within this bureaucratic world and the institutional ethic that it imposes. In so far as moral dilemmas are recognized and acted on, then they are subordinated to an organizational logic which demands fealty to a pragmatic code of corporate survival and occupational careerism rather than to an ethic of personal responsibility:

For most managers . . . the real meaning of work – the basis of social identity and valued self-image – becomes keeping one's eye on the main chance, maintaining and furthering one's own position and career. . . . Corporate managers who become imbued with this ethos pragmatically take their world as they find it and try to make that world according to its own institutional logic. They pursue their own careers and good fortune as best they can within the rules of their world. As it happens, *given their pivotal institutional role in our epoch*, they help create and re-create, as one unintended consequence of their personal striving, a society where morality becomes indistinguishable from the quest for one's own survival and advantage.[68]

In their different ways, each of the studies described above stand testimony to the strategic role of modern organization as a dynamic process or mechanism for bracketing or collapsing time/space distances and thus bringing them under administrative control. By ripping social action free from its situational context and stretching it across vast time/space distances, modern organization provides a vital mechanism for transforming social relations within complex webs of local/global interconnections. But at the same time that it globalizes and universalizes, modern organization fragments and decontextualizes social action and relations. Rather than subordinating social choice to a universalizing developmental logic which makes political conflict obsolete, modern organization establishes a restructured institutional terrain on which different types of power struggles are pursued. While the quest for the organizational and informational panopticon remains a powerful motivating force underpinning sociotechnical transformation, its realization still remains beyond the grasp of modern management. Indeed, the closer that the latter seem to get to realizing this goal, the more intractable the problem of overcoming human recalcitrance in the face of organizational rationalization seems to become. The greatly enhanced 'control at a distance' which modern organizational practices facilitate through their capacity to monitor and correct the conditions under which they are reproduced, is paralleled by a continuing struggle to shape and direct the values and interests which underpin institutional transformation.

## CONCLUSION: BEYOND THE FRAGMENTS

This chapter has provided an overview of the major strategies for future theoretical development currently being advanced in organizational analysis. It has also supported one particular way forward and suggested how it can be advanced. As such, it has attempted to identify and elaborate the 'progressive narrative' which needs to be pursued within organizational research and analysis at the present time – a time when fragmentation and polarization seem to be the dominant motifs.

This strategy has been advocated as a way out of the impasse into which organizational analysis seems to have moved in recent years. On the one hand, its development has been shaped by 'schools of thought' that advocate a very radical form of epistemological and ethical relativism. Within this perspective, the sociology of organizations becomes an expression of economic, political and cultural power which is unable to make any sustainable knowledge claims concerning the nature of organizational reality and the rightness or justice of particular kinds of organizational conduct.

Organizational knowledge is social power. Its historical development and contemporary relevance can only be assessed in terms of its status as a power discourse legitimating changing forms of disciplinary regimes.

On the other hand, this 'radical relativism' has produced a strong conservative backlash which reasserts the primacy and predominance of scientific methodology and practice. It attempts to re-establish and reimpose a privileged epistemological doctrine and programme which will 'deliver the goods' in terms of an applied policy science that directly speaks to the concerns of dominant coalitions occupying key positions within organizational and institutional power structures.

The position advocated in this chapter – and indeed throughout this book – finds neither of these extremes attractive propositions. It maintains that there is a continuing need for the construction of, and dialogue between, intelligible narratives and constituting *the* vital intellectual process sustaining the collective search for a better understanding of 'modern organizations'. The most promising basis for the continuation of this dialogue has been located in Giddens' conception of modern organizations as strategic devices for the reflexive monitoring of system reproduction and change. This view gives particular emphasis to the way in which modern organizations consist of cognitive and social practices which facilitate the collapsing of time and space into simplified and portable representational systems – such as information technology, bureaucratic processing and cultural codes. The latter provide the mechanisms through which social relations can be manipulated in such a way to facilitate effective organizational control at a distance' – that is, over vast time/space distances which had previously defeated the control aspirations of older, more traditional, forms of administrative power which lacked the 'reach' that the modern organization provides.

However, this capacity to 'control at a distance' is never total and is always contested in some form or another by those who constitute its primary targets. In this way, the detailed operation of modern organizations as representational and administrative technologies facilitating reflexive monitoring and control becomes a resource or an agenda that is struggled over by various groups and classes, rather than an accomplished fact. Organizational analysis has a vital role to play in furthering our understanding of 'organization' as constituting the strategic social technology and institutional site in which the interplay between the micro-politics of control and the macro-politics of power is worked through to prosecute the radicalization or globalization of modernity.[69] It will only be in a condition to fulfil this objective if it begins to tell a new story that critically engages with older narratives, which are in need of substantial overhaul but continue to relate to present problems and projected futures. Thus, the search for narrative understanding and dialogue can only be sustained if the shared sense of historical and intellectual continuity between current concerns and past achievements is retrieved from the collective amnesia or forgetfulness which is encouraged by recently fashionable modes of discourse and analysis.[70]

The interparadigmatic 'Star Wars' of the 1970s seem to have exhausted themselves. The 1980s were dominated by an ethos of intellectual playfulness and disciplinary fragmentation. The 1990s seem set to witness a substantial move away from the polarized thinking that has shaped the agenda for too long and towards a search for intermediation between competing, but nevertheless communicating, perspectives, programmes and narratives. This development signals the pervasive strength of those intellectual traditions out of which the sociology of organizations has been forged – traditions that are continually, and critically, reworked to speak to changed realities. In so far as this book has contributed to the renewal and regeneration of that continuing search for an improved understanding of such a vital institution as modern organization, and its contribution to the remaking of the modern world, it will have done its job.

### REFERENCES

1. Cooper, R. and Burrell, G., 'Modernism, Post-Modernism and Organizational Analysis: An Introduction', *Organization Studies*, vol. 9 (1), 1988, pp. 91–112; Power, M., 'Modernism, Postmodernism and Organization' in Hassard, J. and Pym, D. (eds), *The Theory and Philosophy of Organizations: Critical Issues and New Perspectives* (Routledge, London, 1990), pp. 109–24; Gergen, K., 'Organization Theory in the Postmodern Era' in Reed, M. and Hughes, M.D. (eds), *Rethinking Organization: New Directions in Organization Theory and Analysis* (Sage, London, 1992), pp. 207–26.
2. Reed, M., 'Scripting Scenarios for a New Organization Theory and Practice', *Work, Employment and Society*, vol. 5 (1), 1991, pp. 119–32.
3. Reed, M., *Redirections in Organizational Analysis* (Tavistock, London, 1985); 'Introduction' to Reed, M. and Hughes, M. (eds) *op. cit.* (1992).
4. Child, J. 'Organization: A Choice for Man' in Child, J. (ed.) *Man and Organization* (Allen and Unwin, 1973), pp. 234–57.
5. Donaldson, L., *In Defence of Organization Theory: A Reply to the Critics* (Cambridge University Press, Cambridge, 1985).
6. Benson, J.K., 'Innovation and Crisis in Organizational Analysis' in Benson, J.K. (ed.), *Organizational Analysis: Critique and Innovation*, Sage Contemporary Social Science, issue 37 (Sage, London, 1977), pp. 5–18 (p. 16).
7. Morgan, G. (ed.), *Beyond Method* (Sage, Beverly Hills, 1983).
8. Reed, M., 'The End of Organized Society: A Theme in Search of a Theory?' in Blyton, P. and Morris, J. (eds), *A Flexible Future? Prospects for Employment and Organization* (De Gruyter, Berlin, 1991), pp. 23–37. Also see Chapter 5 of this book.
9. Whitley, R., 'East Asian Enterprise Structures and the Comparative Analysis of Forms of Business Organization', *Organization Studies*, vol. 11 (1), 1990, pp. 47–74.
10. Clegg, S.R., *Modern Organizations: Organization Studies in the Postmodern World* (Sage, London, 1990), pp. 98–106.
11. Thompson, J.D., *Organizations in Action* (McGraw-Hill, New York, 1967).
12. Gouldner, A.W., 'Organizational Analysis' in Merton, R.K., Broom, L. and Cottrell, C. (eds), *Sociology Today* (Basic Books, New York, 1959), pp. 400–28.
13. McNeil, K., 'Understanding Organizational Power: Building on the Weberian Legacy', *Administrative Science Quarterly*, vol. 23 (1), 1978, pp. 65–90.

14. Clegg, S.R., *Power, Rule and Domination* (Routledge and Kegan Paul, London, 1975); Pfeffer, J., *Power in Organizations* (Pitman, London, 1982).
15. Morgan, G., *Organizations in Society* (Macmillan, London, 1990).
16. Power, M., *op. cit.* (1990), pp. 109–24.
17. Gergen, K., *op. cit.* (1992), pp. 207–26.
18. Donaldson, L., *op. cit.* (1985).
19. Mintzberg, H., Waters, N. Pettigrew, A. and Butler, R., 'Studying Deciding: An Exchange of Views', *Organization Studies*, vol. 11 (1), 1991, pp. 1–16.
20. Donaldson, L., *op. cit.* (1985), pp. xi–4.
21. Donaldson, L., 'The Ethereal Hand: Organizational Economics and Management Theory', *Academy of Management Review*, vol. 5 (3), 1990, pp. 369–81.
22. For a much more cautious, not to say, critical review of recent developments in economic theory and their implications for organizational analysis see Perrow, C., *Complex Organizations: A Critical Essay* (Random House, New York, third edition, 1986), pp. 219–57.
23. For a further elaboration of this point and a critical riposte see Donaldson, L., 'Redirections in Organizational Analysis' and Reed, M., 'Deciphering Donaldson and Defending Organization Theory', *Australian Journal of Management*, vol. 14 (2), 1989, pp. 243–60.
24. Donaldson, L., *op. cit.* (1985), pp. 7–8.
25. *ibid.*, p. 9.
26. Hinings, C.R., 'Defending Organization Theory: A British View from North America', *Organization Studies*, vol. 9 (1), 1988, pp. 2–7.
27. Aldrich, H., 'Paradigm Warriors: Donaldson versus the Critics of Organization Theory', *Organization Studies*, vol. 9 (1), 1988, pp. 19–25.
28. Child, J. 'On Organizations in their Sectors' and 'Letter to the Editor', *Organization Studies*, vol. 9 (1), 1988, pp. 13–19 and pp. 143–4; Donaldson, L. *op. cit.* (1989), Reed, M., *op. cit.* (1989).
29. Burrell, G. and Morgan, G., *Sociological Paradigms and Organizational Analysis* (Heinemann, London, 1979).
30. Gioia, D.A. and Pitre, E., 'Multiparadigm Perspectives on Theory Building', *Academy of Management Review*, vol. 5 (4), 1990, pp. 584–602; Jackson, N. and Carter, P., 'In Defence of Paradigm Incommensurability', *Organization Studies*, vol. 12 (1), 1991, pp. 109–28.

31. Morgan, G. and Burrell, G., *op. cit.* (1979), pp. 397–8.
32. *ibid.*, p. 398; for an elaboration of this strong version of paradigm incommensurability and its implications see Reed, M., *op. cit.* (1985), pp. 183–89 and pp. 205–9; Donaldson, L., *op. cit.* (1985), pp. 35–46.
33. Jackson, N. and Carter, P., *op. cit.* (1991), p. 111.
34. Gioia, D.A. and Pitre, E., *op. cit* (1990).
35. One example which they provide of this bridge-building across transition zones is the way in which Giddens' concept of 'structuration' has been developed by a number of researchers operating from very different paradigmatic bases to form a *shared* collective focus on the processes through which organizational structures are reproduced and changed over time.
36. Burrell, G., 'Modernism, Postmodernism and Organizational Analysis 2: The Contribution of Michel Foucault', *Organization Studies*, vol. 9 (2), 1988, pp. 221–35. On 'actor network' theory see Latour, B., *Science in Action* (Open University Press, Milton Keynes, 1987).
37. Wolin, S., 'On the Theory and Practice of Power' in Arac, J. (ed.), *After Foucault: Humanistic Knowledge, Post-Modern Challenges* (Rutgers University Press, New Brunswick, 1988).
38. Reed, M., *op. cit.* (1985), pp. 63–93.
39. See Chapter 4.
40. Burrell, G., *op. cit.* (1988), pp. 224–33.
41. Wolin, S., *op. cit.* (1988), p. 184.
42. Thompson, P. and McHugh, D., *Work Organizations: A Critical Introduction* (Macmillan, London, 1990), pp. 47–85.
43. Gioia, D.A. and Pitre, E., *op. cit.* (1990), p. 599.
44. Willmott, H., 'Beyond Paradigmatic Closure in Organizational Enquiry' in Hassard, J. and Pym, D., (eds), *op. cit.* (1990), pp. 44–62 (p. 49).
45. See Chapter 3.
46. See Chapter 1.
47. Giddens, A., 'Time and Social Organization' in Giddens, A., *Social Theory and Modern Sociology* (Polity Press, Cambridge, 1987), pp. 140–65.
48. See Chapter 1.
49. Giddens, A., *The Consequences of Modernity* (Polity Press, Cambridge, 1991).
50. *ibid.*, pp. 27–8.
51. *ibid.*, p. 20.
52. The other agency or site crucial to future organizational and institutional development is social movements. For analyses of

the latter see Scott, A., *Ideology and the New Social Movements* (Unwin Hyman, London, 1990).

53. Sabel, C., *Work and Politics: The Division of Labour in Industry* (Cambridge University Press, Cambridge, 1984).
54. Zuboff, S., *In the Age of the Smart Machine: The Future of Work and Power* (Heinemann, London, 1989).
55. Jackall, R., *Moral Mazes: The World of Corporate Managers*, (Oxford University Press, Oxford, 1988).
56. Sabel, C., *op. cit.* (1984), p. xiii.
57. See Chapter 5.
58. Sabel, C., *op. cit.* (1984), pp. 226–31.
59. Zuboff, S., *op. cit.* (1989), pp. 5–7.
60. *ibid.*, p. 23.
61. For further development of this point see Cooper, R., 'Formal Organization as Representation: Remote Control, Displacement and Abbreviation' in Reed, M. and Hughes, M.D. (eds), *op. cit.* (1991).
62. Zuboff, S., *op. cit.* (1989), p. 322.
63. *ibid.*, p. 333.
64. *ibid.*, p. 361.
65. Jackall, R., *op. cit.*, (1988), p. 6.
66. *ibid.*, p. 13.
67. *ibid.*, p. 192.
68. *ibid.*, pp. 202–4.
69. On this point see Giddens, A., *op. cit.*, (1990).
70. On the 'forgetfulness' of postmodernist thinking in social science see Clarke, J., 'Enter the Cybernauts: Problems in Postmodernism', *Communication*, vol. 10, 1988, pp. 383–401.

# GLOSSARY

The purpose of this glossary is to provide short definitions of key terms or concepts which are used extensively throughout the text. They are central to the various debates and developments which are reviewed and assessed within the text. They also inform the analysis of those debates and developments which the author provides.

## BUREAUCRACY

A form of organization based on hierarchical authority structures and a highly specialized functional division of administrative labour. The authority structures and administrative arrangements are assumed to reflect the diffusion of a form of decision-making rationality in modern societies characterized by systematic calculation and planned coordination of resource allocation and distribution. This decision-making rationality reinforces the drive towards forms of socio-economic, political and cultural organization in which efficiency and effectiveness are the dominating norms and values informing social action. The growing emphasis on bureaucratically determined conceptions of organizational efficiency and effectiveness pushes alternative or competing value systems – such as cooperation, trust, integration and stability – on to the margins of socio-economic, political and cultural life within modern societies.

CONTROL

A process or mechanism for realizing the effective monitoring and regulation of social action within forms of organization based on competing and conflicting interests and values. Control processes or mechanisms provide dominant individuals and collectivities with the means by which they can ensure that their interests and values shape the behaviour of others whose action is crucial to the former's realization. In this respect, control processes and mechanisms are directly tied to institutionalized patterns of domination and subordination within societies and the underlying conflicts of interest and value which they necessarily reflect.

DISCIPLINARY TECHNOLOGIES

An interrelated set of techniques and practices which achieve a level of self-discipline and control that is eventually accepted as 'normal' and 'natural' by those who are subject to their embrace. These techniques and practices are most appropriately thought of as the accumulated products of ways of thinking and acting which categorize individuals in such a way that they can be placed in general classifications which are amenable to administrative manipulation and control. Considered in these terms, disciplinary technologies are the outcome of a long-term historical process of organizational maturation and development which has a pervasive influence on the nature and structure of society. Their relationship with the proclaimed or unstated 'projects' of dominant groups or classes is always subject to a significant degree of historical and organizational, or social, indeterminacy. The development of the human or social sciences is closely bound up with the growing sophistication and reach of disciplinary technologies.

DISORGANIZATION

A condition in which centralized bureaucratic structures in all spheres of socio-economic, political and cultural life are in the process of fragmenting and disintegrating. Thus, the relatively high degrees of social stability and integration associated with bureaucratically organized socio-economic systems are put in jeopardy by various economic, technological, social, political and cultural transformations which push in the direction of much more highly decentralized, dispersed and autonomous structures. This incipient decay of social stability and the breakdown in cultural integration, once facilitated by bureaucratic order, is presumed to generate an underlying 'disorganizing dynamic' that systematically and irreversibly transforms the institutional structures of modern societies in the direction of 'postmodern' forms.

## DISCURSIVE HISTORY

A form of historical narrative and repository which stores information and knowledge about categories of individuals, groups and classes that may be useful for managerial purposes. These purposes, and the discursive histories in which they are embedded, are focused on the production of 'governable subjects' who will largely follow the scripts that their organizational positions specify. Consequently, historically sedimented knowledge becomes a political and administrative resource which organizational elites gather and deploy to achieve disciplinary power and control. However, the latter is always incomplete and likely to produce consequences which escape the manipulative concerns of dominant groups.

## EXPERT SYSTEMS

Systems of technical accomplishment and professional expertise which are geared to the lifting of social relations out of immediate local contexts and stretching them into universally applicable forms of knowledge and practice. These systems provide the cognitive and technical basis for organizing large domains of the material and social context in which individuals live their everyday lives. As such, they establish the theoretical foundations and practical techniques on and through which modern social life is made possible – from fixing a burst water pipe to a transatlantic air flight. As the organizational complexity and functional specialization of modern social living becomes greater, so 'our' dependence on expert systems – to make that living possible – deepens. Thus, the inevitable expansion and escalating power of expert systems within modern societies raises some fundamental questions about the distribution of power and control that confront nominally 'democratic' polities.

## FLEXIBLE SPECIALIZATION

A type of production organization which combines product specialization and technical flexibility within an integrated management system. Production organizations which operate on the basis of flexible specialization – such as speciality steels, precision machine tools, speciality chemicals and luxury consumer goods – exemplify three mutually inter-dependent characteristics: first, a highly differentiated product range; second, flexible utilization of widely applicable – rather than product-specific or functionally dedicated – technology; third, the creation of regionally based socio-political arrangements which balance cooperation and competition amongst firms so as to encourage continuous innovation and adaptability. In this sense, flexible specialization constitutes a production regime that breaks with all the constitutive features of mass production systems and their associated managerial structures.

## LABOUR PROCESS

The work process through which raw materials are transformed into products for social use and, under capitalist economic systems, into commodities to be exchanged on the market. Approached in this way, the labour process under capitalism is necessarily bound up with the transformation of 'labour power' – that is, the *potential* for work – into 'labour' – that is, actual productive effort of the required scale and intensity. Thus, the labour process within capitalist systems is necessarily imbued with the conflicting interests of owners in profit maximization or capital accumulation and workers in effort minimization and wages maximization. This conflict has to be regulated if capitalist production and capital accumulation on a continuous basis are to be made possible. Such conflict regulation is achieved through the design and deployment of various control processes and practices which ensure – in a rough and ready kind of way – that the organizational and ideological prerequisites necessary for profitable production are sustained over time and institutionalized in accepted social and cultural forms.

## LOGICS OF ACTION

The underlying rationales which inform and direct social action. These rationales embody forms of calculation and evaluation which structure social action and justify the ends to which it is oriented. In the case of organized or administrative action, they would include theoretical concepts and associated modes of calculation such as profit maximization, legal rationality, accounting procedures, technological and scientific reasoning, and professional expertise. As 'logics of action', these cognitive and technical systems are directly implicated in the mechanisms which organizational elites develop to secure and retain control over the environments in which they operate.

## MODERNITY

The cultural experience of modern social life and the institutional forms through which it is articulated and communicated. This cultural experience is characterized by the dynamism, innovation, experimentation and uncertainty endemic to modern living when compared to the habituated routines and stability associated with life in traditional societies. It is also characterized by the emergence, and eventual dominance, of organizational systems and structures that homogenize individual experience into standardized and routinized forms of mass communication and consumption. Thus, the culture of modernity is communicated by bureaucratized forms of production and consumption in all walks of life – that is, in family life, at work, during leisure pursuits and in politics.

## MODERNIZATION

The processes of material and institutional development through which pre-industrial societies are transformed into industrial capitalist systems. Within the latter, a particular configuration of institutional and organizational patterns emerges which characterizes the social structure of 'modern' societies. This configuration consists of a series of interrelated organizational clusters in which the capitalist business enterprise, large-scale factory production and rational state bureaucracy are the strategic social units. The interrelated development of each of these organizational clusters entails a dramatic expansion of administrative power in economic and political institutions which was unavailable in traditional societies.

## ORGANIZATION

A social unit and a related set of social practices which assembles collective action into sustainable institutional forms that can be stretched or transported across vast time/space distances. As strategic social units for the storing and mobilizing of administrative power in modern societies, complex organization possesses the *potential* for 'global' surveillance and control which would have been unimaginable in traditional societies. However, the inherently fragmenting impact of administrative power exposes it to challenge and breakdown which mitigates against the 'totaliz-ing' forms of organizational surveillance and control en-visaged by some – currently influential – commentators.

## POSITIVISM

An epistemological doctrine which insists that the 'received model' of natural science methodology has universal ap-plicability for all forms of knowledge gathering and develop-ment. This doctrine has been particularly influential in organizational analysis in so far as it has justified the search for 'laws' of organizational change and development that necessarily press in the direction of certain types of ad-ministrative structure.

## POST-INDUSTRIALISM

An interpretation of recent changes to the economic, political and cultural systems of modern societies which takes them beyond the material conditions and institutional forms associated with 'industrial society'. Thus, the shift from a manufacturing to a service economy, the increasing political and administrative power of a 'knowledge elite', and the emergence of an information society are seen to have an accumulated impact that takes modern societies into a post-industrial condition.

## POST-FORDISM

A view of contemporary socio-economic developments and their longer-term implications which suggests that the core components of 'Fordist' production regimes – mass pro-duction systems for mass markets coordinated through bureaucratic control mechanisms – are in the process of breaking down under the accumulated weight of economic, political and social crisis. Alternative production regimes are beginning to emerge based on a qualitatively different 'organizational logic' which radically departs from the core principles on which Fordism was built and implemented.

## POSTMODERNISM

An analysis of underlying developments and trends in contemporary cultural, political and social conditions which maintains that we are at the beginning of a fundamental rupture or break with the institutional trajectories modern societies have followed since the eighteenth century. Associated with this rupture, postmodernist writers have identified a complex cluster of cultural, technological and ideological transformations which are indicative of a collective mood or state of mind in which incoherence, inconsistency and irony characterize the prevailing ethos. Both the epistemological and organizational foundations of modernity are seen to be eroded, if not destroyed, by the constantly shifting balances of cognitive and cultural power which are characteristic of the postmodern epoch.

## POSTSTRUCTURALISM

An approach to cultural and social studies which rejects the structural determinism or reductionism characteristic of mainstream science and the belief of a knowable human rationality on which it is premised. In direct contrast to the deterministic predilections of mainstream socio-cultural studies, poststructuralist writers have focused on the extremely diverse cognitive codes and technological systems that have shaped everyday life into cultural and social forms which constantly threaten to collapse under the weight of their *inherent* plurality, indeterminacy and ambiguity. Their research has presented a formidable challenge to the rationalistic foundations on which mainstream work has been based.

## REFLEXIVE MONITORING

The continual monitoring and correcting of the conditions under which social systems are reproduced and transformed through time and space. This process is facilitated through the development and deployment of various representational technologies which permit 'control at a distance', such as the vastly extended possibilities for information storage, retrieval and manipulation made available by advanced information and communication technologies.

## RELATIVISM

An epistemological and moral doctrine which argues that there are no universal cognitive or cultural foundations on which scientific and ethical judgements about competing explanations or justifications can be formulated. Its advocates maintain that there is no permanent, ahistorical and trans-cultural framework of procedures or values available for determining truth or rightness. Instead, we are placed in a position where the criteria which inform both scientific and ethical judgements are equally dependent on a pragmatically negotiated compromise between conflicting norms and values.

## SURVEILLANCE

The deliberate monitoring and supervising of objects and persons through the deployment of administrative practices and mechanisms associated with information management, behavioural control and normalizing judgement. The most developed form of the processes and practices associated with surveillance is to be found in formal organization. The latter represents the development of continuous surveillance through bureaucratic mechanisms in its most elaborate and sophisticated form.

# INDEX